Christianity and World Religions

Christianity and World Religions

Disputed Questions in the Theology of Religions

Gavin D'Costa

WILEY-BLACKWELL
A John Wiley & Sons, Ltd., Publication

This edition first published 2009

Blackwell Publishing was acquired by John Wiley & Sons in February 2007. Blackwell's publishing program has been merged with Wiley's global Scientific, Technical, and Medical business to form Wiley-Blackwell.

Registered Office
John Wiley & Sons Ltd, The Atrium, Southern Gate, Chichester, West Sussex, PO19 8SQ, United Kingdom

Editorial Offices
350 Main Street, Malden, MA 02148-5020, USA
9600 Garsington Road, Oxford, OX4 2DQ, UK
The Atrium, Southern Gate, Chichester, West Sussex, PO19 8SQ, UK

For details of our global editorial offices, for customer services, and for information about how to apply for permission to reuse the copyright material in this book please see our website at www.wiley.com/wiley-blackwell.

Library of Congress Cataloging-in-Publication Data

D'Costa, Gavin, 1958–
Christianity and world religions : disputed questions in the theology of religions / Gavin D'Costa.
p. cm.
Includes bibliographical references (p.) and index.
ISBN 978–1–4051–7674–3 (hardcover : alk. paper) – ISBN 978–1–4051–7673-6 (pbk. : alk. paper) 1. Theology of religions (Christian theology) I. Title.

BT83.85.D36 2009
261.2—dc22

2008049751

A catalog record for this book is available from the British Library.

Set in 10.5/13pt Minion by Graphicraft Limited, Hong Kong
Printed in Singapore

1 2009

For Kitty

Contents

Preface

After twenty years in the field of "theology of religions," Christian engagement with the great religions of the world and newer religious movements, I am struck at how fast the field is developing in response to the cultural situation in the West. Christianity is a minority religion in Europe and possibly becoming even more marginalized. However, Christianity is growing fast in Africa, South America, and the United States, and constitutes a stable small minority in Asia and an unstable, diminishing, and often persecuted minority in the Middle East and Arab countries. This means that, in 50 years' time, huge changes might have transformed the face of Christianity, especially in Europe. According to some theorists, Europe will be "Eurabia," a collection of states with a Muslim majority population; the West might witness a clash of two great civilizations, the Christian and Muslim. Further, given the demographic shifts, the Latin European cast of theologizing might give way to local theologies of great diversity. This is a challenging picture. Just over 50 years ago, looking back rather than forward, European Christians were recovering from the shock of two bloody wars, the near destruction of the Jews, and a very uncomfortable history of imperialism where, some argue, the torch and sword worked rather too closely together. Mission and imperialism allegedly destroyed indigenous cultures while seeking to change heathen souls. Capitalism changed ancient cultures overnight so that Coca-Cola and Microsoft now constitute the new universal culture. These two contentious snapshots work together to give a picture that means there is hardly an audience for this book in Europe. So why write it? One obvious answer would be: it is my job. I am a professional university theologian. There are three other more interesting answers.

First, I think that Christianity witnesses to the truth that changes the world in the most profound way possible: that God has become man in Jesus Christ for the redemption of the entire earth. Numbers do not finally matter, but the importance of explicating this good news in an intellectually rigorous and robust manner does. This can only be done in the contexts in which we find ourselves. My context is as a lay Roman Catholic working in a secular university in Bristol, England, as a professor of Roman Catholic theology. Bristol, like the United Kingdom, is religiously diverse, and many theological and social questions arise out of this situation. Further, my context as an Indian whose parents lived in India – but whose ancestors were originally converted by the Portuguese in the sixteenth century – born in East Africa, migrating to England in 1968, means that religious and cultural pluralism has been part of my story. I write this book as it reflects the personal, social, and intellectual struggles and joys that constitute me.

Second, to understand our contemporary situation requires an enormous amount of patience and hard work because, as I shall be arguing, our very understanding of what "theology" is, what "religions" are, what constitutes "public debate," what "truth" is, is deeply problematic. Thus, part of this book is devoted to untangling this conceptual thicket to offer a particular way of looking at these issues and to conceptualize the problems that arise. In arriving at a view on these matters, I try to remain aware of the situatedness of all narrations (which makes me a postmodern), the relatedness of all contexts (which makes me a modern), and the universal claim made arising out of the particular Christian narration (which makes me a pre-modern Christian). To write on any topic that relates to disputed questions also requires a telling of how these disputes came about (looking at genealogy), before being able to move forward in suggesting solutions and new questions. If a reader interested in the questions "What is the theology of religions and what are the big issues in this field?" finishes this book with a sense of the complexity of issues as well as hearing a distinctive answer, then all is well. I hope to draw maps and suggest routes through them. Readers clearly have to find their own way.

Third, it is difficult to think of a more important question facing Christianity in the twenty-first century. Christianity's very existence in part depends on how it relates to the world religions. This is a matter of survival and more importantly a matter of plausibility: how do Christians relate to their tradition, which so many think has related so negatively to the world religions? The questions are not simply theological and pastoral (Can a non-Christian be saved?), but also very practical and political (How should Christians relate to the religiously pluralist public square? Should they join with Muslims, for example, to campaign for religious schools?). These are my questions in my context, but I think many will be shared by readers in differing contexts. This book seeks to build an approach toward answering these and other questions, while showing readers the many alternatives and contested ways of formulating the problems and giving different solutions.

That accounts for why I wrote the book, but now to the "what" of the book. Let me briefly tell you what the plot line is so you can use this book usefully. The book is divided into four parts, with each part containing two related chapters. Part I, "Charting the Territory: Theology of Religions," looks at the theological debate that has taken place among Christian theologians. In chapter 1 I cover the period from soon after the Second World War until the 1980s. I inspect the way maps were drawn in response to the questions raised by other religions. The key dogmatic issues are the doctrines of God as trinity, the nature of the incarnation as unique, the character of the church, the meaning of mission, and the ethical/social challenges that Christians face in encountering religious pluralism. I try to show how some of these questions are deeply interrelated so that if you answer one question in a particular fashion, that might determine your response to a whole range of further questions. We will also see that certain tradition-specific ways of approaching issues and problems come to the fore almost as much as the actual questions being discussed. In chapter 2 I draw the map further into the present day, which shows a revolt against the earlier mapping, new maps being produced, and significant areas of continuity in terms of questions and concerns from the earlier period. Most significantly, the social and political dimensions of religion in the public square become far more central, without eclipsing a range of doctrinal issues that continue from the previous era. Further, an interest emerges in religions for their own sake, rather than as fodder for theological evaluations. These two chapters should act as a reasonably comprehensive map to the field of theology of religions in the twentieth century. They also serve to show where I locate myself on the map and readers should try and do the same. It will help their journey through the book.

Part II, "The Making and Meaning of Religions," touches on a very important question about how "we" view "religion," for if "religions" are what Christian theology is to engage with, we need to clarify what they are. The drawing up of the terrain is so controversial that I decided to tell two stories, one in chapter 3 and another entirely contrary story in chapter 4. Chapter 3 takes up the narration of religion as modernity has told it through some of its chief architects. It is a story that most Europeans will know like the air they breathe. It tells of the wars of religion, the internal strife in Europe among Roman Catholics, Lutherans, and Calvinists, and then other denominational groups. It also tells of the rivalries between Christianity and Islam, and Christian anti-Semitism. It tells of the only route out of this tense and violent history: the hard-fought, slow emergence of a public square where religions might co-exist with a basically neutral state that upholds the freedom of all religions. Religion must be honored as a free choice that allows a person and communities to follow their traditions of cultic worship without interference and persecution. The alternative story told in chapter 4 tells instead of the emergence of the nation state, which replaced religion as the center of society. Further, the nation state slowly took on all the features of public religions, and its struggle for total power and the construction of the public square was related to the preservation of its own privileges. The emergence of the nation state better explains the "wars of religion," not inter-denominational rivalry *per se*. I further argue that the nation state has caused the construal of religion to focus on "doctrines," "worship," and "cultic practices," which are deemed by modernity to be the domain of religion. This means that the debate about religious pluralism has not even begun, as the "religions" that constitute this pluralism must first conform to modernity's "religions" before they can participate in the public square. The picture is far more nuanced and complicated of course, but I suggest that we should instead view religions as cultural configurations of power and discipline, which brings into focus a wider range of questions where doctrine and social practices are profoundly interrelated. Through each narrative, I attend to the academic study of religion and how it evolved in the light of these political social patterns.

Part III picks up the arguments from part II and addresses the much debated question about the role of religion in the public square. After 9/11, as it has been iconically baptized, the London bombings of July 2005, the murders of Theo van Gogh and Pim Fortuyn in Holland, unjust imprisonment at Guantanamo Bay, and the questionable invasion of Iraq, political religion has returned to our culture with a vengeance. In chapter 5 I ask the question, "In whose public square is European religious pluralism envisaged?" I look at some major European and American social theorists regarding public discourse such as Rawls, Rorty, Fish, Stout, and MacIntyre to argue that the various forms of modern and postmodern thinking on this matter spell an end to socio-political religious expression. Why? Because the public square cannot admit "religious reasoning" and demands that religions either provide universally acceptable reasons, or translate and change their discourse before engaging in public debate. I argue that this exalts secular discourse to the status of a new authoritarian religion incapable of dealing with real religious plurality. In chapter 6 I turn to Catholicism and various forms of Islam (for there is no such thing as "Christianity" or "Islam") to see how these traditions construe public space, other religions, and reasoned debate. The outcome of this investigation is that Catholicism and various forms of Islam might better facilitate debate between religions in the public square than might secular proposals. The real clash of civilizations is not between Christianity and Islam but possibly between modernity/postmodernity and religious cultures.

In part IV I turn to a doctrinal question left hanging from part I: how is it intelligible that the just who have not been evangelized might nevertheless be saved, without denying the necessity of Christ for salvation? This is taught by mainstream Roman Catholic tradition, the Orthodox, and certain strands of Reformation theology. To deal with this question I turn to the article in the Apostles' Creed: "he descended into hell." I show how the resources of the Creed can be utilized to answer this difficult question and, indeed, how every level of the descent tradition bears upon the question. The descent is traditionally understood to relate to hell proper, the place of the damned, as well as the limbo of the just, the limbo of unbaptized infants and purgatory. This complex mythological world, which conjures up Dante and a cosmology that seems outdated and quaint to most moderns, nevertheless yields rich theological insights into God's grace, mercy, and justice in relation to our question. Without requiring the reader to accept the cosmology underlying these different circles of hell, I argue that the descent helps to explain how someone with no conceptual knowledge of God here on earth might nevertheless share in the beatific vision, the bliss of eternal life in adoration and worship of the blessed trinity, which entails conceptual knowledge. I focus especially on the limbo of the just in chapter 7 to establish this point. In chapter 8 I show how the doctrine of purgatory profoundly complements the limbo of the just in a manner that is open to the riches and depths of non-Christian religions. I steer clear of granting non-Christian religions salvific status. I also argue against the theology of Hans Urs von Balthasar, whose theology of Holy Saturday, the descent into hell proper, is claimed to solve the problems I seek to address. This solution facilitates a relaxed pastoral approach to non-Christians, rather than an anxiety about their salvation, without undercutting mission.

There are so many more questions that deserve attention that I can only justify my selection by saying that these seemed to me the most urgent and pressing ones. I may be wrong. Many might have desired separate chapters on trinity, incarnation, church, mission, and so on. I hope those readers will find that these topics informed what has been discussed.

Special thanks are in order to people who commented on draft chapters or on presentations of chapters in public lectures. The book would have been the poorer without the advice of: Dr Amir Akrami, Professor Karl Josef Becker SJ, Professor Frank Clooney SJ, Dr Oliver Crisp, Dr Joe DiNoia OP, Professor Paul Griffiths, Professor Savio Hon tai-fai SDB, Augustine Holmes OSB, Rev. Tessa Kuin, Dr David Lauber, Dr Muhammad Legenhausen, Professor Edward Oakes, Dr Reza Shah-Kazemi, Professor Gerard Loughlin, Dr Alyssa Lyra Pitstick, Dr Daniel Strange, Professor Francis Sullivan SJ, David Tollerton, Professor Paul Williams, the monks and audience at Pluscarden Abbey, Inverness, where parts of this book were delivered as the Pluscarden Pentecost Lectures for 2008. Special thanks to Abbott Hugh for his generous hospitality. Thanks also to my editor at Blackwell, Rebecca Harkin, who has been a delight to work with. I am grateful to the Arts and Humanities Research Council for a grant that helped me complete this book, as well as the School of Humanities at the University of Bristol, who granted me study leave to work on the book. My wife and children, Beryl, Roshan, and Sachin, have put up with a distracted and sometimes preoccupied husband and father. My special thanks to them for their support and love. I dedicate this book to my sister Kitty, who was raised a Roman Catholic and has now become a Buddhist. I have learnt much from her; not least, from her humor and love.

PART I

Charting the Territory: Theology of Religions

1

Early Map Making

Introduction

While there are disputed questions *in* the theology of religions, there is in fact a more primary question: what *is* the theology of religions? In these first two chapters I will provide a survey of how the field of theology of religions is currently understood in contemporary theology by different groups that have a stake in the issues. During the survey, I will present arguments for why certain approaches are better than others. My critical analysis is of necessity underdeveloped, but this mapping is intended to help the reader gain a good overall picture of various developments, controversies, and discussions going on in this field. Further, these chapters will also help locate the various disputed questions I pick up in the rest of the book. However, I need to say a few words about the way I understand "theology" so that readers will appropriate the context of my criticisms and constructive proposals.

What is theology?

First, all theology is tradition-specific. That is, it is practiced by a theologian or theologians working within a particular/denominational Christian community, within a particular context, such as a university, seminary, or other religious educational setting. Admittedly, some theologians today do not associate themselves with ecclesial bodies, but most do, and nearly all I examine in this book do. Second, being tradition-specific shapes the manner of our theologizing, its methods, presuppositions, goals, and objectives. Fortunately, there is significant overlap in the manner of theologizing between different Christian denominations, but their differences will always also affect what they hold in common. For instance, a Baptist, a Lutheran, a Catholic, a Greek Orthodox all hold scripture as authoritative, but the latter two might add to this other "authorities," such as tradition (the teachings of the great theologians through history and councils) and liturgy (the prayers and formal liturgy of the church), which are not necessarily accepted or recognized by the first two as regulative authorities in the practice of theology. Further, to tradition and liturgy, theologians within Catholicism will certainly add the authority of the teaching magisterium, including papal authority, although there will be significant differences of interpretation regarding the scope and process by which papal authority is exercised. Thus, within a tradition-specific context, say Catholicism, we have some internal plurality. The limits of Catholic plurality are determined by the teaching office of the church, even when contested by theologians. The limits of plurality in another denomination might be more loosely or more tightly articulated.

Third, tradition-specific argumentation is conducted with what might be called "controlling beliefs," so that creative, innovative, responsive, and faithful theological thought must remain within these controlling beliefs as specified by that community. Theological reflection is always controlled by certain parameters. When people refuse these parameters, for example the Creed, they might form new non-creedal groups (for example, the Quakers) or leave the Christian tradition entirely. Fourth, it is sometimes difficult to argue against those who do not necessarily share one's controlling beliefs and authoritative sources, because the types of authority accepted in the process of theological thinking are quite different, as are the controlling beliefs. Matters are complex, and coming to decisive theological judgments is difficult without at least sharing closely in the tradition-specific manner of doing theology. Fifth, I need to declare my tradition-specific orientation so that the reader can understand the way I handle arguments and assess positions other than my own. I am a Roman Catholic who believes theology is an ecclesial discipline, accountable first to God (in His revelation to us), the church (traditions, councils, magisterium, the sense of the faithful, reason), and finally to all women and men who show any interest in what the church is about ("people of good will" is the novel jargon in official documents in the twentieth century). Hence, in what follows, I will assume that denying the Creed and its trinitarian dogmas is inadmissible. Just as I have never found reading Calvinists, Lutherans, Anglican, or Orthodox theologians a problem or that they are un-ecumenical by writing from within their tradition, I hope the reader will grant me the same freedom.

Christianity in a world of religious plurality

Christianity was born into a religiously pluralist world and throughout its history developed in that context. Sometimes it has been a persecuted minority (in its earliest days, and today especially in the Middle and Far East, in Asia and East Asia, and parts of Africa – see the "Christian monitor" website: www.christianmonitor.org – all websites cited checked in June 2008). At other times it has been part of, or allied to, strong political powers: initially through Constantine (ca 274–337); in the Middle Ages through powerful princes and kings or at times equally powerful popes and bishops; more recently it has been sometimes associated with European expansionism and imperialism. The mandate to go and preach the gospel to the corners of the earth (Matthew 28:19 – "Go therefore and make disciples of all nations, baptizing them in the name of the Father and of the Son and of the Holy Spirit") has always ensured an active engagement with world religions, with very different theological and socio-political attitudes to be found in Christianity's 2000-year history. These attitudes range from the mass enslavement of thousands of non-Christians in South America for not accepting the gospel (even though they knew no Latin, the language in which the gospel was preached to them); to the care of outcasts, the dying, and sick, and development of schools, colleges, hospitals, and infrastructures that were central in the independence movements of many colonized countries; to the partial conversion of whole continents or countries (the western Mediterranean world, southern America, and large swathes of Africa); and, some argue, to the attempted liquidation of the Jews in the Second World War. What should be apparent from this brief list is that we are talking not only about theology but about its social and political embodiments at different times in history.

A cursory look at some statistics may help, although their reliability is a problem, no less than their interpretation. Compare, for instance, a roughly 500-year gap: the difference between 1491 and 2001. In 1491 approximately 19 percent of the world's population was Christian, while 2 percent of the non-Christian world was in contact with Christianity, and 79 percent remained entirely ignorant of its existence. Some 93 percent of all Christians were white Europeans. Compare these figures with 2001, when 33 percent of the global population were Christians, with 40 percent of the non-Christian world being aware of Christianity, while only 26 percent had no contact with Christians and the gospel. The numeric basis of Christianity has also radically shifted so that the largest Christian community is now to be found in Latin America, only then followed by Europe, with Africa third (and growing much faster than Europe), followed by North America and then South Asia.

To get a sense of the broader picture regarding "world religions" it will be helpful to briefly survey the figures for 2001 regarding the numerical strengths of world religions. After Christians (33 percent of the world's population), Muslims are the largest religious group (19.6 percent), followed by Hindus (13.4 percent), with Buddhists at 359 million (5.9 percent). In terms of the traditional five major religions, Judaism is in fact smaller than Sikhism (0.2 percent compared with 0.4 percent) and both are smaller than new religions, admittedly difficult to categorize at 1.7 percent. In terms of future projections, in 2050 it is estimated that the percentage share of the five major religions will be Christianity at 34.3 percent, Islam at 25 percent, Hinduism at 13.2 percent, Buddhism at 4.8 percent, and Judaism at 0.2 percent (Barrett 1991, 32–3; and Barrett *et al.* 2001, 4). Clearly, the number of Hindus is related to India's population growth alone, whereas the numbers for Christianity and Islam relate to population growth and mission in a number of different countries.

There have been many different Christian theological responses to the world religions. To limit ourselves to the post-war period only makes things slightly easier. No set of categories is adequate to analyze and deal with the complexity of the topic, but it may help to label five types of theological response to other religions for heuristic purposes only. I will later be questioning the adequacy of this typology. The typology also historically reflects the movement of the debate through the last half century. There are of course considerable differences between theologians belonging to the same "camp" and many features of overlap between different approaches. Nevertheless, I shall call these five approaches pluralism, inclusivism, exclusivism, comparative theology, and postmodern postliberalism. I shall deal with the first three in this chapter and the next two in the following chapter.

1 *Pluralism*: This comes in three varieties. (a) *Unitary pluralists* hold that all religions are, or can be, equal and valid paths to the one divine reality. "Unitary" indicates a single unitary divine being behind the different plural religious phenomena. (b) *Pluriform pluralists* hold that all religions are, or can be, different paths to different plural divine realities. (c) *Ethical pluralists* hold that all religions are related to the divine insomuch as they contain certain ethical codes and practices, and religions should not be judged according to the conceptual pictures of divine reality they profess. All three

varieties hold that Christ is one revelation among many different and equally important revelations; the religions can learn about the divine from each other; the days of religious imperialism and chauvinism are over, and mission is understood in terms of dialogue.

2 *Inclusivism*: There are two types of inclusivism alleged in the literature. (a) *Structural inclusivists* hold that Christ is the normative revelation of God, although salvation is possible outside of the explicit Christian church. Salvation is, or may be, available through other religions *per se*, but this salvation is always from Christ. This type of inclusivism contains the pluralist legitimation of other religions as salvific structures while also holding to the exclusivist claims of the causal saving grace of Christ alone. (b) *Restrictivist inclusivists* hold that Christ is the normative revelation of God, although salvation is possible outside of the explicit Christian church, but this does not give legitimation to other religions as possible or actual salvific structures. These theologians are careful to restrict the sense of God's inclusiveness to people and elements of their culture, but not their religions *per se*. In both, Christ is ontologically and causally exclusive to salvation, but not necessarily epistemologically. This is *solus Christus* without the *fides ex auditu*.

3 *Exclusivism*: This comes in two basic flavors. (a) *Restrictive-access exclusivists* hold that God elected some for salvation and others for damnation. Because God is exclusively revealed in Jesus Christ (*solus Christus*), we can at least tell that non-Christians (and varying numbers of Christians who are unfaithful – and destined to be so) are destined for damnation. This restricts the number of saved and damned based on God's election. (b) *Universal-access exclusivists* hold that because God is exclusively revealed in Christ, only those who profess Christ can be saved, who hear the gospel (*fides ex auditu*) and confess it in their hearts. The major difference within this latter group is between those who insist that this opportunity to confess Christ must take place for all before death, and those who argue that this can take place at the time of death or after death. Both types of exclusivists hold to *solus Christus* and *fides ex auditu*, and the former can also include *solus ecclesia* (salvation through Christ solely via his church).

Pluralism and structural inclusivism are recent developments in the history of Christian thought. It is for this reason that I shall give them special attention in what follows. All three positions mentioned so far have grappled with central dogmatic questions concerning creation, sin, God, Christ, the trinity, the church, sacraments, mission, and eschatology; in short, the contents of systematic and dogmatic theology. More recent positions, examined in the next chapter, extend the scope of the debate and broaden the agenda most interestingly.

4 *Comparative theology, not theology of religions*: Comparative theology and postliberalism emerged in the late 1980s for three discernable reasons. First, in reaction to the central focus on the question of salvation that has dominated and characterized the debates between pluralism, inclusivism, and exclusivism, these recent movements have moved the agenda to address questions of readings of texts within other religions and their impact on Christian reading and practice, as well as the socio-political aspects of inter-religious meeting. Second, in reaction to the question of the validity (or otherwise) of other religions being discussed in abstraction from those religions, these movements have stressed the particular and contextual engagement with particular religions, avoiding generalizing from one particular to the general. Third, these shifts have also reflected changes in philosophical background beliefs and specialist interests. For example, specialists in the history of religions have shaped comparative theology, and the cultural–linguistic turn (with its neo-Wittgensteinian and pragmatist roots) has shaped many postliberals who have now entered the debate. Comparative theology holds that we should abandon the enterprise of trying to provide overall frameworks *about* religions. Instead, we should engage specifically with a religion in its particularity, not to judge it, but to see what Christianity learns from engagement with those particular sacred texts and practices. We do not need a theology *of* the religions, but multiple theologies *in* engagement *with* religions. The scriptural reasoning movement can be closely aligned to this movement, although its pragmatist orientation is quite different.

5 *Postmodern postliberalism*: Postmodern postliberals are to be distinguished by their drawing on both these philosophical traditions. They generally eschew overarching theological theories about how religions are related to Christianity and focus on the particular social and political engagement, but splinter into two distinctive groups. (a) *Ethical deconstructionists*, like ethical pluralists, want to shift the terms of engagement into politics, in part because some think theology is politics, while others think every theology entails a politics. (b) *Radical Orthodoxy* or *rhetorical out-narrationists* tend to argue that every theology entails a politics, although the two are not reducible to each other. The focus should be on theo-political engagements with a view to rhetorically showing Christianity to be the truth because of its beauty, constantly out-narrating other religions. It contends that only Christianity can produce and underwrite civic peace. Mission, not dialogue, is enjoined. I am sympathetic to some aspects of the latter group.

Pluralism

Pluralism is a very recent phenomenon within Christianity. This kind of approach has its strongest supporters among "liberal," liberationist, process, and feminist theologians – and some "postmodern" theologians too. Although it has been prominent in Anglo-American circles, there are an increasing number of Asian and Southeast Asian theologians developing this approach. To illustrate the three types of pluralism, I will briefly inspect three illustrative representatives, without presuming that they encompass the rich diversity and tensions within the group they represent. My basic argument is that this position is inconsistent with orthodox Christianity and some of it is neo-Christian in its basic presuppositions. The good intentions of the various writers are never in question.

The unitary pluralism of John Hick

John Hick (1922–), a British Presbyterian, initially argued that the *solus Christus* assumption held by exclusivists was incompatible with the Christian teaching of a God who desires to save all people. There are many millions who have never heard of Christ through no fault of their own, before and after the New Testament period – the *inculpably ignorant.* It is therefore un-Christian to think that God would have "ordained that men must be saved in such a way that only a small minority can in fact receive this salvation" (1977, 122). Hick argued that it was God, and not Christianity or Christ, toward whom all religions move and from whom they gain salvation. Hick therefore proposed a God-centered (*theocentric*) revolution away from the Christ-centered (*Christocentric*) or church-centered (*ecclesiocentric*) position that has dominated Christian history. Hick's emphasis on *God* at the center of the universe of faiths is a unitary pluralism, a theistic center, but what then of Christ? Hick argued that the doctrine of the incarnation should be understood "mythically" – as an expression of devotion and commitment by Christians, not as an ontological claim about the unique and exclusive action of God in this particular man, Jesus (1977, 165–77). Hick stressed an all-loving God over the *solus Christus* principle. Hence Hick's initial pluralism is unitary theism, not trinitarian or Christocentric. Technically, it might even be called theistic inclusivism, indicating the ragged edges of these models.

An important later development in Hick's position came in response to the criticism that his theological revolution was still *theocentric* and thereby excluded non-theistic religions. Hick developed a Kantian distinction between the noumenal and phenomenal: between a divine noumenal reality "that exists independently and outside man's perception of it," which he calls the "Eternal One," and the phenomenal world, "which is that world as it appears to our human consciousness," in effect the various human responses to the Eternal One (1989, 233–52). These responses are then seen as including both theistic (e.g., trinity, Yahweh, or Allah) and non-theistic (e.g., *nirvana* or Nirguna Brahman) conceptualities and images. In this way Hick tries to overcome any underlying theistic essentialism or unitary pluralism. However, Hick is not a pluriform pluralist, because what unites both theistic and non-theistic representations for him is a deeper unitary reality, the noumenal Real, beyond theism and non-theism. It is this noumenal Real that forms the unitary pluralism of Hick.

Other unitary pluralists, who are basically theistic, are the English Anglican Alan Race (1983), the Canadian Protestant Wilfred Cantwell Smith (1962), the American Jesuit Roger Haight (1999), and the German ex-Catholic, now Anglican, Perry Schmidt-Leukel (2008).

Critical comments on Hick's unitary pluralism

Hick's motivations are noble. He is keen to offer a fair and balanced philosophical appraisal of how to resolve conflicting religious truth claims, to bypass the "I am right, you are wrong" mentality, to overcome Christian triumphalism and imperialism. He has pioneered work in this area and has generated much reflective argument. But the first question to be asked is whether his unitary pluralism is not in fact a new form of triumphalism and imperialism, albeit of an agnostic type.

I contend that Hick is led into agnosticism when we press his Kantian distinction between the Real in itself and its various phenomenal manifestations in religions. Kant had similar problems with the relation of the noumenal and the phenomenal, which he had to make subject to the categorical imperative, so that religion eventually became a matter of ethics. There is a similar pattern found in Hick when he cannot specify doctrinal criteria for the truthfulness of a religion, but only ethical criteria. Hick's sharp distinction between the noumenal Real and the phenomenal images raises the question of whether there is any real relationship between the two. Hick is so concerned to deprivilege any normative or ontological claim made by Christianity, or any other religion, that he insists there can be no real relationship between the noumenal and phenomenal:

> It follows from this distinction between the Real as it is in itself and as it is thought and experienced through our religious concepts that we cannot apply to the Real *an sich* [in itself] the characteristics encountered in its [various manifestations]. (Hick 1989, 246)

This inability to speak of the Real or allow "it" the possibility of self-utterance leads into a cul-de-sac regarding any valid or normative reference for the Real. Agnosticism is the inevitable outcome of the trajectory of Hick's flight from particularity, a flight helped by his use of "myth": first, from the particularity of the incarnation; then from the particularity of a theistic God; and then from the particularity of any religious claim, be it Christian or non-Christian. The outcome of his escape from particularity leads to nothing in particular. Further, is it not "imperialist" to impose this "Real" upon all religions, even if they insist that the Ultimate Reality is ontologically theistic or non-theistic? Clearly, this is not Hick's intention, but it is an inevitable outcome, despite his stated aims.

A second criticism is that Hick's notion of "myth" employs a purely instrumentalist, rather than also referential, model of language. Take the statement: "Jesus is divine." According to Hick it is mythologically true because it evokes "an appropriate dispositional attitude to its subject matter," such as imitation and devotion, not the claim that Jesus *is* divine (1989, 248). Basically an instrumentalist view of language replaces a referential view. Even if one were to read Hick differently, at best the instrumentalist view that God *is* acting in Christ is emptied of any *sui generis* referential quality so that the incarnational claim relates to a general referential quality shared by all claims that God is acting in history. Hick rules out *a priori* the very possibility claimed by the entire Christian tradition: God becomes man uniquely and exclusively in the incarnation of Jesus Christ. But even this theistic referential view is undermined in Hick's later work as noted above – and that is when his position collapses into agnosticism. For further elaboration on Hick, see D'Costa (2000, 24–30).

The burden of my argument is that Christian language about God is necessarily rooted in the shape of Jesus' life, death, resurrection, the outpouring of the Holy Spirit, and the formation of the Christian community centered on the risen Christ. In theological terms, the trinity is the foundation of the church, or more elaborately: Christocentricism, pneumacentricism, and ecclesiocentricism are inextricably related. This in no way implies that God's activity is restricted to these events or to the Christian church. Orthodox Christians do not compromise the incarnation in acknowledging God's activity in history, but argue it is of a different order to the incarnation – as I shall show. Further, Hick is left with a "pick and mix" divine, without the control of any authoritative revelation. One can simply choose which parts of which tradition one likes. Thus, like Kant, without any authoritative revelation, Hick ends up with authoritative ethics and principles – and, like Kant, with no adequate metaphysical grounding for either. Finally, in the process of deprivileging any and all revelations, Hick ends up mythologizing both theistic and non-theistic claims. Ironically, in his attempt to accommodate the world religions on an equal status within his pluralist outlook, he ends up accommodating none of them as he can only accept them within his system on his, rather than their, terms. This type of pluralism fails in relation to its own goals (granting truth and respect to all religions) and in its non-conformity to orthodox Christian dogmas regarding the incarnation and trinity. Clearly, the latter are not accepted parameters for Hick, although others like Schmidt-Leukel and Haight struggle (unsuccessfully in my judgment) to conform to them.

The pluriform pluralism of Raimundo Panikkar

The Roman Catholic Raimundo Panikkar's (1918–) early work (1964) represents the best in inclusivism. However, after 1973 he develops what I will call pluriform pluralism. Panikkar (1987) argues Christianity must shift in its view of other religions and uses the motif of three rivers to symbolize this: the Jordan, the Tiber, and the Ganges. The Jordan represents Christianity in its earliest days, fighting for survival, with a traditional exclusivist outlook. The Tiber represents the eventual imperial expansion into an inclusivist outlook. The Ganges, today, requires a new baptism in Asian waters, a crossing over into pluralism that makes Panikkar denote himself a "Christian-Hindu-Buddhist." How can he be all three and a Catholic priest?

His answer lies in the cosmotheandric reality that underlies all things, in which the divine, the human, and the earthly are held together indivisibly, yet distinctly. The trinity is Christianity's way of framing this reality, but the reality of the trinity is certainly not exclusive to Christian revelation. Panikkar writes that it is "simply an unwarranted overstatement to affirm that the trinitarian concept of the Ultimate, and with it the whole of reality, is an exclusive Christian insight of revelation" (1973, viii). This is an apparent inversion of Augustine's *vestigia trinititas*, as Panikkar wants to say that Christianity itself has vestiges of this reality that is far greater and deeper than Christian revelation. Other pluriform pluralists are the American Baptist S. Mark Heim (2001) and the process theologians Methodist John B. Cobb (1982) and David Ray Griffin (2005, 3–66).

Panikkar wants to hold a robustly orthodox Christology that Jesus *is* the Logos incarnate, for he has no desire to dilute or water down central confessions of the faith. However, he also wants to steer clear of some implications "read into" this orthodox claim. First, he rejects that the Logos is restricted to Jesus Christ, for this makes the incarnation subject to a type of "Christo-idolatry." This is the danger of exclusivism. Second, he rejects that all salvation comes from the historical Jesus Christ, such that other religions cannot be "saving" in any way. While Panikkar is deeply aware that "salvation" is a Christian term, he wants to speak of the reality of the divine transforming religious traditions, without imputing Christian realities present in a hidden way. This he does by means of a typological exposition of the trinity, not as the object of special revelation, but as a mode of divine action that is trans-Christian. Emphasis on the Son alone, which is currently a problem in the theology of religions debate, is as imbalanced as if theologians were to emphasize the Spirit or Father exclusively. In this cosmotheandric reality "it is our way of looking that causes reality to appear to us sometimes under one aspect and sometimes under another," and Panikkar is happy not to fix God into a single aspect (1973, 75). He wants to emphasize all three modalities together as mutually correcting.

The Father represents the apophatic truth that the divine is utterly other, such that nothing can be properly said of "it" and silence is the purest way of responding to this unfathomable mystery. Allied to this path are the ways of mysticism and asceticism, which strip down the pretensions of the self in the light of the "nothingness" of the divine. This brings about a deep self-surrender or self-forgetfulness, and thus a profound compassion, love, and service. However, for Panikkar, there is always a danger of indifference to the world in this mystical path. He sees various strands of apophatic mysticism within Christianity, and most profoundly within Theravada Buddhism and Advaita Hinduism. The Son is an icon compared to the utter mystery of the Father that is beyond all forms. The Son represents the path of devotion and personalism, the ecstasy of love and joy, mercy and forgiveness, personal reconciliation and humanity. Indeed, Panikkar reads the *kenosis* of Christ, the self-emptying, in terms of the *sunyata* and *nirvana* of Buddhism. He also sees theistic Hinduism within this spirituality. If the danger of the Father's path was worldly indifference, the danger of the Son's path is anthropocentricism, making the human the measure of all things or, in its divine form, assuming God to be a "person" writ large. The Spirit represents the unseen mediator, which is only seen in its powerful effects. This path is also associated with power and charism, and Panikkar relates this to the Shaivite Sakti tradition in Hinduism and within the Tantric Buddhist and Hindu traditions that map the deep powers within the human in which the divine resides, the *kundalini*. The danger of this path is that of idolizing works or rites.

Panikkar is content to allow the reality of each tradition to fructify and transform the others, while recognizing that none has the whole truth and all have some truth, a truth that is pluriform, not unitary. The trinity offers a model of this cosmotheandric reality.

Critical comments on Panikkar's pluriform pluralism

Panikkar's writings constantly defy easy classification. He writes out of a rare spiritual sensibility and has been an inspiration to many. His attempt to penetrate the depth of meaning within other traditions and to find parallels within Christianity is very attractive, as is his searching criticism of Christianity and other forms of religion. He sees the immensity of wisdom and goodness in all religions, as well as the dangers of myopia. However, there are three problematic areas in Panikkar's work.

First, Panikkar inadvertently prioritizes the transcendental Logos over the particularity of Jesus Christ, because for him the scandal of particularity belongs to the age of the river Jordan, not the Ganges. This is a stark change in his book, *The Unknown Christ of Hinduism*, from its first edition (1964) to its second edition (1981). In the first edition Panikkar wrote that the Logos is revealed in Jesus Christ, thus Christianity is "the place where Christ is fully revealed, the end and plenitude of every religion" (1964, 24). In 1981 he changed this: "When I call this link between the finite and the infinite by the name of Christ, I am not presupposing its identification with Jesus of Nazareth" (1981, 27). In this move Panikkar equally disposes of the ecclesiocentric dimension of his early Christocentricism. There is no problem about acknowledging the activity of the Logos in history, in creation for example, as St John does in the prologue (John 1:1–3), but it is deeply problematic to sever the inextricable relationship between the eternal Logos and the incarnate Logos in Jesus Christ. This allows Panikkar to argue that wherever the Logos acts, the risen Christ is not necessarily present. St John's prologue goes in the opposite direction to

Panikkar, as does most of the Christian tradition, for the economy of revelation discloses the immanent relations within the divine reality. These relations are not known prior to revelation, such that it can be said that Jesus is one example of the link between the finite and infinite and that there are many other such links. Augustine, for example, would see vestiges that are anticipations of that reality known in the trinity. Panikkar instead sees images of the different aspects of the divine reality of which the Christian trinity is a vestige.

Second, this subordination of the "historical Jesus" to the "Christ principle" also finds a parallel in Panikkar's subordination of the historical revelation of the trinity to the cosmotheandric principle. This is borne out in Panikkar's unambiguous statement that the trinity is not a unique truth of the self-revelation of the triune God but an insight into a reality that is also equally, but differently, penetrated by the Eastern religions. One must be very clear here. It is permissible, in principle, to argue that the Eastern religions bear vestiges of the trinity, and in this sense, which is not Panikkar's sense, his project might be fruitful. However, it is an altogether different matter to argue that, were the trinity not known in Christianity, then it would be known in these different religions – which Panikkar admittedly never argues explicitly, although it is the implication of his position.

Third, a related objection would be that Christianity and the other religions are being viewed from a place outside of any of the particular traditions through the forging of a kind of religious Esperanto that bears the name of "Christian-Hindu-Buddhist." In some respects, if the control conditions for theology are so dramatically changed, there is nothing to say that within this new paradigm of religious confession such statements as Panikkar makes are problematic. Certainly, Panikkar is not the only Christian to claim such multiple belonging, so the problem is far more complex (see Cornille 2002). At least from the viewpoint of current Catholic orthodoxy, Panikkar's position presents serious Christological and trinitarian difficulties. Paul Knitter, another Catholic, sees the difficulties of unitary and pluriform pluralists and develops an ethical pluralism.

Paul Knitter's ethical pluralism

Knitter, like Hick, is dissatisfied with the usual approaches to other religions and is keen to overcome the alleged "imperialism" of starting with the church, Christ, or God. Like Hick, Knitter started out an exclusivist, went through a Rahnerian inclusivist phase, then a Hickian theocentric phase, and currently holds a liberationist ethical stance. He is dissatisfied with unitary and pluriform pluralists for trying to resolve the problem on theological–philosophical grounds, and criticizes Hick's emphasis on reality-centeredness as it posits a "common essence" to all religions and is therefore prone to the imperialism of imposing a commonality, a oneness, despite real religious differences (Knitter *et al.* 1990, 47–8).

Instead, Knitter argues that all religions are to be judged by their truthfulness, their real responsiveness to what Christians call "God," insofar as religions promote the "kingdom" through their social struggle for the values of "justice," "peace," "tolerance," and "equality." Because the kingdom is characterized by the fruits of the Spirit (for Christians), this pneumatological emphasis bypasses the Christological focus that has been so restrictive for Christians in granting equal status to non-Christian religions. One might say that Knitter takes the ethical emphasis in Hick as his foundational starting point but gives it a Spirit/kingdom basis. Knitter calls his position soteriocentricism, and sees it as an important move beyond Christocentricism, ecclesiocentricism, theocentricism, Hick's realocentricism, or Panikkar cosmotheandricism. While recognizing that the terms "kingdom" and "Spirit" are derived from his own Christian tradition, Knitter is confident that the reality denoted by the kingdom – the struggle for justice and peace – is not an exclusive Christian possession or derived exclusively from Christ or God (1990, 33–48). For example, when religions promote the oppression of women, they are to be judged as being against the kingdom. When they tackle the marginalization and exploitation of the poor and the weak, they promote the kingdom. For Knitter no religion is better than another except by these criteria, and under these criteria they are all in need of reform and mutual help.

Many Asian theologians, such as the Roman Catholics Aloysius Pieris (1988), Felix Wilfred (1991), and also Michael Amaladoss and Samuel Rayan, emphasize the imperialist and colonial patterns of exclusivism and inclusivism, but their basic position is similar to Knitter's in its liberationist orientation. Rosemary Radford Ruether, also Roman Catholic, has further argued that these imperialist patterns have been turned upon the Jews in Christian anti-Semitism, culminating in the Holocaust (1980).

Critical reflections on Knitter

Knitter is to be applauded for bringing the political and ethical dimensions of theology of religions to the fore, for restlessly thinking through the issues and having the courage to change his position in the light of such discussion. But does Knitter's ethical stance bypass unitary and pluriform pluralism? What does soteriocentricism amount to? There are three problems in Knitter's solution.

First, soteriocentricism cannot escape the question of normativity, the framework of meaning that informs "soteria" and the ontological grounding of ethics. Knitter is aware of this, but seems to find "imperialism" on behalf of the poor and marginalized more acceptable than "imperialism" that acts on behalf of correct doctrine (1987, 26). Is this plausible? I think not. First, because Knitter is striving for a common place where differences of doctrine are bypassed, he fails to account for the way in which the paradigmatic and normative sources of a tradition shape the understanding of what "the human condition" is and what it ought to be, and what constitutes "liberative" actions. Hence, "promoting human welfare" is an unhelpful common denominator, as it specifies nothing in particular until each tradition defines the terms. For one tradition it can mean proper adherence to *jati* (caste), for another, it means obeying the most authoritative interpretation of *sharia* (Muslim law), for another, it means adhering to non-contraceptive forms of sexuality, and for another, it might mean opposing all of the above as contrary to liberative justice. In this sense there is no way in which theory can bypass praxis or vice versa. They are always in mutual interaction. And if theory cannot be bypassed, Knitter has not escaped the theoretical problems he found so intractable.

Second, Knitter's emphasis on ethics is deeply reminiscent of the Kantian ethical golden rule employed by Hick. Bluntly summarized: as we cannot agree on religious truths, let us agree on moral truths. The assumption here is that universal moral truths are easy to establish and religious truths deeply contested. However, this relies on two certain presuppositions. First, that there is such a thing as praxis without theory, or a priority given to practice that is able to establish justice. Second, Knitter's view presupposes that ethics is about acting on apparently self-evident right causes: equality, justice, liberty, and so on. This ethical stance is called into question from an Aristotelian virtue–ethics approach in which the relationship of action, theory, and goods is very differently construed. In the Aristotelian view, the *telos* of action is understood in terms of the goods that are internal to particular types of activity, not in terms of their outcome, which leads to consequentialism and pragmatism. Ethics is thus part of a cosmological narrative, inseparable from ontology and complex questions regarding the "good." There is, in effect, no such thing as "action" without "belief," a narrative form that makes it a "good" action.

Third, Knitter's emphasis on the "kingdom" cannot bypass Christ through an emphasis on the Spirit instead. This emphasis on the Spirit as a way of endorsing other religions as God-given and inspired, without having to have an anonymous Christ present, is to be found in Haight and the work of Greek Orthodox George Khodr (1991). It is a problematic strategy for four reasons. First, it introduces a rupture within the trinity that is not to be found in the classical tradition: that somehow the Spirit is ontologically independent of the Son, and the Son's actions are somehow independent of the Spirit's activity. There is a danger of tritheism here. Second, it introduces separability between the kingdom of God and the person of Jesus, thus rendering the kingdom into an ideological programme or a product of human action alone. This is entirely unbiblical and possibly Pelagian in emphasizing salvation by good works. Third, the criterion for discerning the authentic activity of the Spirit is Christological, such that it becomes impossible to criteriologically identify either of the two persons without the other being co-present. Fourth, it is not clear why an "anonymous Christ" is imperialist and an "anonymous Spirit" is not. For an elaboration of these points see D'Costa (2000, 30–40).

Conclusions regarding pluralism

I have given pluralism extended attention due to its widespread popularity and its novelty within the Christian tradition, and tried to indicate various problems with the three types of pluralism I have considered. Unitary pluralism erases the self-understanding of the religions to which it is trying to relate, it provides a meta-solution that is finally framed and based outside any traditional religion – betraying its possibly secular presuppositions: in Hick's case, his Kantianism; in Knitter's, his Marxism. Pluriform pluralism either falls into a covert Christian inclusivism, which is contrary to its intentions, or ends up encoding other religions' ultimate *teloi* within its own single *telos*, thus erasing the self-understanding of the other religion and finally thereby collapsing into a type of unitary pluralism. Ethical pluralism fails to escape from theory, for there can be no ethics or practices without metaphysics or ontology. Practice and theory are indivisible. So pluralism in its three varieties potentially fails according to its own standards and goals. It also seems to fail in violating the controlling beliefs of orthodox Christianity.

Inclusivism

Structural inclusivism is quite novel and has become increasingly popular since the mid-twentieth century. Restrictivist inclusivism has a longer lineage in the Christian tradition insomuch as grace has been acknowledged to operate outside the confines of the visible church. A fair number of Roman Catholics, Orthodox, Reform, and Protestants adopt it. The main differences between the two forms of inclusivism revolve around: first, whether a person can finally come to salvation apart from explicitly confessing Christ; second, whether non-Christian religions can be said to have salvific structures, insofar as it is acknowledged that non-Christians can be saved as non-Christians. On this second issue, structural inclusivists affirm non-Christian religions as "salvific"; otherwise, on the first question we obtain varied answers from both types of inclusivist. I will first focus on the major twentieth-century structural inclusivist, Karl Rahner, a German Jesuit.

Karl Rahner's structural inclusivism

Rahner's (1904–84) theological anthropology shapes his brand of inclusivism, although he also argues his case from various doctrines. In the first case (1968) Rahner argues that the precondition of finite (categorical) knowledge is an unconditional openness to being (*Vorgriff*), which is an unthematic, prereflective awareness of God – who is infinite being. Our transcendental openness to being constitutes both the hiddenness of grace and its prethematic presence at the heart of our existence. Men and women therefore search in history for a categorical disclosure of this hidden grace. In Jesus' total abandonment to God, his total "yes" through his life, death, and resurrection, he is established as the culmination and prime mediator of grace. Therefore Christian revelation is the explicit expression *of* grace, which men and women experience implicitly in the depths of their being when, for example, they reach out through the power *of* grace in trusting love and self-sacrifice or in acts of hope and charity. Rahner attempts to balance the *solus Christus* principle with the doctrine of the *universal salvific will of God*, so as to maintain that Christ is the sole cause *of* salvation in the world, but that this salvific grace may be mediated through history without explicit knowledge of Christ. The *fides ex auditu* is missing from Rahner's position.

What of his second approach (Rahner 1966)? His theological arguments for the same conclusion draw on the history of Israel, which Rahner calls a "lawful religion" prior to the time of Christ. Rahner maintains that Israel remains a lawful religion for those who have never been confronted historically and existentially with the gospel – in effect, the inculpably ignorant. But for Jews who have heard the gospel historically and existentially and rejected it, Israel can no longer be judged "lawful," and such people would be in a state of sin. However, by "historically" and "existentially" Rahner means that although a person might hear the gospel being preached historically (the preacher and the preached to being in the same time and place), that person may not have existentially been addressed for all sorts of reasons (e.g., the preacher's life is dissolute and dishonest, so the hearer does not take the preaching seriously). Hence, the hearer cannot really count as having "heard" the gospel existentially, although historically speaking they will have heard it. If they reject it, they may still not be culpably rejecting it. To return to the argument: if Israel in a certain context had a "lawful religion" prior to Christianity, may it not in principle be the case with other religions of the world prior to their adherents being presented with the gospel? Rahner answers this affirmatively.

Rahner argues that if salvific grace exists outside the visible church, as he believes it does in the history of Israel, in creation, and through conscience, then this grace is causally related to Christ (always and everywhere – as prime mediator) and to his church. Rahner argues that Christology and the doctrine of God cannot be separated from the church, as Christ is historically mediated through the church. This means that Rahner must reconcile membership of the church as a means of salvation and the possibility that salvific grace is mediated outside the historically tangible borders of the church. He does this by employing the traditional Catholic teachings regarding the *votum ecclesia* and the related notion of implicit desire. The *votum ecclesia* (a wish or desire to belong to the church) was understood to count as baptism when for good reason – e.g., being run over by a chariot on the way to baptism, or being martyred before getting to the baptismal font – actual baptism could not be administered but was desired (Rahner 1963b). Furthermore, given the socio-historical nature of men and women, Rahner argues that grace must be mediated historically and socially. The incarnation is paradigmatic of this. Therefore, if and when non-Christians respond to grace, this grace must be normally mediated through the non-Christian's religion, however imperfectly. Hence, non-Christian religions may be "lawful religions" analogously to Israel. Rahner thus coins the terms "anonymous Christian" (this refers to the source of saving grace that is responded to: Christ) and "anonymous Christianity" (this refers to its dynamic orientation toward its definitive historical and social expression: the church).

Because God has already been active within the non-Christian religions, the Christian can be open to learning about God through her non-Christian partner. Furthermore, the Christian is free to engage in active social and political cooperation with non-Christians when appropriate. The structural inclusivist has a firm theological basis for fruitful dialogue. Given Rahner's notion that grace must seek to objectivize itself, mission is clearly important as Christianity is the best expression of grace. Hence, Rahner is able to affirm that Christianity is the one true religion, while at the same time holding that other religions may have a provisional salvific status. On our two questions regarding other religions as provisional salvific structures and the possibility of salvation without explicit confession, Rahner answers that both are possible – the first to be corroborated by the history of religions, the second established through the analogy of implicit faith or *votum ecclesia*.

Objections to Rahner's structural inclusivism

Rahner's influence is enormous and most inclusivists are indebted to him, even non-Catholics such as the evangelical, Clark Pinnock (1992). Rahner sought to correct a historical negative attitude to non-Christian religions and address the same scandal that pluralists rightly react to: that all non-Christians are damned. However, there are five objections to Rahner's structural inclusivism. First, Hans Urs von Balthasar (1994a), a fellow Catholic, argues that Rahner's transcendental anthropology is in danger of conflating nature and grace, and reducing revelation to a predetermined anthropological system. Balthasar is concerned that, by viewing supernatural grace as being part of the very nature of human action apart from revelation, Rahner minimizes both the transforming power of the glory of the Lord that shines forth in Christ's revelation and the character of sin and tragedy. To Balthasar, Rahner has an impoverished theology of the cross.

Second, with respect to his primary analogy of Israel as a lawful religion, Rahner fails to highlight that Israel has this status because it is the "church," not an independent religion prior to Christ, and is heir to the explicit covenant made to God's people. In this respect, Israel should not be seen as an independent religion, nor can it be the basis of an analogy with other religions due to its *sui generis* status in the history of salvation.

Once this is emphasized, Rahner's notion of "lawful religion" collapses, for to allow any other religion such a status would require that it has an *explicit* covenantal relationship with the God revealed in Christ in the way that Israel is in explicit covenanted relationship. This is simply not the case, except possibly in a very deformed sense regarding Islam. Third, and relatedly, there is a further problem in Rahner's application of the *votum ecclesia* tradition to persons in other religions. The "desire for the church" related to those catechemunates who wanted to become baptized and cannot be easily applied to non-Christians who may not even have a belief in God. Catechemunates were saved as their desire for baptism counted as implicit membership of the church. But requisite for implicit membership was explicit knowledge of God and Christ, not an implicit knowledge. Of course theology develops by analogical application and the application of tradition to novel situations, but one must question whether in this application, the point of analogy has been undermined. One can see how explicit theistic belief might be argued to be part of an implicit desire for baptism, as argued by the Jesuits Francisco Suarez (1548–1619) and Juan De Lugo (1583–1660) in the light of the discovery of the "new world" with millions who had never heard the gospel. Based on the minimum requirement of Hebrews 11:6, which calls for the necessity of believing "that God exists and that he is the rewarder of those who seek him," they argued that theism sufficed as an implicit desire for baptism. Hence, one could argue that a Muslim or Hindu theist who has not heard the gospel might have such a desire, and thus could not be counted "lost," but that is entirely different from saying they are saved through Islam or Hinduism *per se*.

Fourth, Rahner was always clear to emphasize the provisional status of other religions as salvific structures, fully recognizing that to do otherwise would posit another revelation alongside Christ's trinity. The removal of this "provisionality" in the work of the neo-Rahnerian, Jacques Dupuis, is one reason Dupuis' book was questioned by the Congregation for the Doctrine of the Faith (CDF 2001). If revelation is the triune God, then the triune God must be proclaimed explicitly in other religions if Rahner is correct. But it is not. Further, the *preparatio evangelica* tradition taught that elements within a philosophy or religion held truths that led a person not to reject the gospel but to be receptive to it, not that those truths were the gospel. They were preparations for the gospel. Even though the *preparatio* was rarely applied to religions other than Israel and primarily to Greek philosophy, there is no theological reason why it should not be so applied. The same goes for the *semina verbi* (seeds of the Word) tradition, whereby Justin and other fathers saw elements of truth found outside the gospel. Justin of course argued that any such religious truths were in fact unacknowledged borrowings from Israel, and any other truths were accessible to reason, leading such people to see the truth of the gospel when confronted by it (see part II for more on this). On these grounds one must question other religions as provisional salvific structures, which is not to say that they are demonic, bad, or incapable of bringing adherents to some relationship with God, but as a whole they are not properly speaking "revelation" and thus a means to salvation.

Fifth, Rahner's own work in other contexts shows that he holds that salvation *is* the explicit beatific vision, and in earlier writings he developed a complex notion of the pancosmic soul, a communal redemption process *after* death, which has some parallels to DiNoia's position (see ch. 2). What is significant is Rahner's ambiguous position on this matter. He both requires explicit faith for the beatific vision and seems not to. Which is it? I would contend that when pushed, Rahner could not hold that the anonymous Christian who has never heard the gospel is "saved" in the proper eschatological sense, but is on the road to salvation. If he allowed that they were saved in the full eschatological sense, he would have to then provide some explanation as to how someone cannot know and yet can know at the same time the triune God in the beatific vision.

None of these objections are definitive, nor am I disallowing the prospect that God saves whomever he wishes to. One cannot restrict the freedom of God. The objections are based purely on tracing the contours of what scripture permits us to say: *as far as we know* the conditions of salvation require *solus Christus*, *fides ex auditu*, and *extra ecclesiam nulla salus*. Second, I am not suggesting that non-Christians are damned. I have made this clear above. Third, I am not arguing that other religions are worthless and have no theological interest. They do, as they are capable of transmitting truth, goodness, and beauty, three transcendental qualities all rooted in the divine nature.

Restrictivist inclusivism and objections

Restrictivist inclusivists hold that Christ is the normative revelation of God, the ontological and causal grounds of salvation, and that baptism is the normal means of salvation. However, they also hold that, because not all have had the opportunity to hear the gospel, a just God makes provision that all might freely accept or reject God through varying means: the natural law inscribed in the universe and in the heart through conscience, or the good, true, and beautiful *elements* within non-Christian religions. They do not accept that other religions *per se* can be salvific means (for reasons given above in my criticism of Rahner), but at their best are preparations for the gospel. Christ is ontologically and causally exclusive to salvation, not epistemologically. This position is apparently advanced by many Roman Catholic, Orthodox, Reform, and Protestant theologians and is sometimes (wrongly) attributed to their respective ecclesial bodies. This position is subject to the first, third, and fifth criticisms advanced above against Rahner. The fifth criticism is the most important: final salvation requires not only an ontological and causal, but also an epistemological relationship to Christ. If the beatific vision requires explicit knowledge and enjoyment of the triune God, then it is not strictly correct to say that such non-Christians are actually saved by these various means. Rather, these means are positive preparations. This is perfectly compatible with saying that these people are destined for salvation. Below, I shall be arguing that the mainstream churches are better seen as exclusivists in precisely this respect, for they clearly stipulate the final epistemic necessity of faith (*fides ex auditu*). One further criticism might be introduced. Restrictivist inclusivists want to affirm the possibility of salvation outside the visible church, which is why they are sometimes called inclusivists (they include non-Christians in the scope of salvation). The objection would be that certain exclusivists allow for this and better explain the epistemologically necessary relationship to Christ that is required as a final means to salvation. Further, positive preparatory status to other religions is entirely compatible with some forms of exclusivism. If both these are the case, the argument amounts to suggesting that the classification is problematic: restrictivist inclusivists are better grouped as universal-access exclusivists, for their aims and goals are fully attained under that heading. Whether this is the case or not will be seen in what follows.

Conclusions regarding inclusivism

I have given structural inclusivism extended attention due to its widespread popularity and relative novelty in the history of theology. I have argued that structural inclusivism becomes either a form of pluralism (as Dupuis so rightly notices in calling his own position inclusivist pluralism), or temporally limited pluralism (in Rahner's case). Both are unsatisfactory because they fail to explain how religious truths that are not the truth of the trinitarian God in Christ can be the means to salvation. Both fail as there is, strictly speaking, no analogy to Israel, for Israel is part of the explicit covenant history of the church. While restrictivist inclusivists do not fall foul of these criticisms, they are still subject to the basic criticism underlying these: they fail to explain how non-explicit Christological means can bring about Christological knowledge that is requisite for salvation. Exclusivism is the only position that seems to hold together all that is required.

Exclusivism

Some argue that exclusivist theology leads to racism, imperialism, sexism, and Eurocentricism. Traces of this dark history cannot be denied, although the causal link is complex. There are persuasive arguments that much missionary work was not in fact pursued in tandem with empire building, but actually resisted it (Stanley 1990). Further, missionaries were central in developing respect and understanding for cultures, partly because of the importance of translating the Bible into indigenous languages, thus enriching local cultures rather than denigrating them. Lamin Sanneh (1987) criticizes the Western "guilt complex" underlying much European theology, which fails to note complex reciprocity. I have highlighted these issues to show the ways in which theological attitudes are indivisible from practices, but with no easily discernable causal links. Exclusivist theologies do not logically and necessarily lead to racist or imperialist attitudes toward non-Christians, although, contingently, they may on occasion. We have seen above how some pluralist theologies can be imperialist! I shall turn to two types of exclusivism, but give more attention to what both exclusivists hold in common, before focusing on the differences.

The exclusivist position was mainstream Christian orthodoxy until the nineteenth century. It is fundamentally concerned to affirm two or/and three central insights. The first is that God has sent his Son, Jesus Christ, to bring salvation into the world and that this salvation is both judgment and mercy to all human beings who are deeply estranged from God. Salvation therefore comes from faith in Christ alone – *solus Christus*. Second, this salvation won by Christ is only available through faith in Christ, which comes from hearing the gospel preached in this life or the next (*fides ex auditu*), requiring repentance, baptism, and the embracing of a new life in Christ. This second axiom distinguishes inclusivists from exclusivists. Third, because Christ is the cause of salvation, the church must also be the means of salvation (*extra ecclesiam nulla salus*). This third view is more emphatically held by Catholics, although it is to be found among some Reformers. There is an important difference between exclusivists that gives rise to restrictive-access exclusivism (RAE) and universal-access exclusivism (UAE).

Restrictive-access exclusivists

RAE is held mainly by strict Calvinists, but also by non-Calvinist evangelicals. One of the best exponents is Carl Henry (1991). RAE has the following differences from UAE. First, it is held that salvation is restricted to those who respond to the preaching of the gospel in this life, which is seen as stipulated in the Bible. The concomitant is that those who do not hear the gospel are lost. Clearly, there is a great urgency for mission, for it is the sole means to salvation. Second, Christ dies only for the elect, not for those destined for perdition. This is the distinctly Calvinist contribution. Third, neither of the above can be deemed to be incompatible with the justice and mercy of God, which is the typical objection introduced by pluralists: an all-loving God could not consign the majority of people to perdition through no fault of their own. Hence this position contradicts God's mercy and justice. Henry replies to this in three steps. First, God's justice is not compromised because justice actually requires that all be damned and none saved, given the fall and rebellion of humans. All are justly damned. Second, God's mercy is seen in Christ's death for the elect sinners, who deserve damnation but are actually saved. We should stand in awe and thanks at God's merciful, free, undeserved gift of his Son. Henry says that the unevangelized are like the fallen angels, destined for damnation because of their rebellion.

There is a further defense on the matter of God's distributive justice, provided by a philosophical retrieval of the doctrine of God's "middle knowledge" in the work of William Lane Craig (1989). Middle knowledge combines a strong view of God's omniscience and an indeterministic view of human freedom. Divine knowledge has the following characteristics. First, God knows all that *could* happen in any possible world. Second, this means that God knows what free persons will choose in any possible situation, without compromising their freedom. Third, God knows all that *will* happen in this world before it has happened. God simply knows all possible outcomes of every possible free choice. Middle knowledge allows God's omniscience to be "expanded" without compromising human freedom. Craig thus argues that God knows that some will reject the gospel, whatever their circumstances, even though they are truly free. So if one claimed a good God could not damn a pre-Christian Amazonian who had never heard the gospel and sought to do the good, Craig responds that this man would never have accepted the gospel even if he had heard it, so it is just, not unjust, that he is damned. "God in His providence has so arranged the world that anyone who would receive Christ has the opportunity to do so" (Craig 1989, 185).

This makes for a clean type, but it should be noted that RAE shades into UAE at certain points, because of various exceptions to the above. Calvin, the alleged master-type of RAE, in fact argues against the rigidity of the rules guiding this model as it would be a constraint on the freedom of God. He argues that the truly elect could be among the non-evangelized and, if this were the case, God would make sure that this person would receive the message of the gospel somehow (Sanders 1994, 57). Henry, for example, more significantly allows that pious Jews before Christ and unbaptized children before the age of reason will also be saved: the first because they have belonged to the "channel" of revealed religion; the second because "they are embraced by covenant theology as members of the family of faith." He argues, rather unconvincingly (given his initial premises), that "Other communions hold that, just as children are counted guilty in Adam without volition of their own, so God accounts them justified in Christ without personal exercise of faith" (1991, 247; better arguments are provided by William Shedd on this matter – see chapter 8).

Critical reflections on restrictive-access exclusivism

It is important not to caricature RAE, for there is no theologian I know who actually argues that God damns people against their will or that God damns people other than because God is just. Rather, what is at stake is a broad set of presuppositions involved in this basically Calvinist/Reform starting point, established at the Synod of Dort (1618) and given the delightful mnemonic of TULIP by J. I. Packer (1983, 4). TULIP stands for the five fundamental points established at Dort: Total depravity (justly damned), Unconditional election (some mercifully saved), Limited atonement (Christ only dies for the elect), Irresistible grace (God's sovereignty is paramount), Preservation of the saints (his restricted saving will must be accomplished). These are challenged from within the Reformed fold. For example, Arminians emphasize human freedom and responsibility in what is called a "libertarian" view of human freedom, which will not allow that God "causes" human decisions. Further, the middle-knowledge claims have been criticized for their curtailment of human freedom (a form of philosophical Arminianism), or because God denies himself such knowledge, or because there is nothing for God to know before a free decision is actually taken (see Hasker 1986; Adams 1977). I am unable to assess these intra-Reform/Calvinist debates except to say that there is a compelling logical force in RAE as outlined above, and it is difficult to resist except in refusal of one or other of its TULIP petals. As a Catholic theologian, I am compelled to reject two in particular: total depravity and limited atonement. I will focus only on the second as, if it falls, then RAE is severely weakened.

Catholics and others reject RAE on the basis of scripture, tradition, and the teachings of the magisterium. I will simply indicate a few aspects of this rejection. According to 1 Timothy 2:3–6:

> God our Saviour *wants everyone to be saved* and reach full knowledge of the truth. For there is only one God, and is only one mediator between God and mankind, himself a man, Christ Jesus, who sacrificed himself as a ransom for them *all*. (My emphasis)

According to Luke 5:31–2, "It is not those who are well who need the doctor, but the sick. I have not come to call the virtuous, but sinners to repentance." These passages are read to imply that Christ's atonement is for all and is not limited. The Reformers protested that, because universalism is false and God's will cannot be thwarted, these verses do not refer to "all" meaning the damned, but "all" meaning all the elect. However, many of the early fathers, councils, and the magisterial tradition interpreted them otherwise. Ambrose certainly follows this line. The Council of Orange in 529 excluded the possibility of God predestining anyone to evil (Denzinger 1955, 200). Pope Innocent X condemned as heresy the proposition that Christ suffered for the predestined only (Denzinger 1955, 1096), and Alexander VIII refused the assertion that Christ had sacrificed himself for the faithful alone (Denzinger 1955, 1294). The controversy against Jansenism consolidated this position. This alternative reading does not permit universalism, but refuses to hold that God's love and mercy is restricted, while allowing human freedom its tragic dimension. This does not mean that God's will to save all is thwarted, because God also wills men and women to choose him freely. I noted at the outset that some differences between Christian positions were shaped by controlling beliefs, and here it is beyond my scope to argue against the controlling beliefs of RAE. My starting point indicates the outline of a wider critique and means (in line with other denominational groups) that UAE is actually required to preserve the truth of revelation.

Universal-access exclusivism

This position is best defined through four rules, some or all of which are adopted by various UAEs and all of which can lead to optimistic or pessimistic outcomes regarding the majority of the unevangelized. The first is that, because not all have heard the gospel, but the *fides ex auditu* requires that all have this opportunity, there will be a chance to respond to the gospel and enter into salvation for all people at the point of death (Catholic: Boros 1965), after death in a post-mortem state (Protestants: Lindbeck 1984; Davis 1990; Fackre 1995), after death in a reincarnation as another person (Protestant: Jathanna 1981), or in purgatory (Catholic: DiNoia 1992). The second rule relies on a middle-knowledge form of argument, which runs like this (Lake 1975). Because God's middle knowledge allows God to know who would and would not accept the gospel among the unevangelized, God simply "applies that gospel even if the person never hears the gospel during his lifetime" (1975, 43). Lake's argument is analogous to the implicit-faith argument, without in any way attributing positive import to any elements within other religions. A third rule simply acknowledges that we cannot and do not know how God will reach the unevangelized who are to be saved, and we cannot exclude such a possibility, but he will do so and it is a legitimate mystery. The evangelical John Stott (Stott and Edwards 1988) occupies this position along with the Calvinist Paul Helm who speaks of "opaque exclusivism" (1991, 274), as does the bishop of the church of South India, Lesslie Newbigin. The fourth rule is that explicit faith and baptism are the normal means to salvation; there can be other means that act as a preparation (*preparatio*) to salvation, which will eventuate in final salvation. How this might happen (the means) varies: through natural revelation in nature (natural law – objectively), in following the good through conscience and reason (natural law – subjectively), or through elements within a religion, but not through that religion *per se*. This would conform to restrictivist inclusivism were it not for the qualification of a *preparatio* status and the further qualification that salvation entails a specific knowledge and full participation in the life of the triune God. These two qualifiers properly complement the restrictivist inclusivist position (but making it UAE as a result) and grant the possibility of a positive status to elements of non-Christian religions. This is the official Catholic position (as I shall argue in part IV) and the position of a wide number of Catholic, Orthodox, Reform, and Protestant theologians. I shall look at one Lutheran and one Catholic to flesh out these rules in the work of actual theologians.

The American Lutheran George Lindbeck, for example, argues that because becoming a Christian is a process of being included into cultural–linguistic practices, then it follows that

> there is no damnation – just as there is no salvation – outside the church. One must, in other words, learn the language of faith before one can know enough about its message knowingly to reject it and thus be lost. (1984, 59)

This position is deeply dependent on the postliberal emphasis on the cultural–linguistic construction of social reality, such that people are shaped by the sign-worlds within which they are raised and that they then subsequently shape. The relationship between different cultural–linguistic worlds is ambiguous. Lindbeck initially spoke about the incommensurability of different worlds, which some have taken to imply a deep relativism in his position. While this is an unresolved debate, I think Lindbeck's position implies that we cannot simply judge one world X, from the perspective of another world Y, in terms of that judgment being *meaningful* to those in X. Hence, what is required is that a Y learns the language of an X, like an Englishwoman might learn German, or better a Christian learns the language and practices of a Hindu so that they can understand the inner logic, the practices that are entailed by various beliefs, the way in which beliefs and practices evolve within the rules of the Hindu tradition. In this way a Christian might be able to make evaluative intra-traditional judgments about Hinduism (and vice versa). In terms of the metaphor of learning languages, in this process, both languages are being enriched, at least for person X. If Lindbeck really held religions as cultural–linguistic forms to be incommensurable, it would be impossible to understand another religion at all. It would make no sense for him to even suggest learning another language. It is very important for various aspects of our debate to understand this point. With no damnation outside the church in place, Lindbeck suggests a program of real engagement between Christianity and other religions in the spirit of open learning and mission. Lindbeck also holds out a hope, not a certainty, for the salvation of all and suggests a post-mortem confrontation with Christ (thereby satisfying the *fides ex auditu* principle) to allow that all non-Christians who have not heard the gospel in this life have a chance of salvation. Lindbeck claims the benefit of this position is that it does not entail a negative judgment on non-Christian religions, nor does it imply that "below" or "above" their own self-knowledge, which is thoroughly cultural–linguistic, something else non-cultural–linguistic is going on, such as hidden grace or "anonymous Christianity" (Rahner). I find Lindbeck's position deeply attractive and will develop it in part IV, closely following Joseph DiNoia.

The Roman Catholic DiNoia develops Lindbeck's position in two ways. First, in terms of the doctrine of purgatory (a process of purification after death and prior to the beatific vision, which is the final eschatological enjoyment of the blessed trinity in heaven in communion with the redeemed) as the means whereby the non-Christian who has already responded positively to God in this life will be purified and will hear the gospel, thus satisfying the *fides ex auditu*. Second, DiNoia leaves it open as to whether other religions play a role in God's plan of salvation – they may and they may not, but their different aims and means must be seen clearly for what they are. DiNoia is resolute that Rahner's way of affirming another religion as a possible anonymous Christianity, as a possible means of salvation, is problematic in neglecting the explicit stated goals and the means for achieving these as taught explicitly by that religion. Rahner imposes a goal upon a non-Christian religion in calling it "anonymous Christianity," which is "not the aim fostered by their distinctive patterns of life but that fostered by the Christian pattern of life" (DiNoia 1992, 77). DiNoia develops this point quite differently from Lindbeck due to his knowledge of Buddhism and also in his careful argument that Buddhism, for example, might be understood to be providential (indirectly contributing to final salvation) though not salvific (directly contributing) (1992, 92).

What unites Lindbeck and DiNoia is their concern to facilitate universal accessibility, not universalism, that satisfies the epistemological, ontological, and causal necessity of Christ for salvation, the necessity of baptism into the church (in differing manners), a respectful listening to other religions to see how they envisage reality and the means to attain that reality, and the possibility of affirming elements of both means and goal, but always recognizing that this involves Christian interpretation and appropriation.

Some criticisms of universal-access exclusivism

I support the first and fourth types of UAE and also, as argued, a modified form of restrictive inclusivism, which is best transformed into UAE. I am unhappy with rules two and three. I disagree with Lake's position, not on middle-knowledge grounds, but because it does not clarify itself from restrictivist inclusivism (which it could) and more importantly does not actually show why we cannot articulate the way this salvation might happen given a rich biblical and historical set of speculations (which it could). If it does do this, then it will move into either the first or the fourth rule-group. I disagree with Stott, Heim, and Newbigin on the same grounds. The premature resort to mystery is rather like the traditional Orthodox resort to mystery in explaining the change in the Eucharist when affirming "Real Presence." If one cannot give reasons for asserting mystery as an answer, then it is probable that mystery is a premature answer.

Between types one and four there is an important disputed question that I shall explore in part IV of this book. On the one hand, if a person's destiny is fixed at death and they can make no choice after death affecting their destiny, which is the teaching of the Catholic church, then what of the *fides ex auditu* principle? This is a particular problem for Catholic theologians. On the other hand, if a person's destiny is not fixed at death, allowing for a post-mortem "conversion" and thus satisfying the *fides ex auditu*, then what of the necessity of mission and the strong Augustinian tradition that a person's destiny is fixed at death? This is a particular problem for Reformed theologians. In part IV I shall suggest a resolution that allows for the *fides ex auditu* as well as the Augustinian prohibition that a person's destiny is fixed at death.

Conclusions regarding exclusivism

I have argued against RAE on inconclusive grounds regarding basic shaping doctrines. I have affirmed UAE on positive grounds, especially in terms of its forms in rules one and four. I have claimed that I shall attend to a serious issue among UAEs in the final part of this book and I have claimed that UAEs properly hold together a wide range of doctrinal teachings that constitute orthodoxy, while allowing for the salvation of the unevangelized without affirming other religions as means of salvation. UAEs can also affirm positive elements within other religions and acknowledge what is good, true, and beautiful within them. UAEs best advance the authenticity of the Christian tradition and in fact the position of the Catholic and Orthodox churches, and a number of Reformation communions.

This takes us to the end of our mapping exercise and discussion between the three emergent positions in the early period of the late twentieth century. I have also argued that all major forms of pluralism and inclusivism are problematic in serious ways – which justifies the extensive treatment granted to them. No argument against these positions is decisive, as space has restricted the scope and extent of argument. I will be developing my form of UAE throughout this book, and extending its scope into social and political dimensions of religious pluralism. Let us now turn to more recent discussions in the theology of religions in the past twenty years to see how this map has been filled out or, indeed, been discarded.

2

Changing the Angle: Recent Maps

Some Criticisms of the Threefold Typology

Before proceeding, it is time to register some problems with the threefold typology of pluralism, inclusivism, and exclusivism. The typology has been useful, like a raft crossing a river, to get to where we are now. But is the raft still useful? There are two main issues. First, the threefold typology fails to deliver on the question of the salvation of the unbeliever in a precise enough sense. For instance we find that Barth, Rahner, and Hick, traditionally classified as exclusivist, inclusivist, and pluralist respectively, can all be regarded as holding forms of universalism. Hick and Barth hold universalism as a certainty rather than a hope, as does Rahner. This means that all hold virtually similar views about the outcome of salvation for the world, but in the threefold typology they are categorized in very different ways. Or, to use another example, we have seen that so-called inclusivists like Rahner, when pressed, have to admit a *fides ex auditu*, a face-to-face relationship with Christ, which undercuts the effects of their argument that a person finds salvation through a provisionally lawful religion. What we find is that at a certain point on the inclusivist spectrum the distinction between inclusivist and exclusivist becomes vague or blurred. Similarly, at the other end of the inclusivist spectrum, it is difficult to distinguish the difference between pluralism and inclusivism, which is what causes Dupuis to call himself an inclusivist-pluralist, holding to Christ's salvific efficacy in all cases, but allowing other religions to be substitutive salvific means.

These examples show the difficulties of precise categorization, but they also indicate the possible need to construe differing positions along a different axis. From the discussion so far, I would suggest a seven-graded classification on the precise question of how a person is saved. This will really help us make significant distinctions between positions and focus precisely on the *means* and the *goal* of *salvation*. This will also allow us to see positions where the goal is the same but the means differ, and note positions where the goals are different. In the latter case, if the goal is not the beatific vision, we can safely judge this is not a Christian position. Clearly, there will be significant overlap where different positions can share the same goals, but differ on some means, though not all; and positions holding the same means might emphasize them in very different ways. The seven means/goals would be: through the trinity (trinity-centered), through Christ (Christ-centered), through the Spirit (Spirit-centered), through the church (church-centered), through God not conceived of in a trinitarian fashion, but in a theistic fashion (theocentric), through the Real that is beyond all classification (reality-centered), through good works (ethics-centered).

A second reason for abandoning this threefold paradigm is that the terminology conceals the fact that all the different positions are exclusive in a very proper technical sense. The pluralisms of Hick and Knitter are indebted to agnostic liberalism, thus imposing upon all religions an exclusive hurdle which they must conform to if they are to grow up from their parochial adolescence. Unwittingly, Hick and Knitter stifle real religious differences, which are now encoded within their exclusive narrative about how things should be to be truthful to reality, a narrative that stops religions pursuing their own agendas in their own terms. They are reality-centered and ethics-centered exclusivists. It is also quite right to claim that they are hard-line exclusivists for agnostic liberalism (or in Panikkar's case, for a gnostic triadic "real" called "trinity"). This is also true for inclusivists, for they too are exclusivists in the sense of holding an exclusive criterion for what constitutes truth. Hence, Rahner holds to the exclusive truth of Christ and nevertheless allows for the provisional validity of non-Christian religions until they are historically and existentially confronted by the true religion. If they are not confronted in this life, Rahner in other writings not related to religious pluralism still holds that they will be confronted in the next, in some manner; otherwise they will not be able to share the beatific vision. In this sense, his provisional inclusivism is eschatologically a strong exclusivism. I think it would be possible to analyze every theologian in the previous chapter and show that they are operating with an exclusivist singular particular notion of truth. Their differences lie not in this structural foundational similarity, but in their way of developing their position out of their particular notions of truth. Some of these positions are not rooted in the trinity and Christ and can therefore be called post-Christian or neo-Christian theologizing. We have to make theological judgments about the adequacy of these positions in relation to the traditions they represent and the intra-traditional arguments that then come into view.

I am suggesting it would be more fruitful to stage an argument between a liberal Protestant exclusivist and a transcendental Thomist exclusivist than to stage the argument between a pluralist and an inclusivist, for to stage it in the former terms allows us to see more clearly what is theologically at stake in the differing construals, not just isolate one question (the salvation of the non-Christian) as if it were the only question constituting the theology of religions. It is not, as we shall see below. The point I am making is that, by shifting attention to the seven categories, we helpfully lose the rhetorical and polemical heat from the terms pluralist, inclusivist, and exclusivist (as if the first were generous with God's salvation, the second more grudgingly so, and the last plain mean) and focus instead on the substantive theological issues that must be resolved in fidelity to the Christian tradition.

The seven "centricisms" act as shorthand. I would contend that the first five are required for Catholic orthodoxy, and the first three are required for Protestant/Reformed orthodoxy. If the last three are used normatively at the expense of the first four, this results in heterodoxy. For example, if God is emphasized, as in the early Hick, this bypasses the self-revelation of that particular God in Jesus Christ. Or, if reality is emphasized, as in the later Hick, it is in danger of floating free from any God, let alone that confessed in Christianity. If ethical practices are emphasized, as in the later Knitter, their grounding, their authority and shape, become hidden, such that a secular liberal agenda can easily be smuggled in as normative to all religions. Further, of the first four, if any single one of the means to salvation is emphasized exclusively at the cost of the others, various imbalances will set in. For example, when Christocentricism is rigorously emphasized, the universal action of God's Spirit can be dangerously downplayed, as we saw in Carl Henry. If the Spirit alone is emphasized, it can conceal the Christological dimensions that must always be implicit, as we saw in Knitter. If the church is emphasized on its own, it can lead to maintaining that all those who die outside its visible boundaries are doomed to perdition, a teaching rejected by the very groups (some Catholics, Orthodox, and Lutherans) that are deeply ecclesiocentric. And if the trinity alone is emphasized, we see that it can be detached from the community of practice within which it is confessed and which it shapes, such that it could lead to a type of gnostic triad as in Panikkar, which can never be definitively anchored in history.

Let me summarize my argument so far. Our three positions have been generated in relation to the question of the salvation of the non-Christian, a clear pastoral and theological issue. I have basically argued that universal accessible exclusivists have the best theological arguments insomuch as they keep with four required tenets: salvation comes from the triune God through faith in Christ and his church, through the power of the Spirit. These four tenets are non-negotiable (which of course requires more argument, but certainly has the mainstream western and eastern Christian traditions behind it). This does not entail the denigration of non-Christian religions or any negative outcome regarding their eventual individual and communal salvation. While many elements of pluralism and inclusivism are important, the various types of models that I have inspected compromise on one or more of the three tenets that I consider central. I have also argued it is time to contextualize or to jettison the threefold paradigm, and instead focus on the seven dogmatic issues revealed in digging through this field. I have left myriad issues unexamined and can only claim tentative status for my argument so far, but I hope this survey will have left the reader with a vivid sense of the vitality of the debate between the 1950s and 1980s. We can now turn to more recent developments, which have not meant a unilateral shift in the debate, but rather new types of interlocution and challenges.

Comparative Theology

The following constitute a loose and evolving group, some tightly clustered around Boston, USA: Francis Clooney, Jim Fredericks – both Catholic priests – and Protestant colleagues John Berthrong and Robert Cummings Neville; and others elsewhere such as David Burrell, Leo Lefubre, Pim Valkenberg, Michael Barnes, and John Keenan with Western backgrounds; and Sebastian Painadath, Joseph Pathrapankal, and Francis Veneeth from Asia. Their internal diversities are significant, but they tend to be united on seven points. First, as Fredericks put it, "all three options [pluralism, inclusivism, and exclusivism] inoculate Christians against the power and novelty of other religious traditions" (1999, 167). Why? Fredericks argues that theologies of religion have been fixated on the question of the salvation of the non-Christian and had very little interest in the religions as such. It is time for this to change. The dialogue between religions must become the center of the stage as it reflects the real situation of religions in modern society. Second, dialogue must precede theology of religions, for dialogue is "a process or practice, not a theory" and thus we "must first learn *about* non-Christians" "from" them, before theorizing "about" them (Fredericks 1999, 9). Third, in this approach, the specific religion in a particular context becomes the focus, so that comparativists tend to be specialists in a religion: Clooney, Veneeth, and Painadath in Hinduism; Fredericks, Lefubre, and Keenan in Buddhism; Valkenberg and Burrell in Islam (and Burrell triangulates with Judaism as well).

Fourth, and relatedly, the grand theories of theologies of religion generated by the threefold paradigm must now make way for a theology in engagement with religions, thus comparative theology, not theology of religions. Comparativist close readings of specific texts and practices are grounded on the assumption that one cannot speak in generalized ways about religions ("Hinduism is theistic," "Buddhism excludes worship as there is no God," and so on), but that the religions become known only through close engagements with their texts and practices and historical contexts. This in part is a cultural–linguistic point, that meanings are generated through the practice of texts and cannot be divorced from the cultural–linguistic world within which they are given. For example, saying that Hinduism is theistic immediately assumes that "theism" in Hinduism is cognate with "theism" when used in Islam or Christianity. "Theism" is shaped by texts and practices as Clooney (1993) shows of Hinduism and Christianity, which might cause us to draw back from abstract comparisons and start moving back and forth between these texts exploring how our Christian reading and practice of "theism" might be transformed in the process.

Fifth, this process differs from comparative religions insomuch as it is a theological engagement with the other as well as a theological self-transformation in light of this engagement with the other. Comparative religion traditionally sought understanding of similarities and differences without assuming involvement and transformation of the comparativist's own religion. Finally, for a minority, such an engagement might lead to "multiple identities" where, for example, Panikkar says he left Europe as a Christian, found himself as a Hindu and returned as a Buddhist, while always remaining a Christian. This multiple belonging is not only the preserve of remarkable individuals, but is also found among cultures, as in Japan and to a limited extent in Sri Lanka (see Van Bragt 2002; and Harris 2002, respectively). However, multiple belonging is not representative of, or the goal of, comparative theology, the latter of which is to be transformed by the novelty and power of another tradition while being deeply faithful to one's own religion, which leads to the sixth point. Fredericks is very critical of pluralists who mythologize Christ as a pre-requisite to dialogue for it is precisely difficult differences and loyalty to tradition that make dialogue engaging. All the comparativists want to uphold strong doctrinal claims and represent Christianity in its orthodox form. Seventh, comparative theology is a call for multiple theologies in engagement, not a singular theology of religions.

Allied to the comparative-theology movement, there has been a promising Jewish–Christian–Muslim dialogue through the inspiration of the Virginia-based Peter Ochs' scriptural-reasoning project. David Ford at Cambridge has been the champion of the project in the UK. Either two or three of the traditions come together to read each other's sacred scripture and discover how, for example, friendship or usury is understood by each tradition. In this process, there is also attention to the forms of reasoning generated in the reading of scripture, which develops a dialogue between the traditions that began in medieval Spain and late-medieval France and Italy. This is an open-ended process that is keen to build communities of friends and cooperative readers. The London Central Mosque Trust and Islamic Cultural Centre published a *fatwa* (legal decision) in 2002 requiring equal leadership and partnership in every practicable way as a condition of engagement in this movement, because of the history of improper power balances in such dialogues and because of the sacred status of the Quran. While scriptural reasoning as it exists is dependent on Ochs' indebtedness to Charles Pierce's philosophical pragmatism, which may cause some concern to some religious persons in its dependence on democracy (see Lamberth 2008; and chapter 5 of this book), the way this movement will develop is difficult to predict. Interestingly Ochs contrasts his own reading strategy in the context of Semitic interfaith engagement with two others, one of which we have already met in pluralism, and the other of which we have already met in exclusivism and will meet again in the work of John Milbank (see below). It is worth citing in full:

> Liberal theologians may argue that Christians, Jews, and Muslims must reinterpret their scriptures in the interest of universal principles of human rights, justice, and peace. Radical Orthodox theologians may argue that universal peace can be guaranteed only through the truths disclosed in Christ, who *is* peace. Postliberal theologians [Ochs' own position] may argue that the inter-Abrahamic study of scripture should both strengthen each of the three Abrahamic traditions of faith and disclose scripture's rules for cooperative reasoning among the three traditions. (Ochs 2005, 659)

Some criticisms of comparative theology

I am in basic agreement with some important claims made by comparative theologians. First, they are right to emphasize the importance of particular and contextual engagement between religions. This avoids generalizations about religions and enables one to be more sensitive to historical intra-religious diversity. This is important, for both Christianity and other religions have been construed as monolithic entities, which they are not, and each engagement generates very different concerns, which may not be the concern of a future generation. Hence, a meeting between modern Jews and Christians in the United States may have an agenda that has little or no resemblance to a meeting between medieval or fourth-century Jews and Christians in Spain or in Egypt respectively. Second, it is right to highlight the significance of allowing close textual and practical engagement with another religion to transform our Christian self-understanding, as can be seen in the recent Jewish–Christian dialogues that have been shaped by the Holocaust and the subsequent Christian retrieval of its Jewish roots. In this process, Christians are called to engage with this aspect of their sometimes repressed tradition. The scriptural-reasoning movement generated by Peter Ochs also provides a good example of this taking place among Christians, Jews, and sometimes Muslims. Third, comparative theology rightly draws attention to other questions than the salvation of the non-Christian, and looks at varying conceptions and practices of God (in Clooney's work), mediation (in Fredericks' work), and rationality and tradition-specific ways of argument (in Burrell's work). Fourth, comparative theologians are right to emphasize the theological nature of their enterprise in contrast to the comparative religions' tradition, which is committed to comparing and contrasting, not making judgments about truth and not concerned to grow traditions through the process of dialogue. However, might comparativists have perhaps failed to achieve their own goals? I shall be criticizing comparative theologians for not being concerned enough about the process of judgment and the issue of truth, but focusing on inculturation out of relation with mission and dogmatics.

First, Fredericks perhaps overstates the case in arguing that dialogue must precede theology. As in my argument with Knitter above, I think that practice and theory cannot be rent asunder. Indeed, if one is going to argue with a particular type of pluralist, inclusivist, or exclusivist that they should be open to the "power and novelty" of other religions, one has to do so theologically. If an exclusivist held that other religions are of no interest except in terms of mission, one would have to challenge the theological axioms that generate this attitude, not simply rule out this starting point as invalid. On this Clooney and Fredericks differ, as Clooney thinks inclusivism is best flushed out in comparative theology:

> Inclusivism's insistence that salvation is in Christ alone and yet universally available is a perplexing double claim which, if merely stated, may suggest incoherence. Yet now, in the context of [comparative theology] this complexity appears as part of its vitality. (Clooney 1990, 73)

It is noteworthy that, technically, Clooney's description of inclusivism conforms to my description of universal-access exclusivism and both forms of inclusivism – which serves to indicate that Clooney's inclusivism (and he has not written enough on this to differentiate his form of inclusivism further) and forms of exclusivism would be consonant with comparative theology, contrary to Fredericks' claim. This also explains my own enthusiasm for the project, despite my reservations about inclusivism. Indeed, there may be a conflation of categories in Fredericks' criticism of the threefold model, for there are particular dogmatic tasks that must be addressed, as well as further questions regarding mission, inculturation, and so on. Fredericks conflates different questions that require attention independently of dialogue and also in relation to dialogue. Stephen Duffy (1999) has characterized this difference as one between *a priori* theologies (theology of religions) and *a posteriori* theology (comparative theology), which takes the sting out of Fredericks' critique and also illuminates the manner in which Clooney rightly dovetails the two projects. I will return to the slight problem with Duffy's definition below.

My second question will use Clooney's position as an example, but is addressed to comparative theologians as a whole. While it is very good to stress the self-transformation involved in the exercise of engaging with the other (their texts and practices), what of questions of truth in the engagement with another religion's text? Clooney's response is subtle. He does not want to occlude the question of truth, but wishes to stress that with his respect for context, the tension between intra-textuality and inter-textuality, one cannot jump out of one context (Christianity) to criticize a textured practice and belief in another context (Hinduism) by alien criteria (from Christianity). As it stands, this could be simple cultural relativism, but Clooney is not eschewing the question of truth, insisting instead that it requires a long patient engagement with the embodied, textured nature of the claims. What is perplexing is the interesting phenomenon that none of the comparativists seem willing to make these types of judgments concerning questions of truth. These are too early days to judge the comparativists, but one might raise two tentative ancillary questions. If there are no challenges and questionings of these other texts, but simply a self-referential transformation, can this be called "comparative," "dialogue," or even Christian? Mission, intrinsic to Christian witness, seems to have no place in the theological project except a deferred role. To put it differently, inculturation (which is another term for the transformation that Fredericks and Clooney speak of) is divorced from mission and this may reflect that it is contextually defined by academic practice, not ecclesiological witness. Further, if comparative theology is allied to real engagement with living religious people, although obviously it need not be in terms of some of its explicit goals, then are these texts not susceptible to critical questioning in respectful and reverential study, both intra-textually and inter-textually? Compare the two editions of Panikkar's classic study, *The Unknown Christ of Hinduism* (1964; 1981). In the first edition Panikkar undertook what I take to be comparative theology of the type I would advocate. The detail of his first edition is helpful to understand my contention.

Panikkar tries to grasp Hinduism in its own terms and then asks whether Hinduism in any way anticipates the God-Man, Jesus Christ. This question is only answered by a thorough grounding in the Hindu texts he will consider, in their own context (intra-textually). Panikkar then tries to answer "yes," intra-textually, through an exegesis of the celebrated passage in the *Brahma Sutra* 1.i.ii, which reads "janmadi asya yatah," which is traditionally rendered "Brahman is that whence the origin, sustaining and transformation of this world comes"; in effect, "Brahman is the total ultimate cause of the world." Through the centuries this important text has been interpreted differently by the many philosophical commentators in their *bhasyas* (commentaries). For Sankara's Advaita Vedanta, a major Hindu monist school, the problem in interpreting this text was to retain the absoluteness of Brahman, the unconditioned reality. Bridging the gap between Brahman and the world was, and is, a major problem in Hindu philosophy. The followers of Sankara felt that Brahman's unconditioned and absolute nature would be compromised if Brahman was admitted as the cause of the world and consequently held that this cause was not properly Brahman, but Isvara, the Lord. However, the text maintained its integrity if it was understood that Isvara, the personal God, was in fact the unqualified Brahman in his personal, qualified aspect. Therefore, Isvara becomes the link between the undifferentiated Brahman and the created world. It is at this point in the exegesis that Panikkar suggests that the solution to the antinomy of the One and Many, Brahman and the world, is solved if we realize that Isvara is none other than Christ, the Logos, the Mediator between God and Man. Panikkar is claiming that this is a genuine intra-textual question, conducted on proper intra-textual grounds, but becomes charged in a dynamic inter-textual context, when Hinduism and Christianity meet. His Christological *bhasya* concludes:

> That from which all things proceed and to which all things return and by which all things are (sustained in their own being) that "that" is God . . . not God the Father and source of the whole Divinity, but the true Isvara, God the Son, the Logos, the Christ. (1964, 126)

Panikkar is intervening within a Hindu debate regarding the question of the supremacy of Brahman and Isvara. To further support his argument he draws upon the *Bhagavad Gita* and *bhakti* (devotional) schools where the notion of a personal God is privileged. He is aware that, in popular worship, followers adore Krishna, Hari, Siva, Rama, and other gods, but he notes that in reflective stages the devotionalists often recognize that it is the same Lord that they worship, even if in different forms. Drawing on this *bhakti* tradition then, Isvara is seen to be the bringer of grace, revealer of Brahman, the destroyer of *maya*, allowing souls to recognize their true relationship with Brahman, and although distinct from Brahman, Isvara is also identical to Brahman. Panikkar ends this stunning and careful exegetical exercise drawing out its very clear theological rationale. In Hinduism

> Christ has not unveiled his whole face, has not yet completed his mission there. He still has to grow up and be recognised. Moreover, He still has to be crucified there, dying with Hinduism as he died with Judaism and with the Hellenistic religions in order to rise again, as the same Christ (who is already in Hinduism), but then as a risen Hinduism, as Christianity. (1964, 17)

This too is comparative theology, but in a mode that is not at all present in the work of the comparative theologians I have examined. It exhibits all the positive characteristics of the present movement, but in contrast is also able to really engage with the other, asking penetrating questions, putting challenges, engaging in mission at the very same time as really trying to understand the other in their own terms. No one has criticized

Panikkar of reading into texts or inadequate indological training, but in the process Christians have learnt deeply about Hinduism as it is and about certain *aporias* that beg a response. I see no theological or cultural–linguistic reason why comparative theology cannot move in this direction. The reticence, besides a healthy humility, might be a psychological reaction to the charge that such readings of Hindu texts are imperialist. Fredericks says of Rahner's position "that it puts Christians in a position of claiming to know more about non-Christians that they know about themselves" (1999, 31). I do not find this criticism convincing. Panikkar's exegesis, which comes from a Rahnerian approach, claims no such thing. It asks the question, it probes and pushes and suggests. It reads the Hindu texts with Hindus, never forgetting that this reading is both intra-textual (in the plural, as Sankara and Ramanuja are at loggerheads about the reading of the *Brahma Sutra* 1.i.ii) and inter-textual (Panikkar the Christian is now reading these texts). It poses questions to the Hindu self-understanding in terms of the Hindu tradition itself and it daringly suggests that internal problems within Hinduism are better resolved within the Christian tradition, or a Christianized form of Hinduism. It is thoroughly sensitive to contexts and texts within the Hindu tradition and the context of the reading operation from the Christian tradition. If imperialist charges are leveled at this process by Fredericks, they can equally be turned back on published comparative readings in two ways. First, such comparative exercises are often done in the absence of a Hindu dialogue partner (except in the form of texts). This is not true of scriptural reasoning, which is always done in company. Second, because there is no interaction with, or challenge to, the Hindu community or readers, the Hindu texts simply serve to feed Christian self-development and in this process are taken out of the control of the community that historically "owns" the *Gita* or other Hindu scriptures.

I do not want to discuss Panikkar's second edition of the book as this has been done in chapter 1. I mention this change in Panikkar only to indicate why I am slightly uneasy about Duffy's distinction between theology of religions (*a priori*) and comparative theology (*a posteriori*). Panikkar's book indicates that there are porous boundaries between these two terms for, in doing comparative theology, one's theology of religion might change and vice versa. We saw Knitter's change from exclusivism to inclusivism and eventually to ethical pluralism through dialogue and reflection over the years, and likewise Panikkar's. Indeed, through the process of dialogue and reflection, I have moved from being a structural inclusivist to a universal-access exclusivist. I would prefer to see theology of religions and comparative theology as complementary, as aspects of dogma on the one hand, and missiology and inculturation on the other. In the latter, the reality of other religions must be confronted and its exact contours responded to in terms of apologetics, proclamation, dialogue, and learning from, and one must be attentive to the ways in which some of the new findings might generate fresh dogmatic questions. An example of the latter comes in part IV of this book. One other interesting lesson to draw from Panikkar's change is to show that comparative theology can dovetail with any of the old three paradigms or, in effect, any of the seven criteria for a new theology of religions. Each would bring out different dimensions and, in consistency with my earlier argument, I would suggest that the emphasis on trinitarian ecclesiocentricism is both the most traditional and the most innovative manner of moving forward (see further D'Costa 2000).

Postmodern Postliberalism

Postliberalism has shaped an entire cluster of theologians in interestingly different and related ways. We have seen this in comparative theology and scriptural reasoning in the work of Lindbeck and DiNoia, and will now see it, mixed with postmodern influences, in ethical deconstructionism and Radical Orthodoxy. These more radical postliberals seek to redefine the agenda for this field because they offer new conceptualizations of theology, one of which I will reject and the other, critically, accept. I will first turn to the ethical deconstructionist wing of this new group.

Ethical deconstructionism

The Roman Catholic Henrique Pinto's *Foucault, Christianity and Interfaith Dialogue* (2003) is indebted to the French deconstructionist philosopher Michel Foucault. Pinto is concerned to view Christianity as a set of practices, rather than an abstract, ahistorical truth "out there," utilizing Foucault's relentless genealogical historicism (tracing the historical production and perpetuation of ideas and concepts) to undermine unitary notions of "Christianity," or indeed, the "world religions." Each of these "religions" can only be analyzed in its specific historical sets of praxis to display both what its language enjoins in terms of practices and what that language generates in terms of fields of discourse and intelligibility, of institutional repressions, oppressions, and pleasures. Pinto is critical of the threefold paradigm, for to him all three positions are based on a unitary model of truth (2003, 30). According to Pinto, exclusivists claim they have the truth and no one else does. Inclusivists claim to have the truth, understood in Christological and/or ecclesiological terms, and that others have bits and pieces, or poorer or brighter shades of that truth. Truth in both models, according to Pinto, is unitary and essentializing, reproducing the marks of imperialist discourse (as defined by Foucault and accepted by Pinto). To Pinto, pluralists like Hick and Panikkar are guilty of this same epistemological fault, for they evade the real differences and historical tensions between religions. Pinto does not recognize the category of pluriform pluralism such as I have defined it, although his own position inadvertently makes out a Foucauldian case for it.

Pinto's own alternative eschews unitary and overarching systems of explanation and instead proposes history and genealogy: the drama of the struggle of forces and power that discipline and punish, that generate communities of practice, that constantly and restlessly are, or should be, open to relentless criticism (both self-criticism and criticism from others). Foucault is sometimes accused of nihilism, not only because of his Nietzschian pedigree, but also because of his claim of having no "position." However, Pinto argues that Foucault is not a nihilist but an ethicist of freedom, struggling to keep open every position to criticism and suspicion, including his own. Pinto seeks to overturn fundamental epistemological models operating in mainstream theology (his definition) that draw a clear line between the divine and the human, between the unique truth of religion and the contingent truths of history, between the transcendent God and the limitations of creation. In dissolving these binaries, Pinto argues that religions, and thus interfaith dialogue, are drawn into the groundless dialogical play of historical becoming. This becoming is not pure constructivism, but the interaction with the Foucauldian "More," a "finite infinity," a "bio-historical production," always "exceeding the production of ourselves," not an "eternal *esse indistinctum*" (Pinto 2003, 124–5).

How does this theoretical shift affect interfaith dialogue? Dialogue is now not centralized around any one religion's privileged focus on its *own* "truth," but upon the emergence of ethical practices out of the flux of history whereby the religions allow practices to transform and challenge each other. The human–divine has no single center, and it would be wrong for the theologian to practice theology as an ever-deepening attempt to understand the Word of God found in the inspired scriptures and handed down by the living tradition of the church. In Pinto's interfaith dialogue, such "imperialist" privileging is no longer possible. Pinto is clear that he is not arguing that faith communities abandon reading and practicing their own scriptures, but that to practice and read them properly requires a co-reading with other religious communities that are thrown together in the modern world.

Some criticisms of ethical deconstructionism

There is something to be admired in Pinto's analysis: his critique of the reification of "religion"; his concern to ground religious language in practices; his recognizing the weakness of unitary pluralism; his concern for emancipation; and his stress on reading other scriptures. However, none of these qualities are particular to his position alone and one must question Pinto's allowing of philosophy to dictate to theology so unilaterally. Foucault's "epistemology" dictates the limits and bounds of both reason and theology. Here there are two issues. First, at a methodological level, there is a relentless translation of all theology through Foucauldian lenses, thereby conflating theology into philosophy such that the independence of the former is entirely restricted and controlled by the latter, a certain irony for a position that constantly wants to overcome the imposition of discourses of power and control. For example, Pinto is content to dictate to the Roman Catholic church what theology should be and criticizes the church on the sole theological ground that theologians of the Pinto-type cannot accept the theological premise that "Christ is the ultimate revelation of God." The main objection is not really theological, but rather the Foucauldian analysis disallows any absolute metaphysical statements, any such norming within history. In Pinto's hands, theology has no proper object.

The second objection against Pinto would be that a new norm is smuggled in by adopting Foucault, despite Pinto's and Foucault's claim that Foucault's genealogical project does not contain any norms (Pinto 2003, 84–5). This of course is at the center of the famous debate between Foucault and Jürgen Habermas. I think that Habermas' criticism of genealogy is significant in highlighting Foucault's weakness:

> to the extent that it [Foucault's genealogy] retreats into reflectionless objectivity of a nonparticipatory, ascetic description of kaleidoscopically changing practices of power, genealogical historiography emerges from its cocoon as precisely the *presentic, relativistic, cryptonormative* illusory science that it does not want to be. (Habermas 1987, 263)

Habermas, in this rather breathtaking sentence, nicely locates the way relativists are relativized despite themselves, that a view from nowhere is always a masked view from somewhere. This relativistic crypto-normativity promotes a kind of Kantian negative theology insomuch as no formulation of the divine can be accepted as having any ontological relation to the Real. The effect of this is to change dogmatics into critical philosophy, and "truth" and "salvation" are negated of any positive dogmatic content. This weakness regarding the possibility of speaking truth relates the postmodern Pinto with the modernist Hick, insomuch as epistemologically both sever any ontological link between history, language, and God. Alasdair MacIntyre has argued that the postmodern is purely parasitic upon the modern and cannot furrow a new path, only an anti-path, which inevitably mirrors the path it rejects. This could be one demonstration of MacIntyre's astute insight, and MacIntyre offers many other examples (MacIntyre 1990).

My analysis of Pinto might also explain why Kenneth Surin's (1990) brilliant demolition of pluralism, in more detailed form than Pinto actually offers, is still unable to move toward a positive theological contribution, for Surin, like Pinto, also conflates theology with politics. This perhaps explains Surin's change of discipline to political literary criticism, but theology cannot be conflated with politics, even if it entails a politics. Pinto might perhaps be placed in the pluralist camp because of his relativistic, crypto-normative approach. In the final analysis, it could be argued of him that he simply replaces Hick's Kantian "Real" by Foucault's "More" and his project is then no different from the pluralist figures of Hick and Knitter, except in what Foucault brings freshly to the project. Further, this would also mean that Pinto's theological credentials must be questioned, for he seems to make Christology, trinity, and church all secondary to his Foucauldian framework.

Radical Orthodoxy: John Milbank's rhetorical out-narration

John Milbank, the British Anglo-Catholic, shares some of Pinto's genealogical concerns without transforming theology into genealogy. Milbank has learnt much from postmodernity, but his unique contribution lies in finding a theological voice whereby theology is able to criticize culture and to see how many intellectual disciplines have usurped theology. Milbank tries to show how sociology, politics, and the other disciplines read the world from their viewpoint, often encoding religion within alien reductive categories. His constructive work is to develop an alternative Christian narrative and culture to the world's ways of encoding God's creation without God. Milbank's view of theology of religions can be summarized in six points, the first three of which cover ground that is now familiar and indicates his postliberal pedigree. First, he is suspicious of essentializing "religion" and criticizes the covert modern liberal Christianization that takes place when "religion" is viewed as a genus. Instead, following the cultural–linguistic turn, he views the "religious" as the "basic organizing categories for an entire culture: the images, word-forms, and practices which specify 'what there is' for a particular society" (1990b, 117). He would thus agree with Pinto's criticism of unitive pluralism and certain types of inclusivism that see in others only pale reflections of the self. In chapters 3 and 4 I will return to this constantly recurring problem of defining "religion."

Second, Milbank is deeply critical of the emphasis on ethical practice, as if it were able to avoid theory/theology. He traces the genealogy of this abstraction called ethical "praxis" in the work of Knitter and others to discern, rightly, "the universal discourse in modernity," whereby laws and rules are prioritized over all other discourses and, indeed, police all other discourses. The ethical turn is spurious because it assumes that theory can be bypassed by emphasizing social practices alone, as if they could be practiced or embodied apart from theory. This point will be elaborated in some detail in chapter 5. Third, Milbank points to the imperialism of the pluralist project in showing how Knitter's demands are an imposition of various ethical criteria deriving from secular norms imposed on all religions. Secular notions of "justice," "peace," and "tolerance," which have linguistic echoes with the Christian tradition and echoes with the English translated terms of other religions, are made normative for all religions. According to Milbank, Knitter advances the spurious argument that there is agreement within these religions about such norms. The only agreement comes from secular liberals within each religion who fail to represent the religious tradition in terms of their founding texts and key pre-modern authoritative traditions. Fourth, Milbank contests that the trinity is equivalent to the Hindu divine (mainly with reference to Panikkar and others) by showing how Eastern and Western construals of power, justice, and the good are deeply at variance. In the light of this, Milbank adds the warning that we should be suspicious of modern Hindus keen to engage in dialogue as they are likely to be more representative of liberal modernity (as are Knitter, Hick, and others) than truly representative of their ancient religious traditions. Polemically, but incisively, he suggests that dialogue with ancient dead texts is more profitable than speaking with live moderns who "betray an alienation from the seamless narrative succession of a tradition which never felt the need for dialogical self-justification" (1990b, 178). Milbank's point is important, as he rightfully locates the deep discontinuity between pre-modern and modern versions of many religions. I will develop this point in the next two parts of this book. Milbank's attitude to Judaism is quite different insomuch as he rightly sees it as part of the Christian heritage, and his occasional engagement with Islam (e.g., 2007) recognizes the importance of some family resemblances within the three Abrahamic theistic faiths.

Fifth, Milbank's cultural–linguistic approach does not snag on incommensurability between religions, which is a danger with Lindbeck's approach. Milbank is also clear that there are no commonly accepted norms whereby religious cultures can debate fundamental matters decisively, for all rationalities are tradition-specific embodiments rooted to the authority of a revelation, texts, or teachings within which reason operates to explicate and defend the basic vision of the founding revelation, texts, or teachings. There is no place for rational dialectics in terms of mutually accepted fundamental starting points (the use of reasoned argument to defeat an opponent decisively), although there is a place for limited reasoned criticism, noting internal inconsistencies, poor argumentation, and faithlessness to the sources. On this point Milbank is very critical of what he sees as Alasdair MacIntyre's espousal of rational dialectics. Milbank calls for mission, not dialogue, in the sense that Christians are called to out-narrate other discourses. "Out-narrate" simply indicates that there can be no commonly agreed criteria outside of Catholic Christianity itself whereby Christianity's truth can be "secured," "shown," "established" to a non-Christian. "Out-narrate" suggests that only through the display of Christ can the beauty and truth of Christ be apprehended, thus Milbank's emphasis on mission rather than dialogue. Sixth, nowhere does Milbank give attention to the question of the salvation of the unevangelized and the types of issues discussed within the threefold paradigm, for he has produced a different mapping that invites us to attend to new socio-political questions, because postliberalism and postmodernism have at least established one thing: Christianity is a form of social power. Milbank strategically negotiates this new emphasis with a retrieval of pre-modern Christianity to show that Christianity is uniquely equipped to deal with the modern, the postmodern, and alternative forms of religious discourse, because Christianity *is* the truth. In Ochs' words: "Radical Orthodox theologians may argue that universal peace can be guaranteed only through the truths disclosed in Christ, who *is* peace" (2005, 659).

Critical reflection on John Milbank

Milbank's position is important. I entirely agree with his first three points as outlined above. Regarding his fourth point, while Milbank's criticism of modernity's distorting impact upon religions East and West is germane, his comments on Hinduism perhaps overstate the case. Milbank assumes that all religious traditions are constructed out of a "seamless narrative succession," which is an uncharacteristic ahistorical judgment. Hinduism of all traditions has far from a "seamless narrative succession," for Hinduism displays cultural forms in which, for example, caste has been deeply contested or alternatively fully embedded in what it is to be a Hindu. Or, to give another example, it constitutes profound devotional theism (Madhva) and an austere philosophical monism that also incorporates a vibrant devotionalism (Sankara), it conducts sophisticated philosophical "dialogical self-justification" against the Buddhists (Sankara), and in turn these self-justifications are intra-textually debated (as between Ramanuja and Sankara). Furthermore, one might ask how it is that Milbank can adjudicate between what might be "legitimate" Hindu developments, without any recourse to the complex symphony of Hindu voices, or differing notions of authority within the traditions of Hinduism, and deem himself the arbiter of pristine Hinduism ("we ourselves have to conjure up" real Hinduism from " 'dead' texts pre-dating Western intrusion" – Milbank 1990b, 178). I would not wish to push this criticism too hard, because Milbank is right to raise the problem about the authenticity of discourse. I have been arguing that unitive and ethical pluralism are not forms of Christian discourse, despite their self-description, because they are unable to defend, maintain, or start from the orthodox Christologies of Nicaea and Chalcedon. Further, Milbank's point about neo-Hinduism is supported by an "orthodox" Hindu, Nirad C. Chaudhuri, whom Milbank quotes, even though Chaudhuri's thesis is deeply contested among Hindu and non-Hindu scholars. The matter is complex.

Regarding Milbank's fifth point, he faces the cultural–linguistic dilemma head on. He does not fall into relativism or incommensurability, the easy lures, nor does he assume a common ground of reason. However, I am not sure whether he can justify the call to out-narration (not in its missionary orientation, but in its assumption of no shared criteria) without a lot more argument. While there is no doubt about different embodied traditions within which reason operates, and thus no pure reason that hovers above all traditions, two issues arise. If God creates all men and women in Her image, does the cultural–linguistic entirely eradicate this sense of some common origins and purpose? Notwithstanding the force of sin, both original and subsequent, and its impact structurally, the answer, by Milbank's own criteria, ought to be "let us look and see," not his *a priori* dismissal. To put this differently, while pluralists and inclusivists too often emphasize the commonalities between religions, and exclusivists and postliberals rightly emphasize the difference and discontinuities, it is more appropriate to speak of analogy instead, which does proper justice to both continuity and discontinuity: the recognition of points of contact and similarities, but always within a greater difference. David Burrell (2004) has achieved this analogical imagination in his exploration of faith and freedom within the Christian, Jewish, and Muslim traditions precisely because these three traditions have inculturated the Greek Aristotelian heritage. Burrell shows how Christian reflection on all sorts of themes is deepened through this comparative engagement with Judaism and Islam. This in effect allows Burrell to carry out rational dialectics in a manner ideologically disallowed by Milbank's unnecessarily pushing "out-narration" to its limits. Ironically, Milbank's own project is reliant on rational dialects, when for instance he creatively suggests that "one could attempt to show how the Buddhist commitment to compassion and non-violence inconsistently exceeds the Eastern goals of power and freedom" (1990b, 190). Such a task would have to use rational dialectics and would be analogous to Panikkar's task with Hinduism in his first edition of *The Unknown Christ*. Milbank's major work, *Theology and Social Theory*, is also deeply reliant on rational dialectics or immanent criticisms (showing how positions internally collapse through unresolved lacunae, internal contradictions, or gaping difficulties), and it is unhelpful to emphasize just one aspect of the dynamics that operate when two traditions engage.

While out-narration is required, both in its missionary and in its methodological sense, should it be held in an "either/or" contrast with rational dialectics? Indeed, should discontinuity be pressed so hard by Milbank that it becomes almost inexplicable, when he writes that "we should indeed expect to constantly receive Christ again, from the unique spiritual responses of other cultures" (1990b, 190)? How could one possibly "receive" Christ "from" another culture on Milbank's terms except if there is the possibility of some common ground, even within greater dissimilarities? I am of course touching on the bigger issue of apologetics and the postliberal inclination, following Barth, to eschew apologetics as contaminating theology. Some argue that, if one starts employing the terms and thought-world of non-Christians, one eventually translates Christianity into non-Christian categories, leading to assimilation, not conversion, which is one goal of engaging with non-Christian cultures. While there is an instructive truth here, I do not think it commends itself as a binding rule against careful inculturation, but it is a rule against uncritical assimilation. I have serious reservations about Milbank regarding his rejection of rational dialectics for it misses an opportunity to attain his own goal of "showing" Christianity to be the truth about the world. Further, eschewing rational dialectics is basically inconsistent given Milbank's practice in executing his own project. Otherwise, I share Milbank's orientation and concerns.

Conclusions

The comparativists and postmodern postliberals rightly alert us to the socio-political nature of theology insomuch as the church is in the world and theology is always an embodied practice. This recognition throws up a host of interesting disputed questions in the field of theology of religions – which will be the focus of parts II and III. Any politics that emerges out of theology is always an ecclesial politics, that is, it follows from the Christ-shaped church that is a response to God's revelation, which testifies to the truth of redemption by God, not by human projects and plans. I shall return to this theme in part III. These new movements in the theology of religions also challenge us to recognize a whole cluster of questions that have tended to be occluded from the past 50 years of debate, admittedly for historically explicable reasons. I have already suggested that the comparativist agenda is complementary to the theology of religions, not in a clean *a posteriori* fashion as suggested by Duffy, but nevertheless representing a different stage of reflection. I have also suggested that the comparativist agenda is really a question of inculturation and criticized it for neglecting missiological concerns. In the case of postliberal out-narration, we return to a proper emphasis on mission, but with a neglect of inculturation and rational discussion. Further, with Lindbeck, DiNoia, and Clooney, we see the way postliberalism brings about a close attention to how texts and practices shape us and the viewing of religion as culture, rather than in more abstract categories. Hence, along with our seven dogmatically oriented categories, we might now add two more non-dogmatic ones in the light of the discussion in this chapter: mission (which is a socio-political action) and inculturation (which is also a social and political process). These latter cannot be attended to without close knowledge of the actual culture or religion that is being engaged, both in its historical perspective and in its contemporary shape. The first seven tasks are central to dogmatics, the second two to missiology. My concern to graft theology of religions and the historical study of religions into a traditional theological framework is twofold. First, that the properly theological questions receive appropriate theological attention. Second, that the different aspects of various questions also generated be properly treated within their requisite disciplinary areas, and appropriately related to theology. There is a great danger of theology of religions being seen as some sort of esoteric interest that is not central to the basic tasks of theology.

The rest of this book will deal with some of the new questions raised by these more recent developments (chapters 3 to 6) and some older questions raised by the previous threefold typology (chapters 7 and 8). It is my hope that the reader will have become aware of a huge range of questions that need further attention, ranging from dogmatic issues to social and political ones, and including methodological questions. As we proceed, we will constantly move between these three areas, which, as has become evident in the preceding two chapters, are actually inseparable, even if they are also distinct. Hence, it is possible to address some questions raised in the theology of religions without any knowledge of another religion, and it is impossible to address other questions without detailed and focused knowledge of another religion. The field is an exciting one where dual competences and cooperative endeavor are required, as the dogmatic theologian, the historian of religion, and the political theologian must work together and sometimes be the same person. As with any area of theology, it is demanding, and it also requires learning beyond the traditional boundaries of the theological discipline. Nevertheless, historically, the greatest theologians have often done just this: Aquinas, for instance, in his immersion in the Aristotelian heritage transmitted through the Arabs, injected into theology both new vigor and a profound critique of alternative traditions. Dialogue and mission are indeed part of the same activity.

PART II

The Making and Meaning of Religions

3

Modernity's Story

Introduction

There are a cluster of disputed questions here but the one that will keep us engaged in this chapter will also provide vistas on to later chapters. The single question is: what precisely is a "religion"? To address this question and indicate the complex landscape involved, I am first going to write an answer to this question derived from the work of a number of scholars in the form of a single narrative history. This particular story and various versions of it are deeply embedded in many European societies and in parts of North America. It is the story offered by "modernity," by which I mean loosely the story of history told by those who more or less accept the Enlightenment as a necessary, mainly liberating, immovable turning point in providing our understanding of realities such as "religion," "state," "civic society," "politics," "law," and "tolerance." In the next chapter I will write an alternative narrative, which will unpick the first, trying to advance a different picture of the issues. Admittedly, reality is rarely a matter of either/or narratives, but this will at least highlight some important issues at stake. I have chosen this format, which is quite different from the previous chapter, as the history of the production of "religion" (for there once was no such concept) is so closely tied to a number of other issues, such as politics, economics, capitalism, modernity, and postmodernity, that story-telling allows the interconnections to become more clear. Just as a "character" in a biblical story or novel is only composed by their interrelationships to other characters and contexts constructed within that narrative, so is the character of "religion" in Europe's narrative.

If you think you know what "religion" is and want to skip this chapter, I shall make a claim that will hopefully keep you reading: "religion" was an invention of the sixteenth century, and deeply rooted in the work of the Cambridge Platonists; by the eighteenth century it was more a product of the European imagination than an encounter with an alternative form of power and discipline; and by the twentieth century "religion" became a shadow of its pre-modern self precisely because it was allocated a private, not public, role in the political sphere; a role policed by modernity. It might even help things greatly if we scrapped the word "religion" and instead replaced it with "culture" and asked ourselves about a theology of culture, rather than a theology of religions. Let me turn to the first narrative.

Modernity's Story about Religions

The first stage of the story up until the Reformation needs to be fast-forwarded as it is a basic backdrop to the modern stage with which we are concerned. Christianity, after the fourth century, established a form of Constantinianism. From a minority fringe group that had been persecuted by worldly powers, it became part of the worldly powers with the "conversion" of the emperor Constantine. This conversion owed much to Constantine's mother Helena and was also part of a rather politically astute move to consolidate and unite fractious and diverse territorial rulers. Christianity slowly became the imperially endorsed religion and there was sporadic persecution of Jews, and the often bloody territorial conflicts with Islam. This meant that "religion" was basically related to the big three – Christianity, Judaism, and Islam – and a dying fourth – paganism – which involved other religious and non-religious groups. The successful emergence of the Roman Empire meant that at least for most of what we now know as "Europe," Christianity was the privileged and protected religion. Theologians variously worked out how the civic and armed forms of the body politic had duties to protect and defend the practices of Christianity. Theology and law were intrinsically interrelated; society was basically "Christian."

Act I: the war of religions

Until the Reformation, the Catholic church in the West was only really opposed by Islam and various Catholic princes and rulers who came into conflict with the Papacy, although contesting groups usually liked to claim fidelity to the church as the motivation of their actions. After the fifteenth century, the Reformation brought about dramatic changes. Martin Luther

(1483–1546) and John Calvin (1509–64), in their resistance to the Catholic church's corrupt practices and problematic theology, initiated internal wars in Europe that would cost the lives and liberty of thousands of citizens, as Catholics and Protestants battled for supremacy. The religious wars were bloody and protracted, the first starting with Charles V's attack on the Lutheran states in 1547, which only ended with the Peace of Augsburg in 1555. Augsburg recognized the existence of Catholicism and Lutheranism (but not Calvinism) in Germany, and provided that the people should follow the religion of their local ruler (*cuius region eius religio*). This "Peace" continued as the basis of the ecclesiastical settlement in the Empire until the later Treaty of Westphalia of 1648, concluded after the last and most bloody of the religious wars. In the meantime, in France for example, such barbarities as the St Bartholomew's Day massacre took place, where thousands of Protestants were murdered by Catherine de Medici in 1572. She sought to eradicate Protestants and wipe out the Huguenot leadership. Finally, between 1618 and 1648, the bloodiest of the wars of religion were fought, in which Emperor Ferdinand II tried to establish a Catholic Habsburg Empire. The Peace of Westphalia signaled the end of the Holy Roman Empire. Westphalia legitimated Calvinism, restraining princes from changing religions, and constricting the power of the Roman see. The latter, not surprisingly, brought a strong denunciation from Pope Innocent X (*Zelo Domus Dei*, 1648), but these were the last flaying movements of an ecclesial spent force.

Europe might at last struggle free from the authoritarian domination of "religion" understood as the power of a single "religion," thus facilitating real religious plurality. Anthony Kenny summarizes the situation thus, and I cite in full because of his succinct and now well established trope:

> In the first half of the seventeenth century Europe worked out, by political and military means, the consequences of the religious reformation. It was the age of the wars of religion. In France, three decades of civil war between Catholic and Calvinist came to an end in 1598 when the Calvinist leader, Henri de Navarre, having converted to Rome and succeeded to the throne as Henri IV, established by the Edict of Nantes toleration for Calvinists within a Catholic state. In 1618 the Holy Roman Emperor Ferdinand II formed a Catholic League to fight the German Protestant princes; it defeated the Protestant elector Frederick V at the battle of the White Mountain near Prague, and re-imposed Catholicism in Bohemia. But this Catholic victory was followed by a succession of Protestant victories won by the Swedish king, Gustavus Adolphus. After his death the Thirty Year War was brought to an end in 1648 by the Peace of Westphalia, which established co-existence in

> the Empire between two religions. In Britain, after the defeat of the Spanish Armada in 1588, and the enthronement of King James I from Calvinist Scotland, there was little serious chance of England returning to Catholicism, despite the fantasies of the Gunpowder Plotters in 1605. (2006, 206)

What would be required to facilitate a religiously pluralist society had already been partly put in place by Luther in his treatise *Temporal Authority: To What Extent It Should Be Obeyed* (1523). Luther established his two-kingdom doctrine, with two arenas of governance: the secular and the ecclesial. While God granted coercive power to the secular body, as society is made up of sinners and requires the rule of law, the ecclesial body must concern itself purely with preaching the Word of God. Its authority was the Word and the power of preaching, not social coercion. It took the genius of Hugo Grotius, who had entered Leyden University at the age of 12, to dismantle the connection between law and theology. Through his groundbreaking *De Jure Belli ac Pacis* (1625), Grotius became the father of international law. Grotius rooted justice in the unalterable law of nature whose source was the social being of humankind, not in any theological vision or datum. This would facilitate the possibility of a lawful society without roots in any specific religion.

Act II: the lessons of the wars and the emergence of free Europe

The religious wars taught many Europeans two very important lessons. First, when religion controlled society, that society was incapable of dealing with religious differences, for it was fundamental to the religious spirit that error should be eliminated, and that meant large numbers of men, women, and children dead. Second, if the concept of society led to bloody conflict when based on clashing religious allegiances, then it should be required that a non-religious, non-partisan form of government emerge to secure peace, freedom, tolerance, and prosperity, a state of affairs containing differences productively and non-violently. It is no coincidence that the emergence of the nation state in the seventeenth century dovetails with the waning public influence of religion. It is for this reason that modern political theorists like the early John Rawls, the early Jeffrey Stout, and Judith Shaklar all concur with Stout's claim that:

> liberal principles were the right ones to adopt when competing religious beliefs and divergent conceptions of the good embroiled Europe in the

> religious wars. . . . Our early modern ancestors were right to secularize public discourse in the interest of minimizing the ill effects of religious disagreement. (1981, 241)

Or, in Shaklar's words, liberalism

> was born out of the cruelties of the religious civil wars, which forever rendered the claims of Christian charity a rebuke to all religious institutions and parties. If the faith was to survive at all, it would do so privately. (1984, 5)

Act III: "religion" applied more widely to the "world religions": the Christianization of the religions

If acts I and II are narrated from the emergence of the secular, act III fills the picture out by plotting Christianity's involvement in the process. We will find three trajectories here, and the third, deism, joins the currents of secularism in the nineteenth century. This conjunction of theological deism and the secular has been charted by Buckley in *At the Origins of Modern Atheism* (1987). An important feature of the seventeenth century is the application of "religion" in relation to what we today call the world "religions" by theologians. The story runs something like this, and I am indebted to Peter Harrison's *"Religion" and the Religions in the English Enlightenment* (1990). Harrison's study is seminal in examining the English Enlightenment's part in the production of "religion." He follows Wilfred Cantwell Smith's thesis (1962) that during the age of reason the name "religion" was given to external aspects of religious life, in contrast to the Middle Ages, which emphasized "faith," the dynamics of the heart, and personal piety. This externalizing process was now related to four "religions": Christianity, Judaism, Mahometanism, and heathenism (as they were called then). However, Harrison contests the often touted nineteenth-century starting date for the scientific study of religion, *Religionwissenschaft* (exemplified in the works of Max Müller and C. P. Tiele), and places the starting date in the sixteenth and seventeenth centuries in England, in the debates between the Protestant Scholastics, Platonists, and deists. Harrison argues that this is the important precursor to the French Enlightenment, because nowhere in Europe at that time were such religious freedoms enjoyed as in England (with the possible exception of the Netherlands). His claim is monumental: "The whole comparative approach to religion was directly related to confessional disputes within Christianity" (1990, 3). What precisely were these disputes?

Just the ones we examined in chapter 1: who is saved? The connection between these two issues is vital and will be clearer as we proceed.

First, a note on the term "religion." The modern expression "the religions" found its way into English vocabulary at about the same time as "religion." The earliest occurrence of the singular form is in Hooker's *On the Lawes of Ecclesiastical Politie* ([1593] 1632, 180), where we find the following usage: "The church of Rome, they say . . . did almost out of all religions take whatsoever had any fair and gorgeous show." With the publication, eighty years later, of the first edition of Edward Brerwood's *Enquiries Touching the Diversity of Languages and Religions through the Chief Parts of the World*, the plural expression, "religions" entered common usage. In his preface, Brerwood explains that there are "four sorts of Sects of Religion" – Christianity, Mahometanism, Judaism, and paganism – making it clear that these "religions" are species of the generic "religion."

Harrison depicts three theological positions in English circles, which were crucial to the origins of "religion": the Protestant Scholastics, the Cambridge Platonists, and the deists, who respectively drew upon the Reformation, Renaissance, and Classical heritages. The Protestant Scholastics came out of the Calvinist and Lutheran traditions in their approach. Because revealed religion (Christ and the trinity) equals the truth that is required for salvation, all non-Christian religions are inadequate. Indeed, while non-Christian religions may have natural revelation present, that which is present to all creation through the use of reason and an examination of the natural world, this is sufficient only to be grounds for their damnation. They know enough to be judged guilty. For the Christian, knowing about these religions serves no real purpose except in defeating the enemy.

It is with the second tradition that "religion" really begins to appear as a discrete object of study, even though constructed and inspected entirely for theological reasons. This is where our theological story gets off the ground and relates to the wars of religion narrative in act I. The Cambridge Platonists were a group of seventeenth-century English theologians and philosophers who were distinguished by their veneration of Plato and Plotinus, their opposition to religious fanaticism, and their preaching of a reasonable religion of holiness. Even so, there was serious diversity between the major figures of Benjamin Whichcote, Ralph Cudworth, Henry More, and John Smith. The Cambridge Platonists found that the Calvinist position rendered salvation a "lottery." Everything seemed to depend on where one happened to be born. More significantly it also called into question the justice of God. The Platonists sought to harmonize the truths of revelation with that of natural religion, rather than pit them against each other as had the Scholastics. This they did by emphasizing virtue and morality over belief and, in so doing, they safeguarded the "justice of God." This meant two things in relation to our question. First, they realized that their claims about the religions required substantiation from actual history, and they turned to "religions" to show that natural religions did render the truths established through revelation. Second, this meant that either they discovered the doctrine of the trinity almost everywhere in other religions, in a mitigated Augustinian form as vestiges (see for instance the work of Cudworth); or they were pushed to play down various supernatural truths not found elsewhere. This latter path was not taken by most of the Platonists, but it would be the low road walked by the deists. Harrison says of the Platonists:

> It may be objected that their efforts were tainted with dubious philosophy and theological bias, but for all this it was their unique theological insights which paved the way for the more objective study of the religions. (1990, 59)

Here then, we get the beginnings of comparative religion or, allegedly, the "more objective study of religion." Harrison is more generous than many who narrate this story. Ninian Smart (1988), for example, emphatically stresses that the "objective study of religions" is incompatible with any Christian theological reading. He argues that theology is a "conceptual albatross around the neck of religious studies" (1988, 8). Harrison espouses this Smartian view in most of his book.

Harrison drives home his point about the Cambridge Platonists being the turning point in European history with regard to the emergence of "religion" when applied to world religions:

> Four aspects of their thought were of prime importance in this process. First was their view that God's activity must be as lawful and universal in the religious realm as in the physical world. Second was their application of a reason unshackled by subservience to institutional or even biblical authority to the problem of religious pluralism. Third was their insistence on the validity of the religion of nature, along with that theory of innate religion. . . . Finally there was the recognition, in Cudworth's writings at least, that "innate ideas" are bound to have an historical correlate . . . making hypotheses about innate religiosity in principle verifiable in the pages of history, and in the religious practices and beliefs of the contemporary world. These changes meant that for the first time, the positive religions become

> important sources for Western theories of religions. Only after these foundations had been laid did the dispassionate study of religion become possible. (1990, 59–60)

For Harrison, dispassionate study is the ultimate *telos* of the discipline "religious studies," which historically had not yet been achieved.

Interestingly, returning to our earlier narrative of the wars of religion, much of the Cambridge Platonists' theological efforts was used to show that Roman papism was a deeper disfigurement of "religion" than disfigurement by any noble savage! Henry More, for example, concludes in his *Antidote Against Idolatry* (1653), "We cannot say . . . that every Idolatrous Heathen must perish eternally," but "we have no warrant . . . to think or declare any of the *Popish* Religion, so long as they continue so, to be in the state of Salvation" (Harrison 1990, 49). The birth of the study of non-Christian "religions" takes place at the same time as the birth of the modern notion of "religion" in European society. The two narratives have an interesting interconnection.

The third group in this period, the deists, take up the same tack, but can be said to secularize Platonism in decoupling reason as a mode of revelation, a central tenet of the Platonists. In the deist view, reason now became a natural property of every man (and eventually woman), a faculty that did not participate in the divine reality as did the Platonized reason of the Cambridge Platonists. For the deists, reason related us to a God who had acted and stood back. The deism of Lord Herbert of Cherbury perfectly exemplifies this move, found in a mature form in *De Religione Gentilium* (1663). Here, morality alone counts, even though morality is based on belief in God, a belief found in all religions. Beliefs and ethics are what "religion" is about. Revelation, in the form of trinity and incarnation, is unnecessary. Central to Herbert's thinking was an epistemological insight. Aristotle held that the mind conforms to the object, whereas Kant reversed this to argue that the object is conformed to the mind. Herbert argued that the objects are received, *an sich*, by the *a priori* forms of the mind. This meant that all people were religious, as all had an *a priori* knowledge of God. The question then was: how did this religious *a priori* get obscured, almost cluttered over, with "rubbish"? Deism explained the "rubbish" accumulation through priestly castes controlling the masses. Some deists also developed a theory of the twofold philosophy, related to the elites and the popular. The populace were in the grip of the priestly castes and the elite were the enlightened forerunners of a new religion. The deists rejected Calvinism and transformed theological Platonism through reaching back into the Classical heritage. Although deists prefigured a fully secularized approach to religion (discarding the initial *a priori* reasoning along with the "rubbish" accumulation), they still had not fully achieved this in their assumption that all religions were theistic. Nevertheless, even this position facilitated a trajectory that viewed all religions as of equal worth, accompanied by critical suspicion of all religions (modern pluralism). A trajectory out of this position, more skeptical and secular in its ideological sense, would find expression in David Hume's *The Natural History of Religions* (1757). Hume viewed all religions as equally illusory and, in the end, equally worthless. Hume provided a thoroughly reductionist naturalist reading of all religions (modern secularism).

We can see, in these three forms, typological anticipations of exclusivism, inclusivism, and pluralism. And we can also see, in this narration, the theological and slowly secularized motivations in engaging with other "religions": the Cambridge Platonists trying to overcome the apparent injustice of God's election in strict Calvinism; and deism trying to overcome the apparent prioritizing of Christian revelation, an injustice of Christians, not God. All these traditions continued into the modern period, but the narrative that we are following favors the deist turn in the road: the attempt to understand religions in their own terms, rather than through *a priori* theological lenses that necessarily disfigure that which is viewed. In what follows, the final act, the story will continue from the eighteenth to the twentieth century, culminating in the present day.

Act IV: the emergence of the "religions" from Christian theologizing and the development of the scientific study of religions

The eighteenth and nineteenth centuries are characterized by the influence of two of the greatest philosophers of that period, who carried forward our two currents: Immanuel Kant (1724–1804) and Georg Wilhelm Friedrich Hegel (1770–1831). Kant best represents the trajectory that struggles to free history from the shackles of theology and the churches, so that other religions can be viewed as they truly are. This paves the way for the kind of pluralist society sought for after the wars of religion. Kant argues that we all view the world through the categories of the mind, which limit, control, and shape our knowing. Kant emphasized the importance of epistemology over ontology. That is, our processes of knowing require attention prior to the question of what it is that we know. Before we attend to our knowledge of God we have to ask the question: how do we gain knowledge? We can thus ask: are our claims about the contents of our knowledge permissible within the limits of reason alone? Kant understood "reason" as both practical (moral reasoning) and pure (speculative), forming the boundaries of our knowledge. This Kantian view had two important effects on later thought. First, some later scholars would be deeply sensitive to the "categories," understood not only in a philosophical manner, but also in a broader cultural fashion. Hence, different cultures and religions would come to apprehend the divine reality in different cultural and religious categories, related to their context and mental constructs. Hick's work is an example (see chapter 1). The point is that no religion now sets the criteria by which to judge authentic religion. Robert Neville nicely unpacks this consequence:

> The objective study of religion then is neither the defence of one's own religion against criticisms (although that is possible) nor the investigation of the various worldviews fostered and inhabited by different religions and cultures. Although personal and cultural biases are difficult to guard against, in principle this study of religions is empirical, investigating what various worldviews are and how they work. (2002, 111)

Kant had provided a very thin version of this project in his *Religion within the Limits of Reason Alone* (1793), in which all religions could be seen for what they are without giving any *a priori* special treatment to Christianity (or any other religion for that matter). Nevertheless, Kant also argued that Christianity was the best exemplification of the highest morality available, which existed, in part, in other religions. He conducted, in Neville's terms, both an objective study and an intrusive judging process, allowing his own cultural and personal biases to enter. However, his favoring of Christianity was not a theological bias but, one might say, a moral bias, for it conformed to the yardstick of true morality that Kant had established through practical reason. As we have already seen, Hume took deist logic to its radical limits so that the study of religion would lose its theological bias.

Hegel's theologized rendering of other religions continued the Cambridge Platonist tradition but brought back the supremacy of Christianity so central to the Protestant Scholastics, without their exclusivism. In his *Lectures in Philosophy of Religion* Hegel produced an imperializing rendition of world history whereby all the world religions were placed in an unfolding dialectic of the Spirit, such that their partial insights and truths led to the final and completed truth, to be found in (Hegel's view of) Christianity.

However, his most important contribution lay in the way historical consciousness now began to permeate all worldviews and academic disciplines, and one of Hegel's legacies would be that one could not think "religion" other than in a historic modality.

In the nineteenth century the story takes off fully with the emergence of the scientific study of religion, *Religionwissenschaft*, which developed an anthropological, sociological, and fully historical way of apprehending "religion." The latter part of the nineteenth century saw a flowering of non-theological objective attention to religions. In the social sciences the massive achievements of sociologists Emile Durkheim (1858–1917) and Max Weber (1864–1920) injected serious energy into conceptually understanding religions on non-theological terms, as did the work of anthropologists Edward Burnett Tylor (1832–1917), Branislaw Malinowski (1884–1942), Ruther Fulton Benedict (1887–1948), and Claude Lévi-Strauss (1908–), who forged various conceptualities through which the data "religion" could be best understood. Philologically, two figures in particular provided systematic translations of key religious texts into European languages and are often seen as the founders of the history of religions school.

Friedrich Max Müller (1823–1900) is seen as the father of "indology." Under his editorship of the *Sacred Books of the East*, a massive 50-volume set of English translations of Eastern classics, Müller brought India to Europe. James Legge (1815–97) did the same for China and is the father of "sinology." Importantly, while both were Christians – Legge was in fact a missionary – they were both fully committed to the scientific study of religion, which meant using tools and conceptualities that could be shared by any scholar, religious or non-religious. Bishop Munro, the Catholic bishop of Glasgow, accused Müller of a crusade against divine revelation in his promotion of the "science of religion," and his appointment to the Boden Chair in Sanskrit was blocked due to his alleged Christian unorthodoxy. Müller went on to hold three different Chairs in Oxford.

The benefits of this new scientific attention to the religions were reaped by the development of comparative religious studies, initially in a phenomenological mode through Chantepie de La Saussaye and later and most influentially by Gerardus van der Leeuw (1890–1950), who was adamant about the distinction between phenomenology and theology:

> theology speaks about God, and this the phenomenologist cannot do. . . . Because God, to be grasped by phenomenology, would have to be subject or object; and he is neither. So to the phenomenologist, though he may study

> religious experience . . . and may observe men and women responding . . . to divine revelation, the revelation itself remains inaccessible. (Fitzgerald 2000, 37, citing Sharpe 1986, 232–33)

Comparative religion has moved out of a phenomenological mode and employed various philosophical and ideological conceptualities, although in England (where I write), Ninian Smart (1927–2001) is perhaps one of the most influential and prolific figures who has developed the discipline in a phenomenological mode under the rubric "Religious Studies." Internationally, Mircea Eliade (1907–86) was a major theorist of the comparative school, with his influential theory that hierophanies form the basis of religion, splitting the human experience of reality into sacred and profane time and space. His theory of "eternal return" held that myths and rituals do not simply commemorate hierophanies, but, at least to the minds of the religious involved in such rituals, actually participate in these hierophanies. In Eliade and many others, we find a liberating attempt at understanding the world's religions on their own terms, free of theological baggage. "Religion" has come of age.

I have not done justice to the internal dissonances within this story or its complex twists and turns, but there are two basic motifs throughout. First, the wars of religion precipitated the shaking off of the yoke of the mono-authoritarian dominance of Christianity in pre-modern times. This move could take a reductive path that views religions as false realities – as Marxism did. It could also take the path promoted in this narrative: the attempt to provide the context for religious plurality where mutual understanding and toleration are possible, without mono-authoritarian religion (as in pre-modern Europe) or mono-authoritarian atheism (as found in the worse days of China and Russia). Both are unhealthy.

Second, at the same time, and with obvious related significance, the study of religions developed. But not as an object of the theological gaze with its obstructing *a priori* reasoning, witnessed most bleakly in the Protestant Scholastics of the English sixteenth century or, more fruitfully but with remarkable obscurantism, in the Cambridge Platonists. Rather it developed out of the desire to understand the religions in their own terms, in their own languages (or in very good translations) and with appropriate attention to the complex interdisciplinary nature of the phenomenon: sociological, anthropological, linguistic, philosophical, and so on. This second goal served the first in the foundation of modern liberal society.

An interlude: some issues arising from this story

Before telling a different story, I want to make two points about "religion" prior to the period I have been focusing on to help our understanding of the two differing narratives being offered in this and the next chapter. First, it is fair to say that prior to the sixteenth century the religions identified in Harrison's narrative did not actually exist as "religions" in the way we understand them today, for both Judaism and Islam were seen as deformations of the true religion, Christianity. In the case of Judaism, it was a family member's failure to accept its own fulfillment and destiny, a failure to grasp the promises made to its own people and prophets. It was like a failed Christianity, a youngster refusing to grow up into its true potential. As for Islam, it was seen as taking up the truth of the Jewish–Christian heritage in its own sacred scriptures, but confusing it with errors, deceit, and a lust for political power. It was like a malformed development out of Christianity, a troublesome adult who has left home and insists the parents are in error. The latter two stories have been told often enough (see Perry and Schweitzer 2005; and Goddard 2001), and their consequences in outbreaks of Christian anti-Semitism and Islamophobia are very important to acknowledge. The causal relation between theological views and socio-political action is complex and I will return to this in chapter 5. I simply want to register the reality that most Christians viewed these "religions" not as "religions" as we understand them today, but as deviations of and from Christianity. It is anachronistic and historically inappropriate to criticize them for this, except when we have evidence that they ignored significant developing knowledge that suggested otherwise.

Second, and relatedly, non-biblical religions that had developed entirely out of contact, or with minimal contact, with the Western Semitic traditions were encountered from the thirteenth century on, when Franciscan and Dominican missionaries penetrated deep into Asia and Marco Polo encountered China. By the sixteenth century Francis Xavier the Jesuit missionary was in dialogue with Buddhist monks in Japan and had already conversed with the Brahmin priests in western India on the coast of Goa.

Several points emerge from this long process of missionary activity. First, through the writings of these missionaries, we have some of the most comprehensive accounts of Eastern cultures (Confucianism, Buddhism, and Hinduism), some of which are still used by scholars for their ethnological value. The French Catholic missionary, Abbé Dubois, is a case in point. His description of Hindu customs is still used in universities today. Brian

Pennington argues that Dubois' descriptions are far more rigorous and accurate than those of his Protestant counterparts whose rationalism meant that they were simply impatient with Hindu worship and failed to pay attention to details that the Catholic Dubois noted carefully. That the Protestant missionaries saw Catholic and Hindu worship as idolatrous is not a matter of chance! (Pennington 2005, 59–101). Pennington is still critical of Dubois for his theological prejudices in interpreting Hinduism, but this criticism requires questioning, as I shall be arguing in the next chapter. It is wrong to argue against theological critical reading, but right to argue that such a reading may be lazy, uninformed, not open to correction by evidence, and so on. The former should not be immediately identified with the latter.

As with the entire industry of criticism of colonial culture, there sometimes lurks an assumption that either a neutral secular description of Hinduism or alternatively a self-description of Hinduism (including its persecuted minorities) is the only acceptable form of description. While Marxists and feminists constitute a large number of colonial critics, ironically they cannot conform to these strictures, for they obviously introduce new biases. This highlights my point that theological interpretation *per se* does not necessarily reduce the value of a descriptive account, for all accounts are interpretative. Protestant rationalist missionaries truncated accounts of worship because they saw these as scandalously idolatrous; their accounts should not be relied on if we are keen to understand what the Hindu worshipper actually believed.

Second, and relatedly, Francis Xavier and other missionaries had to theologically interpret what they were encountering and it was not all negative. Indeed Xavier found in Japan a level of civility and refinement that moved him deeply. Drawing on his Parisian theological education, Xavier saw the operation of the natural law in the hearts (nature) of the native Japanese prior to China's incursions. He commended the Japanese for knowing that killing, stealing, and bearing false witness were wrong. Christian missionaries played a vital part in a new understanding of the importance of viewing religions in their own terms, even if "in their own terms" was only significant as a prelude to effective mission, or a means to successfully translate the Bible, to claim that the natural law was operative in that religion, or, in the modern period, to claim that ethical beliefs are present in such religions. In our first story there is a very strong assumption that Christians engaging with other religions generate distortions, negative images, chauvinism, and other problematic "interference," mirroring the Christian denominational wars. Historically, this assumption is informed by some evidence that I would not contest, but it cannot lead to a binding or plausible general hermeneutical rule. When it becomes one, it is purely prejudice, and should be unmasked as such.

Third, I want to question the idea that in pre-modern time "religion" was an inward piety. This is the influential view of Wilfred Cantwell Smith. He argues that, in the pre-modern period, "religion" designated a "personal piety," an attitude of "faith." Only in the modern period does it become associated with "beliefs, practices and values" and associated with a "particular community" (1962, 15–50, quotations from 48–9). Smith uses this distinction for his own "revolutionary approach" to the world religions, to which I will return shortly. Smith claims that Augustine and Aquinas both viewed *religio* (Latin: to bind) in the first sense above, as personal piety. Smith argues that Augustine's work *De Vera Religione*, usually translated as *The True Religion*, is often mistranslated. It should be translated *On Proper Piety* instead. When Augustine writes retrospectively about this work, he comes "close to saying, the book [*De Vera*] argues 'at great length and in many ways that *vera religio* means the worship of the one true God.' " For Augustine, Smith argues,

> "religion" is no system of observances or beliefs, nor an historical tradition, institutionalized or susceptible of outside observation. Rather it is a vivid and personal confrontation with the splendour and the love of God. (1962, 29)

Two criticisms are in order. First, Smith is too meticulous a scholar to avoid the Latin text, which he cites in a footnote. What does Augustine actually say? Augustine specifies that the "one true God" as cited by Smith is "the Trinity, Father, Son and Holy Spirit" (*unum verum deum, id est trinitatem, patrem et filium et spiritum* – all part of the same sentence, but the latter part omitted by Smith in the main body of his text). There is not only inner piety and theism, but a robust trinitarian confession of belief. To say that "religion" does not include a system of true beliefs for Augustine is simply false. Second, Augustine must be interpreted in the context of his overall approach to the matter of those who do not belong to the visible Christian church. His mature attitude is rigorist to the extent that he is happy to acknowledge that the just, prior to Christ, "belong to the church" from the time of Abel (*ab Abel*). However, after the coming of Christ, Augustine is clear that no one can be saved except through explicit membership of the Church. When writing against Christian heretics and schismatics, he is adamant that

> Whoever is separated from this Catholic Church, by this single sin of being severed from the unity of Christ, no matter how estimable a life he may imagine he is living, shall not have life, but the wrath of God rests upon him. (*Epist.* 141:5)

For Augustine, there is an indispensable and necessary institutional dimension to true worship of God: the Catholic church. So much so that even if a schismatic were to suffer martyrdom in the name of Christ, Augustine is clear that this poor soul will still suffer damnation: "Nor will his baptism be of any benefit to the heretic if, while outside the church, he were put to death for confessing Christ" (*De Baptismo* 4:17, 25). For Augustine any martyr outside the church still faces damnation, as charity is lacking in his schismatic action. Augustine is a major definer and transmitter of *extra ecclesiam nulla salus* (no salvation outside the church); Smith's comment on Augustine is therefore difficult to understand: " 'religion' is no system of observances or beliefs, nor an historical tradition, institutionalized or susceptible of outside observation."

Smith says that for Aquinas *religio* is not a central category, and while sometimes denoting "the outward expression of faith," Aquinas' other uses suggest "the inner motivation towards worshipping God, and that worship itself; and à la Augustine (whom he [Aquinas] cites), the bond that unites the soul with God" (1962, 32). Again, there are problems with Smith's emphasis on inner faith and in his singling out of the soul and God as if there were no materiality involved in that relationship. Admittedly, Smith acknowledges wider uses, so he should not be pressed too hard. For Aquinas, in the *Summa Theologiae* II–II.81, articles 1– 8, *religio* is the virtue that directs the person to the true God, and is also thus sanctity, although religion should be logically distinguished from sanctity, as "religion" denotes specifically the liturgical cultus of the church. Aquinas writes:

> Accordingly, it is by sanctity that the human mind applies itself and its acts to God: so that it differs from religion not essentially but only logically. For it takes the name of religion according as it gives God due service in matters pertaining specially to the Divine worship, such as sacrifices, oblations, and so forth. (article 8)

This institutional emphasis is played down by Smith, but it pervades all three usages cited by Smith. Indeed, if we look at Aquinas' view about worshipping the true God, which Smith interiorizes, Aquinas like Augustine held that after the coming of Christ, worshipping the true trinitarian God was only possible through "explicit faith" and institutional baptism:

> After grace had been revealed, all, both the learned and the simple, are bound to have explicit faith in the mysteries of Christ, especially with regard to those mysteries which are publicly and solemnly celebrated in the church, such as those which refer to the incarnation. (*ST*, II–II, q. 2, a. 7)

The *cultus* is essential; the public and solemn celebrations within the church constitute *religio*.

Two conclusions arise. First, Smith's findings on the use of "religion" in the modern period are very important and I have no quarrel with that part of his groundbreaking work, but his characterization of "religion" in the pre-modern period is incorrect. He is right insomuch as the pre-moderns hardly had the conception of "religion," which we nowadays use, but he is wrong to emphasize individual piety as the heart of "religion." Rather than conduct the search on purely linguistic grounds, as does Smith, I have drawn on wider assumptions and beliefs to illuminate the category of "religion." Second, why does Smith, who is such a notable historian, seemingly skew his materials? It is, in part, because of his promotion of a pluralist theological agenda through his distinction between "faith" (inner piety related to the alleged pre-modern understanding of *religio*) and "cumulative historical traditions" (the modern encoding of *religio* for Smith, which has generated the history of religions and the science of religions). The latter consist of observable manifestations or religions that include beliefs and practices: "temples, scriptures, theological systems, dance patterns, legal and other social institutions, conventions, moral codes, myths" and so on. Smith uses this distinction to argue the unity and equality of all religions (1962, 157). He uses these liberal Protestant, rather than pre-modern, distinctions between "faith" and "cumulative traditions" to argue that all the world religions share the same faith (in a transcendent God), but express it very differently and sometimes even contradictorily in the various cumulative historical traditions. This is no different from Hick's early theocentricism, a point made in Hick's preface to the UK edition of Smith's book (1978, ix–xviii). I have discussed Smith's position in more detail elsewhere (1991), so I will not now pursue this issue.

I now want to tell the second account of the "same" story – a Christian narration, one might say. We will find it is a very different story indeed!

4

An Alternative: The Secular Construction of the Sacred

Modernity as the Establishment of a New Ruling Religion

Act I: the story of the emergence of nation states, not the wars of religion

This alternative narrative does not seek to excuse Catholics and Protestants who murdered each other for denominational reasons, nor suggest that when violence did happen there were always other motives than religious ones involved. The scandal of violence by Christians cannot be avoided. However, I want to retell the story with a different central character, which might seem to some like telling an entirely different story. Imagine *Hamlet* without the prince! My alternative narrative has three goals. First, I want to suggest that the driving motor for the wars in Europe was not "religion," but rather a new character on stage that has almost become invisible to us today: the sovereign nation state. This character had to contain, control, and subordinate all other actors if he was going to be center stage, and he argues with different accents and emphases in his various walks on roles in France, Holland, Spain, England, Germany, and Italy. He usually argues that for the peace, justice, and welfare of all, religions must be subordinate to the sovereign nation state. He would assert himself strongly in the imperial history of Europe, especially in France, England, and the Netherlands (the most vigorous imperialist nations). He would reappear after the empires of these European countries had crumbled, arguing that multi-religious Europe could only be redeemed by his presence, or else revert to the bloody wars of religion. Our princely character argues that peace in Europe requires the privatization of religion, for there cannot be two public sovereigns. Second, I shall argue that the sovereign nation state was thus central in generating the definition of religion that shapes so much thought today: religion is a matter of private choice and should not shape the public square. Recall Stout's words:

> liberal principles were the right ones to adopt when competing religious beliefs and divergent conceptions of the good embroiled Europe in the religious wars. . . . Our early modern ancestors were right to secularize *public discourse* in the interest of minimizing the ill effects of religious disagreement. (Stout 1981, 241, my emphasis)

The way this character unfolded in different European countries (and in the United States) meant important differences in constitution and law (more of which in chapter 5). Nevertheless, the overall structuring of society produced a new public "secular" arena. Any religion that is concerned with social power, as most but not all pre-modern religions were, is a public threat. Third, I shall argue that the "wars of religion," even if they are really wars of state, are dwarfed by the carnage exacted by the wars of the secular modern sovereign state where religion was certainly not an issue. The sovereign state has nothing to be proud about in its very short term of office, for it has generated relentless wars.

I draw heavily upon William Cavanaugh's *Theopolitical Imagination* (2002), whose research supports this alternative narrative (and see also Chadwick 1964; Dunn 1970; Milbank 1990). Let me take two examples offered in the first narrative (chapter 3) to help establish my first point: the wars were the effects of the emerging nation states, and not the inevitable outcome of religion being in competition.

The Catholic emperor Charles V's attack on the Lutheran states in 1547 inaugurates the first great war, but it is more appropriately viewed as a struggle to establish sovereign nationhood. Luther's two-state doctrine was one among many moves in the slow erosion and dismantling of the relationship between law and theology (canon law and ecclesiastical courts). It paved the way for the almost total autonomy of secular society, with the church's role being that of preaching and teaching within its own walls, without any relation to the secular. As Quentin Skinner puts it, in the Lutheran divide the "idea of the Pope and Emperor as parallel and universal powers disappears, and the independent jurisdictions of the *sacerdotium* are handed over to the secular authorities" (1978, 15). In the sixteenth century European rulers were keen to consolidate power through marriages, war, and alliances, and freedom from transnational allegiance that might conflict with the state.

Most troubling within the state's own borders were nobles and citizens whose primary allegiance lay to a transnational church, whose ruler lay out of their jurisdiction. One way of settling this was through concordats between state and church. These were agreements that allowed the church certain "privileges" at the cost of political non-interference. This meant that when concordats were established between state and church to curb the powers of an otherwise supranational church, such as in France and Spain, those countries remained Catholic, as the rulers now had secured power over the church. In England, Germany, and Scandinavia, no concordats existed, and these rulers would often prefer to be allied to the Reformers. Luther's two-state doctrine meant this was an even more attractive proposition, as the rulers could be assured of an obedient local church with no transnational commitment.

Charles, at 20, had a huge empire, thanks to the marrying skills of the Habsburgs. His empire covered most of the American continent, between a third and half of what the Turks had left of Europe, Spain, and later the Netherlands in 1506. Pope Leo X and Francis I of France opposed Charles' election, so the Catholic Charles turned upon the Catholic Francis. Charles' armies, made up of Catholic and Protestant princes, defeated the French in Italy, and then marched on to Rome to fill their coffers so as to pay the disgruntled soldiers. The sacking of Rome, not Wittenburg, followed in 1527 as this Catholic ruler was keen to establish his political power over and above the church. Luther was critical of this action. Charles, though embarrassed, was not unhappy at Rome's collapse, and opportunistically imprisoned Pope Clement VII, who spent the rest of his time trying not to displease Charles. Indeed, Charles insisted that Clement confront Henry VIII, who desired an annulment from Catherine of Aragon, Henry's first wife. Catherine was Charles' aunt.

With the pope in his pocket, Charles now wanted to extend his sovereign national boundaries further. He turned on the German Lutheran states, not as an act of religious bigotry, but simply to expand his political power. That national power was at stake, not religious adherence, is clearly evinced in the fact that the French Catholic king, Henry II, joined forces with the Lutheran princes to oppose and eventually defeat Charles, while the German Catholic princes remained neutral. This is the same Henry II who passed the Edict of Chateaubriand (1551), enjoining civil and religious courts to punish all heretics, and place severe restrictions on Protestants. The outbreak of the first of the great "wars of religion" was really the story of Europe being carved up by increasingly powerful rulers and of their emerging nation states.

The same is true about the second incident, the 1572 St Bartholomew's Day massacre in France, which is often portrayed as the massacre of thousands of Protestants by the Catholic queen mother and bigot, Catherine de Medici. After the Concordat of Bologna in 1516, the French king had the power to make all ecclesial appointments and to control church revenues; the French rulers remained staunchly Catholic and equally centralist. Catherine had as her sole goal the preservation of royal power – at any cost. If it meant supporting the Protestant Huguenots in France in internal disputes, she did it. If it meant marrying her daughter, Margaret of Valois, to the Protestant king, Henry of Navarre, she did it. If it meant proposing the abolition of both the Catholic and the Calvinist churches in her country at the Colloquy of Poissy in 1561, to bring together both under her rule as Elizabeth had done in her state-controlled church in England, she did it. Catherine was startled to discover that the ecclesiologies of both Catholic and Calvinist would not tolerate her statecraft. Almost two-fifths of the nobility and increasing numbers of bourgeoisie had adopted the Calvinist cause; the nobility to take back regional power as was enjoyed by various Protestant princes in Germany, and the bourgeoisie who resented the absolute authority of the crown draining away their revenues. The turning point came in 1572, when Catherine found the growing Huguenot influence over her son Charles, the French king, was undermining her own power over him. Catherine acted swiftly. If Catholics and Calvinists would not unite under her authority, then she would destroy the weaker of the two. Had the Huguenots been more powerful, Catherine would probably have supported their cause. She very likely instigated a plot to assassinate the Protestant leader Coligny and catalyzed the massacre of some 50,000 Huguenots in the St Bartholomew's Day massacre, although the extent of the massacre also reflects Catherine losing control over violent and unruly mob passion. But Catherine was quick to take the applause that came from some Catholic quarters. Catherine's ambitions only declined when her third son, Henry, succeeded to the throne after Charles' death in 1574. This battle between localized and centralized power was only resolved in the eighteenth century, with the French revolution, whereby the sovereign nation state won. The battle was not essentially between religions.

This counter-narrative could continue, taking in Emperor Ferdinand II and the last of the great alleged "wars of religion." In brief, the story again is about the attempt to consolidate and control, and thus shape the Habsburg Empire into a sovereign state. Ferdinand had allegiances with various Protestant powers, the Lutheran elector of Saxony, the Bohemian

Protestant commander, Albrecht von Wallenstein, and was opposed by various Catholic powers. Among these was Cardinal Richelieu, who subsidized an army of 36,000 Swedes in German territory. This alleged religious war ended in an imperial contest of power between the Habsburgs and the Bourbons, two Catholic dynasties, both fundamentally state dynasties, first and foremost. This was hardly a battle between Protestants and Catholics. Further, in almost all cases, these wars were never supported by the common people who were forced into armies through conscription and had much to lose and little to gain (Rothenberg 1973).

Terrence Tilley raises an interesting objection to Cavanaugh's argument. Tilley argues that the

> time lapse between the religious wars and the formation of actual modern nations suggests that any who claim that the wars of religion were really not about religion at all may be overstated at best. (Tilley *et al.* 2007, 27)

France is perhaps the first to become a truly modern nation state through the revolution of 1789, Germany not following until the late nineteenth century, Italy in 1870, with the Austro-Hungarian empire only being carved up into nations after 1918. Two responses are in order. Cavanaugh does not claim that the wars of religion were not related to any form of religious rivalries. Rather, the claim is that this is not the sole or major character in the narrative. Second, Cavanaugh does not claim that there is a perfect correlation between the "religious wars" and the emergence of nation states. The latter, as Tilley rightly notes, take some time to emerge. But do they emerge from the already present chrysalis that I have sought to outline, or are they something quite distinct and different? Mixing metaphors, 400 years is actually quite a short time from gestation to chrysalis to full-fledged Leviathans, which is what we have by the end of the First World War. This trajectory is perhaps most clearly present in the controversy about the European charter (2006–7) and the contested and rejected preamble, which sought to mention the Christian contribution to the shaping of Europe, a point I will elaborate in chapter 5.

In telling this story I hope to have illustrated my first claim, obviously in inadequate detail: the wars of religion are in fact the effects of the emergence of the nation state seeking to consolidate power and thus oppose any and every other power that would claim allegiance from citizens. In order for the state to be sovereign, citizens owe the state total and unconditional allegiance. The churches – especially the Catholic church, being transnational

– were deeply problematic for rulers concerned with obedience. Hence both Catholic and Protestant rulers sought to eradicate the power of the Catholic church over the state and to establish the sovereign power of the state.

This slow and long process came to "fruition" in three distinct ways. First, what we now turn to: the slow privatization of religion in the public square through political theory and related legislation. Second, this "privatization" would take many forms: French, German, English, Dutch, Scandinavian, Spanish, Italian, American, and so on. We cannot recount all these twists in the narrative, but must remember significant variations. Third, in establishing nation states, the bloodshed did not stop, but accelerated greatly, and this was a bloodshed that perhaps exposed the driving engine of the earlier "religious" bloodshed: the nation state seeking ever-expanding power.

Act II: privatized religion and public discourse

We have already seen the early moves that helped establish the autonomy and slow sovereignty of law over and against theology and the church in the work of Luther in 1523 and later in Grotius in 1625. There is a line of trajectory connecting major intellectuals, which runs through from Luther to the modern nation state: the Frenchman Jean Bodin, jurist and political philosopher (1530–96), the Dutchman Hugo Grotius, jurist and philosopher (1583–1645), Thomas Hobbes, the English philosopher (1588–1679), John Locke, another English philosopher (1632–1704), and the French opera writer, novelist, philosopher, Catholic, then Calvinist, then neither, Jean-Jacques Rousseau (1712–78). I cannot here examine each of these figures in appropriate detail, but want to present a very selective story line, for it is these figures that intellectually form the context to the privatization of religion, the rise of the absolute sovereign state, and thus the modern rendition of "religion." This is the private inner religion that Wilfred Cantwell Smith universalizes in his theory of religions.

Bodin's classical definition of sovereignty in his *Six Books of the Commonwealth* is: "sovereignty is that absolute and perpetual power vested in the commonwealth" (Bodin 1576, chapter 8). For Bodin, religious allegiance was always possible within the state, but never if it called the state's sovereignty into question or prompted rebellion against the prince. The St Bartholomew's Day massacre and the Huguenot armed response to it were part of Bodin's backdrop. He argued that political stability would only come with a single power that all obeyed, and that power was the state.

He argued for free choice in religion and supported religious tolerance, but only up to a point. He thought it best that a ruler's subjects remained unitary in their religious belief, which would reduce discord between the populace. Hence, Bodin welcomed the Peace of Augsburg, as it required subjects to follow their ruler's religion. Indeed, Bodin praises the ordinances of Spain and the king of Muscovy, where public discussion of religious issues carried the death penalty (Bodin [1576] 1967, chapter 7). He was keen to empower the state.

We have already seen Grotius establish international law based on human nature, independent of revelation. This move to ground law in human nature was not new, of course, and Aquinas made this central to the Catholic tradition. In Aquinas, however, nature was understood within a theological framework: original goodness and sociality, fall, redemption by Christ, final end as eternal communion with the saints and God. Now the framework slowly eroded and was eventually discarded. The story ran: we have a struggling and warring human nature, tending toward individualism and egotism, in need of law and regulation. Redemption comes through the sovereign state as our final end is peace and defense of the realm (Hobbes), ownership of property (Locke), or following the general will (Rousseau). Religious ends must fit within this framework of the state's final goals. There is a profound change in anthropological, theological, and cosmological vision. Salvation by state or salvation by Christ?

All of Europe was deeply affected by internal wars and England no less, with three civil wars between 1642 and 1651, and estimated casualties between 400,000 and 768,000. England unsurprisingly produced two of the greatest and most influential theorists. Hobbes lived through these three wars. To him, there was only one solution: an all-powerful centralist monarchy, which had the total obedience of the populace. Grant the monarchy this power and, in return, the monarchy would deliver peace, stability, and the defense of the realm. The power and omnipresence of the state and the subsequent positioning of religion within this body politic is starkly outlined in Hobbes' *Leviathan* (1651). Hobbes argued that the natural state of nature would be a state of war, for our lives are "solitary, poore, nasty, brutish, and short" (*Leviathan* I, xiii). There is considerable debate as to what is intended in this phrase. It could mean either that we are naturally self-interested, or that egotism is only a formal description, not a material one. Hobbes' wider writings seem to imply the first definition. If we are to avoid this perpetual strife, individuals must choose to enter into a social contract creating absolute government, preferably a monarchy. For that monarchy to be effective, it must be above the law, it must have sovereign rule, for indeed it is the very creator, interpreter, and arbitrator of the law. Hobbes, it should be acknowledged, does not defend an "unadulterated absolutism" (Baumgold 1988, 164), although he does not allow for the right of rebellion as do Locke and Rousseau after him. Hobbes argues that if the state failed to provide "peace and defence" of its citizens, the social contract would become void and man would automatically return to a state of nature until a renewed social contract arose. Religion is swallowed in part III of *Leviathan* like Jonah is swallowed by the whale; the state is indeed a Leviathan. The original front cover of the book designed by Abraham Bosse, with Hobbes' help, portrays a huge king, whose body is made up of all the people, standing high over his city, with sword and torch in hand. Subsumed within the lower half of the cover are two panels with images of the church, lower than the body politic and clearly under the rule of the king.

In part III of *Leviathan*, Hobbes considers a Christian commonwealth, and here we find even the interpretation of the Bible is now subject to the state. Why? Because revelation cannot be allowed to be higher than civil law, as this would weaken the state's ability to deliver its part of the contract. But Hobbes also advances further arguments that undermine religious authority, or rather make it subservient to civil authority. Because we cannot be sure that another person's word is infallible, we cannot trust individual testimony. However, we cannot undermine the Bible – which might be implied in this first argument as it is the testimony of individuals – so Hobbes turns to the question of the authority of the Bible. But here is no answer, for different Christian sects claim different books to be binding and offer varying interpretations of the meaning of these books. Perhaps miracles can give authority to a position. However, as miracles do not endorse any particular sect, the real question becomes: by what authority can any sect make claims upon any other than its own? Hobbes is very astute in seeing that theology is always imbricated with the question of social power. The only social body that can grant a sect any binding, rather than voluntary, authority is the state. Hobbes concludes:

> He therefore to whom God hath not supernaturally revealed that they are His, nor that those that published them were sent by Him, is not obliged to obey them by any authority but his whose commands have already the force of laws; that is to say, by any other authority than that of the Commonwealth, residing in the sovereign, who only has the legislative power. (*Leviathan* III)

But this is not all, for the sovereign can now carry out offices within the church:

> Christian kings are still the supreme pastors of their people, and have power to ordain what pastors they please, to teach the Church, that is, to teach the people committed to their charge. (*Leviathan* III)

The church sits comfortably digested within the stomach of the state. It is precisely this nominalist–voluntaristic contractualism that prompts John Milbank's judgment that in Hobbes we discover "the kinship at root of modern absolutism with modern liberalism" (1990, 13). Theologically speaking, the church becomes disincarnate as a social body and the authority of Christ becomes incarnate in the sovereign state. Any religion, not just Christianity, is allocated this ingested private space within Hobbes' body politic.

Does Locke's social contractualism ameliorate Hobbes' teleological drive toward absolutism? Certainly, within Hobbes, there is either the dissolution of the contract (and endless strife and war) or the contract with its absolutist tendencies. The scholarship of Peter Laslett and John Dunn has made it fashionable to play down Locke's philosophical contribution and emphasize the contextual occasion for each of his political writings. In contrast, A. John Simmons and Jeremy Waldron integrate this historical dimension with a philosophical appreciation. Locke's influence on modern sovereign states is undisputed, and his thinking affected not only European politics but also the formulation of the United States' constitution (as did Rousseau's). Locke discusses whether it is possible to question sovereign power's obedience to the law. Hobbes thinks not, for the court of adjudication dissolves in such a conflict. Locke, however, allows, in the *Second Treatise on Government* (1689), that state power has limits: the property rights of the individual, which it is, after all, the basic purpose of the state to safeguard. However, there is an interminable debate as to what precisely these property rights constitute. Locke then distinguishes between the executive and legislature, and the latter must be trusted to make final determinations in deciding on disputed questions of property rights. But what of the scenario where executive and legislature are in conflict? If all refuse to accept the sovereign power of the legislature, and are determined to pursue their goals, there is no other option than war. Waldron, in comparing this answer to that given by Hobbes, rightly says:

> *But it is not an answer at all.* Hobbes said that if there is disagreement between sovereign and subject or between subject and subject as to whether the sovereign has broken the law, the matter will have to be settled by fighting. And Locke did not deny that. He was unable to come up with any institutional solution to the dilemma Hobbes had posed: either the matter is settled by an earthly institution, in which case the problem is reproduced when someone accuses that institution of breaking the law; or it is settled outside the political framework, by "an appeal to heaven", i.e. by fighting. [In the *Second Treatise* Locke uses the phrase "appeal to heaven" to indicate there is no earthly judge on a matter, and thus only war; see paragraph 168.] The only difference in this regard between Locke and Hobbes has to do with the value of preserving the practice of accusing the sovereign of breaking the laws, and the estimation of social dangers associated with it. (2003, 195, my brackets)

Locke in this respect is more "liberal," but this is more a matter of emphasis, not signaling a substantial difference from Hobbes.

What about Locke and religion? His famous *A Letter Concerning Toleration* (1689) differs from Hobbes' theoretical position. Locke argues that the acceptance of religious differences within society can act as leaven, for when religious sects are suppressed, these groups can constitute civil unrest in desiring their social freedom. Locke is referring to the many sects within Christianity. But this acceptance of religious differences takes place on two conditions. First, one must "distinguish exactly the business of civil government from that of religion." This distinction works neatly if religion accepts its disembodied, inner sphere of activity. For Locke, government properly promotes external interests, relating to life, liberty, and the general welfare. The church, on the other hand, exists to promote internal interests, such as the salvation of the soul:

> Civil interests I call life, liberty, health, and indolency of body; and the possession of outward things, such as money, lands, houses, furniture, and the like. . . . [T]he whole jurisdiction of the magistrate reaches only to these civil concernments, and that all civil power, right and dominion, is bounded and confined to the only care of promoting these things; and that it neither can nor ought in any manner to be extended to the salvation of souls. (*Letter*)

Luther's two-kingdom doctrine has now been fully established. The state and the church serve entirely separate functions, one worldly, the other internal and otherworldly, and the church must accept this or violate civic order. Locke's second condition is that tolerance cannot be extended to Roman Catholics (and, thus, neither to Muslims) or atheists. This is a very telling exclusion. Locke writes:

> [The Roman] Church can have no right to be tolerated by the magistrate which is constituted upon such a bottom that all those who enter into it do thereby ipso facto deliver themselves up to the protection and service of another prince [the Pope]. For by this means the magistrate would give way to the settling of a foreign jurisdiction in his own country and suffer his own people to be listed, as it were, for soldiers against his own Government. [He analogically applies the same argument to Muslims.] . . . It is ridiculous for any one to profess himself to be a Mahometan only in his religion, but in everything else a faithful subject to a Christian magistrate, whilst at the same time he acknowledges himself bound to yield blind obedience to the Mufti of Constantinople, who himself is entirely obedient to the Ottoman Emperor and frames the feigned oracles of that religion according to his pleasure. But this Mahometan living amongst Christians would yet more apparently renounce their government if he acknowledged the same person to be head of his Church who is the supreme magistrate in the state. [Finally, Locke turns to the different case of atheists.] . . . Lastly, those are not at all to be tolerated who deny the being of a God. Promises, covenants, and oaths, which are the bonds of human society, can have no hold upon an atheist. The taking away of God, though but even in thought, dissolves all; besides also, those that by their atheism undermine and destroy all religion, can have no pretence of religion whereupon to challenge the privilege of a toleration. (*Letter*, my added brackets)

Different Christian denominations are tolerated by Locke. By deduction, toleration would be extended to non-Zionist Jews and those of other religions who had no "ecclesiastical" or equivalent authorities outside England to whom loyalty, or as Locke renders it, "blind obedience," was owed. Locke's thinking is prescient on Islam, for only one sort of Islam would pass his test: a form that denied a transnational *ummah* (the community of the faithful, which can technically sometimes include Jews and Christians). Such an Islam is a contradiction in terms, although in theory the obligations to the *ummah* lead to very different practices. What we are seeing is that with the state policing of the public square, religious discourse cannot play a public role, and religious practice is a private choice that must not ever question the state. This is true for Locke as it is for Hobbes. We see through these thinkers the emergence of the political philosophy determining the marginal place of religion and the center-stage character of the European nation state. The nation state's narration of religion becomes identified with the scientific study of religion: a neutral view beyond religious bias.

Was the third father of another form of the social contract, Rousseau, different from his English predecessors? In one way, yes; and in two other ways, no. His *Social Contract* of 1762 was deeply influential in European and American history. Rousseau is very different from Hobbes and Locke in criticizing the notion of rights arising out of nature. His conception of human nature was dramatically postmodern in one sense for, although he used the vocabulary of natural law, deriving from Grotius, Pufendorf, and Burlamaqui, he thought natural law theorists read back into individual human nature arbitrary universal rules deriving from social relations. Rousseau's individual natural man was neither moral nor immoral, and certainly not rational *per se*, but first and foremost able to preserve himself and exercise sympathy. Rousseau could be read as a Romantic critic of the Enlightenment, who prefigures postmodernism. "Self-preservation" should not be read in a Hobbesian fashion, for Rousseau thought it preposterous of Hobbes to imagine that humans perceived their welfare to depend on the destruction of others. Contrary to Locke, Rousseau also believed that property rights were not part of man's nature. Rousseau's view of human nature, un-fallen and innocent, was condemned by both the Catholic and the Calvinist churches for undermining the doctrine of original sin. Even so, like Hobbes and Locke, Rousseau starts with the individual, natural man, who then forms community; and like both, he realizes that this is when the trouble with religion becomes particularly acute.

Rousseau was closer to Hobbes and Locke in his view of the state's absolute power and religion's private and subservient place within the state. Rousseau's central and deeply contested concept here is the "general will." Rousseau emphasized will, rather than reason – and, here again, he is perhaps a precursor of the Nietzschian postmodern. He argued that the will follows either the passions or reason. The first leads to what he called the particular will, which always favors a part rather than the whole; the second, which is more universal, he called the real will. The real will represents a higher level in not being self-seeking and sectarian. It can, but need not, approximate to the highest level: the general will. This latter seems to represent the true good for all, such that 'whoever refuses to obey the general will will be forced to do so by the entire body. This means merely that he will be forced to be free' (Rousseau 1762, 150). Since the general will could not be automatically identified with the particular or real will, it seemed to clash with many of Rousseau's strongly expressed democratic impulses, and became, like Locke, closely associated with what Rousseau calls the "lawgiver." But, differently from Locke, Rousseau associated this figure with a charismatic leader, who would appear to the rulers to have divine authority, for he must convince them of this "authority of a different order, which can compel without violence and persuade without convincing" (Rousseau 1762, 164). Whether or not Rousseau actually intended an aspect of his work to be made central to its entire reading, I think Lester Crocker has a point when he argues that Robespierre implements the "total collectivist state of the *The Social Contract* in which 'virtue patriotism' would rule" (1968, 120), and that the fascisms of the twentieth century (Hitler, Stalin, and others) are also grounded in the primacy of the "general will," which allows man to be "forced to be free." This is a highly contested reading, and while it may not capture the full balance of Rousseau's corpus, it perhaps highlights a trajectory that is possible once neither nature nor the divine are given dominion.

What of religion? In the *Social Contract*, Rousseau defines three types of religion:

> The first, which has neither temples, nor altars, nor rites, and is confined to the purely *internal* cult of the supreme God and the eternal obligations of morality, is the religion of the Gospel pure and simple, the true theism, what may be called natural divine right or law. The [second], which is codified in a single country, gives it its gods, its own tutelary patrons; it has its dogmas, its rites, and its external cult prescribed by law; outside the single nation that follows it, all the world is in its sight infidel, foreign and barbarous; the duties and rights of man extend for it only as far as its own altars. Of this kind were all the religions of early peoples, which we may define as civil or positive divine right or law. There is a third sort of religion of a more singular kind, which gives men two codes of legislation, two rulers, and two countries, renders them subject to contradictory duties, and makes it impossible for them to be faithful both to religion and to citizenship. Such are the religions of the Lamas and of the Japanese, and such is Roman Christianity, which may be called the religion of the priest. It leads to a sort of mixed and anti-social code which has no name. (Rousseau 1762, book IV, chapter 8)

All three forms are subversive of good government and, interestingly, the least embodied, the first, is especially so (although Rousseau calls it gospel "pure and simple" and "true theism"). Why is it so subversive? For Rousseau, it produced a slave mentality preaching servitude and dependence, thus producing citizens incapable of enjoying the liberty of the republic. Here Rousseau sounds like Nietzsche, with a disdain for the meek of the earth.

The conclusion regarding religion and the state is Hobbesian: the state must control religions, for they are a threat to the state in different ways. Toward the end of this final section of the *Social Contract*, Rousseau defines Christianity conveniently for the purpose of slotting it into its pre-aligned space: "Christianity as a religion is entirely spiritual, occupied solely with heavenly things; the country of the Christian is not of this world." Even with such an emasculated "religion," to ensure social stability and the power of the state, like Hobbes, Rousseau takes the extra step by giving the sovereign supreme power over determining the meaning of religion:

> There is therefore a purely civil profession of faith of which the Sovereign should fix the articles, not exactly as religious dogmas, but as social sentiments without which a man cannot be a good citizen or a faithful subject. While it can compel no one to believe them, it can banish from the State whoever does not believe them. . . . If any one, after publicly recognising these dogmas, behaves as if he does not believe them, let him be punished by death: he has committed the worst of all crimes, that of lying before the law. (Rousseau 1762, book IV, chapter 8)

To conclude this section: from the sixteenth to the eighteenth century we have seen the slow emergence of the nation state and its construing of "religion" in the key liberal theorists whose thought has shaped the constitutional democracies of European, American, and most non-European ex-colonized nations (in Asia, the Middle East, and Africa). My second goal of the narrative had been to show that the sovereign nation state was central in generating the definition of religion that today shapes our thoughts. Hobbes, Locke, and Rousseau are all aware of "world" religions and "Christian religions" as we have seen from their texts. The Catholic, Muslim, Buddhist, and Japanese religions are all incapable of being tolerated in these states because of their dual allegiances. Locke also discounts atheists because their promises cannot be based on any higher belief or authority. These are the presuppositions and positioning of a liberal tolerant society free of religious bigotry.

Act III: state wars: the irreligious reign of terror

My third goal is to question the claim that drives narrative one: religions and religious wars cause bloodshed. Statistics are highly disputed so I do not want to make definitive claims. I use Philip's (2004) and White (2005) for my figures. Since the emergence of nation states in the nineteenth century, and the efforts of each to try and secure and expand its sovereign territories, even if we restrict ourselves to European and American involvement in the twentieth century, the figures are terrifying. The First World War saw 19 million dead (excluding related medical illness, which would bring the total to 100 million more). The Second World War saw 55 million dead. After 1945, the death toll from the Vietnam, Korean, French Indochina, and Algerian wars alone comes to 4.8 million. Between 1946 and 2002 there were 226 armed conflicts according to the definitions of the Uppsala Conflict Data project and most of these were related to colonial powers carving up territorial boundaries that were disputed during and after colonial occupation. Much of the Middle East, Asia, and Africa was subject to these new sovereign boundaries. For example, David Fromkin has argued in *A Peace to End All Peace* (1989) that the European powers created the modern Middle East between 1914 and 1922, and in their boundary creations bequeathed many of today's intractable problems to the Arabs. The Iraq–Kuwait border, which has caused recent international tension, was drawn up by the British high commander Percy Cox, who was intent on keeping Iraq dependent on the British by blocking access to the Persian Gulf. The inclusion of the Soviet Union and China in war deaths during this period brings in a further 71 million dead. None of these wars were fought in the name of religion. They were the wars of irreligion, the wars of the nation state that had replaced God with capital, nation, and state. John Gray sees this secular death drive as the inverse of apocalyptic religion, which it replaced, and which threatens to return (Gray 2007), although Gray paints "religion" with too broad a brush (see Rengger 2007).

It is facile to compare figures between the twentieth century and the so-called "wars of religion" in the pre-modern period, in part because body counting is always unreliable, and possibly more so, the further back we go; and the technological power of modernity, as Zygmunt Bauman (1989) argues, is capable of producing killing machines on an unprecedented scale. Nevertheless, I would like to make three points about the figures and the irreligious bloodbath that our century has witnessed. First, as the eminent British sociologist Anthony Giddens has argued in the second volume of *A Contemporary Critique of Historical Materialism: The Nation State and Violence* (1987), since the sixteenth-century emergence of the doctrine of the state, its sovereignty, and the inviolability of its territorial boundaries, war has been the major means by which territory has been secured and boundaries expanded. War and violence have become the state's prerogative, its monopoly and its main tool, to which the economy is harnessed. If we add to this Bauman's point about modernity and the technologically efficient killing machines, there is a powerful conjunction of forces explaining the inevitability of a war-torn twentieth century. David Fromkin, the American lawyer and historian, nicely reverses the question of the modern irreligious period into: how was peace ever possible? In his *Europe's Last Summer: Who Started the Great War in 1914?* (2004) Fromkin confirms the glorification of violence as the underbelly of the nation state:

> In the opening years of the 20th century, Europeans glorified violence. . . . A panoramic view of Europe in the years 1900 to 1914 would show prominently that the Continent was racing ahead in a scientific, technological, and industrial revolution, powered by almost limitless energy that was transforming almost everything; that violence was endemic in the service of social, economic, political, class, ethnic, and national strife; that Europe focused its energies on an escalating, dizzying arms race on a scale that the world had never seen before; and that, in the centre of the Continent's affairs, powerful dynamic Germany had made strategic arrangements such that, if it went to war, it would bring almost all Europe and much of the rest of the planet into the war for or against it. Given these conditions, does not the question, "How could war have broken out in such a peaceful world?" rather answer itself? Would it not have been more to the point to ask how statesmen could have continued to avoid war much longer? . . . Which is not to say that war could *not* have been averted, but merely that, by 1914, it might have taken extraordinary skill to keep on averting it . . . in a world in which war was considered desirable – even necessary. (2004, 41–2)

As heirs to this civilization, we are confronted with some difficult questions, posed so strongly after the First World War: how could a once Christian Europe tear itself apart in so ferocious a manner? This takes me to my second point.

Aleksander Solzhenitsyn, the Russian Nobel Literature laureate, offered an answer to the question just posed in his 1983 Templeton Prize Address at Buckingham Palace. Admittedly unfashionable and deeply pessimistic, Solzhenitsyn saw 1914 as the outcome of a Europe that had abandoned God and, with that, humanity. The savior state had no other *telos* than the naked power of the nation state's self-assertion:

> The failings of human consciousness, deprived of its divine dimension, have been a determining factor in all the major crimes of this century. The first

> of these was World War I, and much of our present predicament can be traced back to it. It was a war (the memory of which seems to be fading) when Europe, bursting with health and abundance, fell into a rage of self-mutilation which could not but sap its strength for a century or more, and perhaps forever. The only possible explanation for this war is a mental eclipse among the leaders of Europe due to their lost awareness of a Supreme Power above them. (Solzhenitsyn 1983)

Solzhenitsyn interestingly extends his analysis to the Soviet Union and it bears remarkable parallels with the European story, not to be pressed, but certainly to be noted:

> In its past, Russia did know a time when the social ideal was not fame, or riches, or material success, but a pious way of life. Russia was then steeped in an Orthodox Christianity which remained true to the Church of the first centuries. The Orthodoxy of that time knew how to safeguard its people under the yoke of a foreign occupation that lasted more than two centuries, while at the same time fending off iniquitous blows from the swords of Western crusaders. . . . But in the 17th century Russian Orthodoxy was gravely weakened by an internal schism. In the 18th, the country was shaken by Peter's forcibly imposed transformations, which favoured the *economy, the state, and the military* at the expense of the religious spirit and national life. . . . Russia felt the first whiff of secularism; its subtle poisons permeated the educated classes in the course of the 19th century and opened the path to Marxism. By the time of the Revolution, faith had virtually disappeared in Russian educated circles; and amongst the uneducated, its health was threatened. It was Dostoevsky, once again, who drew from the French Revolution and its seeming hatred of the Church the lesson that "revolution must necessarily begin with atheism." That is absolutely true. But the world had never before known a godlessness as organized, militarized, and tenaciously malevolent as that practiced by Marxism. (Solzhenitsyn 1983)

While Solzhenitsyn's style of apocalyptic declamation is not always attractive to European intellectuals, there is something significant in his argument, which brings together the emergence of the nation state with the silencing of religion in the public square, the eclipse of Christianity ("religion" in Europe), ideological secularism (one of whose strongest forms was Marxism), the eruption of endless violence, and a "rage of self-mutilation." If these factors are actually related, as I am inclined to think is the case, then the question of "religions" in the public square is a most pressing issue. Part III will address this issue further. I now need to return to my main concern: the effect that the term "religion" has on its application upon the world religions.

Act IV: modernity's construal of the academic "field" of "religions"

To draw a conclusion to my alternative narrative, I want to develop three more arguments in response to the last part of modernity's narrative about "religion." You will recall modernity's story contained three claims: first, of Christianity's distortion of the other for its own theological interests, emblematic in sixteenth-century England; second, the slow struggle to throw off this theologizing of non-Christian religions; third, the emancipation of the study of religion from theological tutelage that facilitates an understanding of religions on their own terms, the victory of the scientific study of religion. In this section I want to challenge all three claims to tell a different story, which, in brief, runs something like this: Christianity actually provides the best conceptual space to understand another religion in its own terms, followed by an entirely legitimate theological engagement that can entail appreciation, learning, and social collaboration, at the same time as immanent critique (intra-textual criticism) and mission (inter-textual criticism). Modernity, both in its politics and in its allied academic rendering of religions, fails to engage with religion's otherness, but neutralizes it for the sake of control. Second, the attempt to throw off one interpretative framework (Christianity) only results in new interpretative frameworks, which can be criticized by theology for failing to meet their own objectives. Third, the victory claimed by some proponents of religious studies is spurious, for they have brought their own presuppositions into play in understanding and interpreting the religions, which has no more justification than a theological interpretation, but may have more social esteem in a secularized society. In fact, it may have less justification because of the belief that there is no interpretative framework (the spurious claim of neutral objectivity). From a theological viewpoint, it certainly has less justification, as it fails to tell the full truth about the phenomenon in question – the full truth meaning speaking in the light of the triune God who is the fullness of truth. Only from this theological narrative can other religions be truly understood, simply because Christianity is true.

Harrison's narrative actually demonstrates that different types of theology generate differing types of interest in other religions, including those that try and properly describe another religion based on the best available findings, culled from a multi-disciplinary perspective (philology, history, archaeology, and so on). I will assume this type when I speak of theology's interpretation of culture for the rest of this chapter, for this type has developed and mutated, in a trajectory between the Cambridge Platonists, Hegel, nineteenth-century comparative theology (see below), and, to a limited extent, the comparative theologies of today (see chapter 2). Panikkar's early work is a role model of what I seek to develop. While most of the Protestant Scholastics were simply not interested in other religions, the Cambridge Platonists were, and they were intellectually serious about this task. They were motivated by their concern for God's justice, for they felt that the Scholastics in their presumption of damnation regarding non-Christians had compromised God's justice. They were thus called upon to demonstrate their thesis that some truths of revelation were found in pre-Christian religions and they drew upon the ancient *prisca theologia* tradition – it was held that Old Testament revelation affected all pre-Christian cultures, so that traces of divine truth were to be found everywhere. As evidence many pointed to the *Hermetica*, which was believed to originate from ancient Egypt. What is important is the responsive flexibility and appropriateness of categories to the material being investigated, and their engagement with the best scholarship on the religion in question. For example Cudworth, one of the leading Cambridge Platonists, acknowledged that, in the light of Casaubon's historical findings about the *Hermetica*, which dated them much later than previously held, it was no longer possible to view these texts as pre-Christian. The theory of their influence from the Old Testament had to be abandoned. Whether Casaubon was correct or not, we see here a responsiveness to historical claims. After Casaubon, new categories were sought that would serve as conceptual lenses through which different cultures could be better understood. The *prisca theologia* hypothesis was eventually abandoned by many (and reinterpreted by others). New interpretative categories arose with Hegel in the eighteenth century, as we saw above, and with the Anglican divines, Frederick Denison Maurice and James Freeman Clarke, in the nineteenth.

In her important study, *The Invention of World Religions, Or, How European Universalism Was Preserved in the Language of Pluralism* (2005), Tomoko Masuzawa makes some astute observations about Maurice and Clarke's type of theological reading, which she calls "comparative theology." She is unaware of Clooney and Fredericks, for the nineteenth century is her remit. She shows that Maurice and Clarke both made good use of scientific studies as the basis for theological engagement and interpretation of the religions. They concluded, with differences, that there was much that was good and noble in these traditions, and that they would find their fulfillment in Christianity, which alone responded to their desire for true worship (Maurice and Clarke: see Masuzawa 2005, 75–86). It is interesting that Charles Hardwick, writing slightly earlier, came up with a very negative assessment of the religions, but he also took the time to learn about these religions (Hardwick: see Masuzawa 2005, 86–95). The point I want to stress is that regardless of their respective theological verdicts on the "religions," what we see is a growing sense that a good initial understanding is required of what is then theologically praised or criticized, or declared as being bewilderingly complex. Understanding, to the best of one's ability, is a prerequisite to any form of judgment. Of course this understanding is not neutral, as it is structured by particular research questions, interests, and methods. Some philosophers of science agree this is true of any research paradigm (Kuhn 1970) and this has been applied in the arts and social sciences as well (see Polanyi 1962; McGrane 1989; Asad 1993).

Further, because Christianity calls for a critical engagement with *all* human culture, the world religions become a necessary object of theological interest, which requires understanding them as best as possible from the "inside," as they understood or understand themselves, before "outside" interpretation can proceed. This whole area can be illuminated greatly from the debate in social sciences, especially anthropology, regarding insider/outsider observation and participation (McCutcheon 1999). For the moment, however, I shall simply specify the following and then proceed. Insider reporting is a descriptive interpretation that would usually be agreed on by an insider or a well-informed and sympathetic outsider. Outsider reporting is an interpretation of insider reporting, which may be entirely congruent with the insider account, or may diverge. If it diverges, a plausible explanatory framework within the outsider report needs to be provided. It is quite possible that an insider might learn constructively from an outsider reporting process, or indeed contest and argue against it. Or simply ignore it. The question of truth operates in both areas, insider and outsider reporting, but obviously in different ways.

For inside reports to be true, they must be intra-systematically coherent with the beliefs and practices of the insider group, and the question of their referential ontology might be part of the insider report, or it might not. For outside reports to be true, they must be intra-systematically coherent with the world of the outsider reporter, who is of course an insider to her own world, and their persuasiveness to the insider about whom they are reporting is entirely contingent on a whole range of factors. If, for example, a problem is located in the insider's world by both the insider and the outsider, the outsider may claim that it is best resolved by actually leaving that worldview, adapting it in a certain way consonant with an insider report, or adapting it in ways that would create intra-systematic dissonance. This process might happen through rational discussion, rhetorical persuasion, example of life lived, and in a whole range of explicit and implicit ways.

Masuzawa acknowledges the important social impact of these Anglican divines. In its heyday, "comparative theology was a very popular, highly regarded, and respectable intellectual–spiritual pursuit" (2005, 22). This reflected a strong Anglican presence within English universities and among the general public at the time. Masuzawa notes that

> it may be credibly suggested that the popularity of world religions was more a legacy of the religious-evangelical enterprise of comparative theology than of the arcane and scholarly tradition of the nineteenth-century science of religion. If this should be the case, the present-day suppression of – or, at least, what appears to be wilful ignorance about – comparative theology may be an intriguing historical conundrum in its own right. (2005, 23)

The conundrum may be explicable by fashionable prejudice from the history of religions school, both then and now. Masuzawa is aware of this:

> The proponents of the science of religion in the twentieth century and thereafter, however, have been careful to keep their own practice at a distance from [comparative theology] reserving the privileged term "science" for studies based on objective appraisal of empirical data, supposedly unmixed with pious sentiments or partisan denominational interests. (2005, 22)

The problem is that the religious "scientists" simply promoted different interests with alternative "pious" sentiments, not pure objectivity.

I want to suggest that there are two alternative trajectories to the theological engagement when it comes to the description/interpretation of world religions – which bear a close parallel to the political arrangements emerging in modern Europe. The political counterparts will appear in examining the debate about religion in the public square in chapter 5. The first school I shall call ideological secular readings (ISR), which has as its modern father David Hume. His *Natural History of Religions* (1757) viewed all religions as equally illusory and, thus, equally worthless. ISR uses religion to further its own agenda and develop its own vantage point, which historically has been inherently in conflict with the self-understanding of the said religions.

The other school I shall call principled secular readings (PSR), which has as its modern father the founder of the *Religionswissenschaft*, Friedrich Max Müller. Müller tried to describe the religions primarily through philology and historical–critical reconstruction, establishing a "scientific" understanding of the religion, shorn of any religious prejudice. He was more concerned to understand and interpret the religions as they understood themselves, integrating the insider and outsider reporting. Müller and his successors practiced under various terms, with strong internal differences, but they shared the same basic goal. Hence, PSR covers history of religions, comparative religions, religious studies, and scientific study of religions.

Let me examine ISR and PSR briefly in turn to establish my claim that theology does not provide a biased reading of religions *compared* to non-theological readings. Only then will I move to a second claim: that theology provides the truest interpretation of the religions. First, the ISR group. Mircea Eliade (1969, 12–36), in an extensive review of over 50 years of the scientific study of religion, chooses 1912 as his decisive start date, because that date marks the publication or completion of five groundbreaking works that, to Eliade, establish the field: Emile Durkheim's *The Elementary Forms of Religious Life*; Sigmund Freud's *Totem and Taboo*; Carl Jung's *Psychology of the Unconscious: A Study of the Transformations and Symbolisms of the Libido*; Raffaele Pettazoni's *Primitive Religion in Sardegna*; and Wilhelm Schmidt's untranslated *Der Ursprung der Gottesidee*, on primitive monotheism. Durkheim, Freud, and Jung belong to ISR, and Pettasoni and Schmidt to PSR.

Few scholars today would class Durkheim, Freud, and Jung as "scientific." They are rather clearly ideological in holding various presuppositions that construe their interpretations quite radically. Durkheim claimed a positivist understanding, dispassionate and scientific, but actually explained religion in purely sociological terms: as maintaining the social order, providing social cement, such that God is society writ large. He saw religion as originally totemic, with its designation of sacred and profane, such that these distinctions ordered and structured social behavior. Durkheim's "objectivity" was such that he positively argued for a common civic religion in the light of the demise of traditional religions, to serve their purpose of social cohesion. The sociologist Kieran Flanagan is blunt:

> [Durkheim's] solution is untenable and is itself founded on an illusion. . . . A religion without God now functions to sacralise social bonds and to effect a harmonisation between the actor and the collective. Religious rituals now

> function to sustain this collective purpose and to affirm social bonds. But in this account *any* ritual is deemed to work. It need not be religious in intention but could be civil or it could be mass forms of entertainment. But by abandoning what is distinctive about religion, its exclusive functions, Durkheim blunts sociological critiques of religious belief. (1966, 116)

He also paves the way to evacuating the truth with which religion is concerned and recoding it entirely in terms of social function. This is a form of sociological reductionism.

Freud was deeply reductive, both in his early and in his later work, where religion masked various neuroses and psychoses, which a mature personality or group would eventually grow out of into mature adulthood. Jung was far more sympathetic to religions than either Durkheim or Freud, but classed them around organizing psychological themes that he thought were central in reflecting immanent psychological cross-cultural archetypes, rather than relating to any transcendent ontological reality. Jung eventually translates all religions into his own psychological worldview. (See further on these brief readings: Milbank 1990, 61–71, on Durkheim; and Palmer 1997, on Freud and Jung.) With Freud and Jung, it is clear that we are dealing with men of genius and profound insight, whose work has shaped intellectual disciplines and generated important research work on religion. Both remind theologians of an important and sometimes neglected aspect of what Christianity embodies. But it is their psychological reductionism that is problematic, their actual portrayal of religion as *being about* social cement, neuroses, or universal archetypes, without sufficient attention to the fact that they are not at all describing, but interpreting, and interpreting with little reference to the self-understanding of the religious groups in question. The science of religion, in these three instances, inscribes the religious worldview being "studied" into its own non-religious worldview (sociological, psychoanalytical, and psychodynamic respectively) without much appreciation of that culture in its own terms.

It is one of the important achievements of postmodernity to undermine the pretensions of these great "modern grand narratives" (Foucault 1970; Deleuze 2004), by showing how their "objectivity" was actually the cultural adoption of a specific way of viewing things, with all its necessary policing and punishment. Modernity's grand narrative had plausibility because it had social and structural endorsement. Its actual claim to truth in terms of its universality was undermined by locating its particularity. However, some currents in this unmasking established a void as the only real, upon which we scratch our cultural markings, and denied the possibility of metaphysics, a discourse that might enact participation with a divine reality, outside our constructions. The year 1912 simply marks a high point in secularized readings of religion, which is called history of religions in Eliade's comprehensive account. If, and only if, the Christian worldview is discounted or objectively wrong can the objectivity of these views be possible, otherwise a lot more argument is required by ideological secular readings.

Before proceeding, I need to address an obvious objection: "surely Christian readings are guilty of the same ideological character as ISR, although obviously not secularist? Even in your two-tiered strategy of attaining insider-reporter understanding, you finally advocate reading religions in ways those religions might not agree with, from an outsider report." Four responses need to be made. First, drawing on chapter 1, I would argue that one concern of mine is to understand, to the best of our interdisciplinary ability, how a religious culture intra-textually understands itself. This is vital for theology and is the foundation of both mission and apologetics. Without a truthful understanding of the other's difference, the latter two are hampered. Here there is no parallel with ISRs. Second, in the next move, that of theological interpretation, there is admittedly a similar process of outsider interpretation, as with ISR. The only difference will be that insider and outsider reporting may have more substantial common ground (with, say, forms of Judaism, Christianity, and Islam) than the outsider reporting of a Freud or Durkheim where the reporting has little point of contact with the self-understanding of the group. Admittedly, this is a contingent matter and would require explication case by case. Third, the Christian can claim the same epistemic validity as any of these other interpretative strategies, rather than accept the notion that there are some biased and some unbiased forms of outsider interpretation. Fourth, because of the Christian belief that the triune God is the true story of our world, it is a task of theology to argue this case with other alternative claims. In chapter 2 I argued that missionary rational dialectics and out-narration are always part of Christian engagement with other religions.

Principled secularists come in two varieties: modernists (the early generation like Müller, and recent writers like Donald Wiebe); and postmodernists (like Timothy Fitzgerald, Gavin Flood, Jonathan Z. Smith, and Robert Cummings Neville). Some of the postmodernists criticize the modernists just as I have the ISRs, but instead charge them with theological rather than ideological secularist bias! For example, Fitzgerald, in his incisive work *The Ideology of Religious Studies* (2000), starts with Müller and continues his trenchant line of criticism, with textual evidence, against the heirs of Müller: Chantepie de La Saussaye, Nathan Soderblom, Gerardus van der Leeuw, C. Jucco Bleeker, Joachim Wach, Joseph M. Kitagawa, Eliade, right up to Wilfred Cantwell Smith.

As I have argued this of Smith in chapter 3, let me take two other important figures in this group to illustrate Fitzgerald's argument: Müller and Eliade. Müller's theory of the origin of natural religion, "the individual's perception of the infinite in or beyond the finite, and the association of moral feeling," is irreducibly "theological" according to Fitzgerald:

> It implies that the relation between the individual and the Infinite is a universal phenomenon because all humans naturally are born with this faculty, which accounts for the existence of "religions". This is a metaphysical claim that reflects a development of the assumptions of western Christian culture, especially liberal Protestantism, both in its positing of the individual's capacities and also in its concept of the Infinite. (2000, 35).

Likewise for Eliade, Fitzgerald cites the criticism of Ninian Smart (whom I have criticized for falsely claiming objectivity through a modified phenomenological method; D'Costa 2005, 20–5). Smart criticizes Eliade's hidden ontological interpretative categories:

> Now of course Eliade's fixing on the sacred–profane polarity as ultimate involves various other limbs of theory. For the sacred is conceived by him ontologically: what is perceived as sacred in a hierophany reflects an archetype and attests to the primordial ontology, which Eliade characterises as Parmenidean (the real is timeless and inexhaustible), Platonic (archetypal) and Indian (temporal experience is illusory). (Smart 1978, 176)

Two points regarding the modernists in PSR: they all have interpretative frameworks, which take a Christian, Indian, secularist, or some other philosophical stance. This should not be surprising, given the arguments deployed against the ISRs. In this sense, the PSRs fail in their goal (neutrality), without in any way minimizing their huge contributions to the study of religion, their philological, historical, and cultural findings and researches, or detracting from their noble concern to understand world religions without distortion. Second, the only distinction between the modernist and postmodernist PSRs is that of greater reflexivity regarding the interpretative task and its necessary presuppositions. This is seen in the lingering sense of a freedom of interpretation beyond religious readings in some of this latter group, which is worth looking at. Let us keep with Fitzgerald.

Fitzgerald's consistent line is that the very construct "religion" is shored up by various ideological presuppositions held by scholars, primarily religious, not always Christian, but always deeply "Western." In summarizing his argument, Fitzgerald says he seeks to show how "religious studies"

> imposes on non-western institutions and values the nuance and form of western ones, especially in such popular distinctions as those between religion and society, or between religion and secular, or religion and politics, or religion and economics. In addition, and in pursuit of this constructed image of the other religions, it draws up typologies of Judaeo-Christian monotheistic categories such as worship, God, monasticism, salvation, and the meaning of history and tries to make the material fit those categories. (2000, 9)

Fitzgerald has a point. His careful historical work helps to support my own argument about the way in which religion in the West became privatized, and this privatization was then exported to the world ("religions"). Fitzgerald is a healthy reminder to be careful that we do not simply see what we would like to (either negatively or positively). He also reminds us not to smuggle in theological or alien interpretative categories *without being clear* that this is happening. But all this presupposes some vantage point that will allow things to eventually appear as they really are.

Where is this vantage point for Fitzgerald?

> My proposal is that those of us who work within the so-called field of religion but who reject the domination of ecumenical theology and phenomenology reconceptualize our field of study in such a way that we become critically aligned with theoretical and methodological fields such as anthropology, history, and cultural studies. (2000, 10)

And the greatest of these is "cultural studies" or, more precisely, cultural anthropology. It would seem that, at the crucial pressure point, Fitzgerald creeps back into the modernist camp. Why should cultural anthropology provide a non-ideological platform, a pure, rather than interpreted, viewpoint, when Fitzgerald has already earlier acknowledged in his argument that "ultimately all our attempts at understanding are based on metaphysical assumptions and articles of faith" (2000, 43)? But at the final step Fitzgerald does not unfold or admit his own metaphysics and articles of faith, and assumes this the best perch from which to view the world. Anthropology has been strongly criticized for just this evasion by the distinguished anthropologist Bernard McGrane in his *Beyond Anthropology: Society and the Other* (1989). Fitzgerald is aware of McGrane's work and cites it approvingly. He adds, with reassurance, "a great deal of the most cogent criticisms that have been made against the culture concept, and indeed against anthropology itself, have come from within the discipline itself" (2000, 237). This reflexivity does commend the discipline, but it does not show how Fitzgerald is going to escape the trap he has set for every other investigator that he has criticized: their ideological constructivism. He is too intelligent to ignore this, but never shows us the way out, except for commending endless reflexivity, which is of course claimed by most intellectual disciplines within the academy. In the end, Fitzgerald is guilty of cultural, anthropological, ideological reading strategies, ISR *and* PSR.

However, some other postmodern writers acknowledge the "ideological" trap is inescapable; every investigator is theory laden. This is found resolutely in the illuminating work of Jonathan Z. Smith, but he, too, in the end, seems to find a place to stand, which is contrary to Sam Gill's (1998) defense of Smith's strength being the recognition that there is "no place to stand" when we study religions. Smith's self-conscious coming from nowhere is expressed in contrast to Archimedes' "Give me a place to stand on and I will move the world." For Smith, we cannot do this any longer. We can only place things side by side like the modern comparative theologians. He writes:

> The historian has no such possibility. There are no places on which he might stand apart from the messiness of the given world. . . . The historian's point of view cannot sustain clear vision. The historian's task is to complicate not to clarify. He strives to celebrate the diversity of manners, the variety of species, the opacity of things. (1978, 289–90)

But note, despite the important trait of resisting simplification, this historian is particularly inscribed: he cannot have any sense of religious truth; he cannot have any "clear vision" such that a good God created this world, and he foundationally rests with the "opacity of things." Once there was modernist positivist history that promised the dissolution of opacity: the neutral platform. Now there is postmodernist historicism that requires opacity for its authenticity: a new, but not neutral, platform.

Neville allows the possibility of a theological religious study in his *Religion in Late Modernity* in arguing that "we must squarely face the question of the integration of theological studies into religious studies" (2002, 214), as does Flood in his *Beyond Phenomenology: Rethinking the Study of Religion* (1999). Even though Neville and Flood do not practice theological readings themselves, they both recognize that tradition-specific readings of one religion by another are entirely legitimate and, indeed, can be very productive. In this brand of postmodernism we come full circle. We can justify theology's engagement with a chastened self-critical form of religious studies that must serve a theological end.

I promised one final argument to conclude this chapter's alternative narrative: that theology's reading of world religions, in their particularity and complexity, is the most truthful reading available. Perhaps, by now, the gist of this claim will be apparent. It means this: once the multi-disciplinary insider/outsider reports about the doctrine of self and compassion in Tibetan Buddhism in the sixteenth century; or the tradition and practices of *sati* in Hinduism culminating in twentieth-century practice; or the doctrine and practice of *jihad* in Sunni Islam in the modern period in Egypt and Pakistan are closely studied and understood, then, and only then, is theology able to make certain judgments that are internal to theology about these findings. These judgments might be very simple: this is compatible with our faith and indeed might be seen as a stepping-stone toward true faith (*preparatio*, fulfillment); this is not compatible with the faith and, in certain instances, this is evil and to be challenged (discontinuity); this aspect seems compatible with faith, but neither a positive nor a negative relation is presently discernable (don't know, but be attentive); it is impossible to judge whether this is compatible or incompatible with faith, and it may actually be incommensurable for the time being (time-bound provisional incommensurability); this aspect actually helps us understand either a doctrinal or a practical aspect of our faith with a refinement not earlier available, because such resources were never present within the Christian tradition before (for example, Aristotle for Aquinas, or Sankara for Panikkar), or because, contingently, this has never been part of the tradition (meditation by the laity), or used to be present in the tradition but is not much used contemporarily (praying the rosary, use of indulgences that can be prompted when confronted by the analogical use of the "rosary" or "indulgences" in Buddhism). These latter questions deal with the questions of truth that none of the alternatives I have looked at address.

Conclusion

In this and the previous chapter I have tried to trace the contested manner in which "religion" has been understood to show that modernity's discourse on "religion" has powerful theological, social, and intellectual consequences: it rendered religion an increasingly immanent sentiment, a matter of private choice, its role being consequently de-socialized, in part because of the rhetoric that religions always fight with each other, and in part because the sovereign state co-opted the social space of religion. From my alternative narrative, I tried instead to show that what happened was the replacement of one religion by another. The new religion of secularism (in both its IRS and PRS modalities) and its accompanying idol, the sovereign state, required war and violence for its perpetuation and maintenance and the destruction of any loyalties that were transnational or contrary to the state's sovereign rule (Catholicism and Islam being two obvious examples). If a theology of religions is to be developed in the light of this narrative, it is unavoidably political and engaged in a cultural critique that not only requires "religions" to be understood as cultural forms of power, but also the often invisible state and its apparatus, which we take as givens, as cultural forms of power that can be deeply inimical to religious adherence. This is what I hope to show in the next part, addressing a much debated question: the role of religion in today's public square.

PART III

Religions in the Public Square

5

Whose Religion and Which Public Square?

The Public Square

In the previous chapter I tried to show how religious culture has been increasingly privatized, interiorized, and transformed from a social cultural force into domestic ritual practices. Its lifeblood as a socio-political dimension of culture has been thinned and watered down so that its heartbeat in the public square is a faint and even dying pulse in modern Europe. This European view of religion has been exported worldwide through imperialism, trade, education, and the new creation of nation states, often made in the image of the departing empire. It has had a deep impact on educated elites across the globe, who have often become the elites through their Western-based education, and it has taken some grip on the popular imagination through United States media dominance. Nevertheless, the subsequent shape of religious cultures in this complex emerging world order, today christened "globalization," has been chameleon and extremely resistant to corrosive forces. Scott Thomas depicts this in fine detail in *The Global Resurgence of Religion and the Transformation of International Relations*, aptly subtitled *The Struggle for the Soul of the Twenty-First Century* (2005). Thomas argues that, while most political commentators imagined the disappearance of religion in the twenty-first century, the opposite has been the case; indeed, so much so, that international organizations rightly call upon religions to help deal with problems and not, as before and exclusively, on traditional nation states or groupings of nation states and their armed forces. Scott's depiction of the issue as a struggle for the "soul" of the globalized world is compelling, and I shall concentrate on one fragment of that struggle: the European soul. Two dissenting voices are strong in Europe, protesting the shape of the secular public square: certain forms of Christianity; and some strands of Islam. Both resist the carving out of social space to privilege the secular over the religious, and in rare instances express this disagreement through violence. The question I want to focus on in this chapter is the contestation of the role of religion in the public square in Europe. The implications are manifold.

Samuel Huntington's deeply insightful (if finally flawed) thesis helps situate the European interreligious situation on a complex global map. After the drawing open of the Iron Curtain through the collapse of the Berlin wall, ping-pong tournaments and diplomacy, followed by intense trade with China, and the shift of Soviet policy, ideological Marxism is withering, if not dead. Huntington argues that future global conflict will operate on a cultural, not ideological, axis, with religion playing a decisive role. This is a sort of reverse to Scott's thesis. Huntington argues:

> Blood, language, religion, way of life, were what the Greeks had in common and what distinguished them from the Persians and other non-Greeks. Of all the objective elements that define civilizations, however, the most important usually is religion, as the Athenians emphasized. To a very large degree, the major civilizations in human history have been closely identified with the world's great religions and people who share ethnicity and language but differ in religion may slaughter each other, as happened in Lebanon, the former Yugoslavia, and the Subcontinent. (Huntington 1997, 42)

The three cultural–religious clusters identified by Huntington are the Asian (China, Japan, and East Asia), the Western Christian (North America and Western Europe), and the Islamic (the Middle East, Africa, parts of East Asia). In Europe, all three clusters meet, although the Asian religious presence is slight compared to the Christian and Muslim (see Jenkins 2007, 16). While Europe is the great cradle of Christianity, it is presently increasingly secular. Demographically, some influential commentators have argued that, given the birth rates of non-Muslims versus Muslims in Europe, within 50 years Europe will be a Muslim state, Eurabia (Ferguson 2004; but see the more complex picture presented on this by Cesari 2004, 9–18). "Secular" and "Christian" Europeans seem to have lost the will to live and celebrate their civilization. Huntington perhaps fails to depict a fourth cultural element, a religion one might say, secular modernity, which in terms of "practice" is the religion of Europe (Weigel 2005, 43–53; Jenkins 2007, 16, 117). While all these configurations are contested and "belonging" is never so clearly cut, I think depicting such religious groupings heuristically (Christianity, Islam, secular modernity) serves to focus more clearly on our question.

In the first part of this chapter I will turn to secular modernity and briefly isolate three particular currents within that tradition that have partially shaped modern Western Europe and Western societies more widely. Bruce (1992) provides a more complex taxonomy of the contested term "secular." By the term "secular modernity" I mean those individuals, communities, and social structures that might be described as agnostic, atheist, and indifferent to the question of God. This is a contested definition but I hope to justify it as I outline the three currents, and believe that it is already justified in the light of the discussion in part II. I will indicate how secular modernity has positioned Christianity – and indeed, other religions in the public arena, further developing my earlier argument. I will focus especially on the presumption that "religion" cannot shape the "common good." It is argued that would mean the imposition of religious authority upon non-religious people. I will isolate basic operative paradigms and subject them to questions. In the next chapter, I will briefly isolate two stages within Roman Catholicism in response to these currents. I choose Roman Catholicism as a test case because I think it bears some fruitful comparisons with some aspects of Islam and is the tradition out of which I work. I will argue that the Roman Catholic church, after its own teething problems with modernity, provides an alternative between theocracy, rightly feared by secular moderns, and the social privatization of religion underpinning secular modernity. Catholics, like other Christians, have the resources to offer religiously pluralist Europe an alternative to the predicted "clash of civilizations." Only in this mode is intercultural and interreligious engagement possible. I will then argue that what has been claimed of Roman Catholicism is also true of some aspects of Islam. Indeed Islam has something to teach Catholics and, I will suggest, Catholics have something to teach Muslims. It is possible to avoid the clash of civilizations predicted by Huntington. There is a deep theological imperative to so do and instead encourage the flourishing of intercultural and interreligious conversations committed to the common good in pluralist societies.

A Taxonomy of Secular Modernity and Postmodernity

The EU, in 2008, is constituted of 27 nation states, although it started with only 6 in 1951. With this expansion the cultural influences that shape Europe have greatly increased, but it is arguable that they are composed of six significant cultural streams: Greek, Judeo-Christian, Islamic, the Latin

West, the East and Byzantine in the newer EU, and, finally, the offspring of the Judeo-Christian heritage, secular modernity. (See D'Costa *et al.* 1995; Neusner 2006; and, for an interesting insight into Pope Benedict's pre-papal view on Europe, see Ratzinger 1988a, 221–36. Just before becoming pope he urged rejection of Turkey's entry into the EU.) Secular modernity has nearly succeeded in erasing the previous five cultural layers, although it is entirely dependent on those traditions to explain its own genesis. One might say it is the young son, trying to murder its father. This is probably best indicated by two important symbolic events.

The first is the attempt at writing an EU constitution in 2004. In the preamble to the constitution, there was fierce controversy over the exclusion of a single mention of Christianity when referring to Europe's distinctive civilization. The draft mentions the Classical Greek heritage, starting with a quote from Thucydides, and the Enlightenment and the deep commitment to democracy, human rights, and the rule of law. Christianity is not mentioned; 1,600 years of European history are silenced. The Vatican campaigned hard on this matter, as did the Polish government, and less so the Czech Republic, Lithuania, Malta, Portugal, and Spain. France, a founding member of the EU, staunchly resisted any such mention. President Chirac publicly declared: "France is a lay state and as such she does not have a habit of calling for insertions of a religious nature into constitutional texts." Olivier Duhamel from the French Chamber of Deputies argued that any mention of Christianity would be "absurd" as it would exclude Muslims, atheists, and secular European populations (all cited in Weigel 2005, 58–9). Duhamel presumably thought Thucydides a more inclusive reference. It is difficult to see how a historical description of Europe's past can exclude, but the opposition here indicates two currents of secularism: ideological secularism, which insists the state be defined through strict exclusion of religion (Chirac); and principled secularism, which does not insist on any ideological position, but advances a public forum that must, on principle, not exclude any from belonging (Duhamel). The parallels between this and IRS and PRS from the previous chapter will be evident.

The second example is the European debate regarding the public presence of Islam. In the UK this was evidenced in the ferocious political reaction to the Archbishop of Canterbury's public lecture in February 2008, where he argued that it was time to think about developing supplementary, not parallel, *sharia* jurisdiction in limited matters of marriage and divorce settlement, which might be freely utilized by Muslims, if required. He carefully qualified his proposal, showing an awareness of the complex problems surrounding his suggestion. But his point was simple: Christians and Jews already have such a provision in English law; it was time to consider Islam. Such provisions exist in different forms in a number of democratic countries, like the largest democracy in the world, India, which allows Muslim *sharia* personal law as supplementary; and the world's largest Muslim-populated state, Indonesia, is based on Suharto's *Pancasila*, a remarkable blend of theism with a separation between state and religion. Williams' lecture was roundly criticized by the three mainstream political parties and savaged in the English media, including the intelligent newspapers (see Beattie 2008; Madood 2008; Williams 2008). Some evangelicals within Williams' church called for his resignation. A very similar story can be told about Ontario's attorney general, Marion Boyd. She wrote a 150-page report in 2004, with 46 closely reasoned recommendations for employing Islamic principles in settling marital and inheritance disputes for Ontario's 4,000 Muslims. Her recommendations helped protect and develop the rights of Muslim women, and provided for greater state legal oversight and accountability in the way the laws might be applied, and for proper checks on freedom to use such provisions. Boyd, like Williams, was keen to encourage conversational multi-culturalism. But her report was rejected through a media barrage that associated *sharia* law with amputation, stoning, and lawless barbarity. In this, it prefigured some of the British media reactions.

Rational arguments and rhetorical gestures are also to be found in various political debates in Europe regarding the *khimar* or *hijab* (headdress worn by some Muslim women), or indeed any public wearing of religious symbols of identity. France once more is in the forefront in its opposition to such religious infringements of public space. In March 2004 Chirac carried the Stasi Commission's recommendations into law. This law banned all religious symbols being publicly worn in French primary or secondary schools and was widely understood to be aimed at Muslims. The law was passed despite advice to the government from the highest legal body, the Conseil d'Etat, in 1989, that it is only public servants, not the consumers of public services, from whom the principle of secularism obliges religious neutrality (for more discussion on the headscarf in Europe, see Cesari 2004, 75–88). What we see in these discussions is a hint of straightforward Islamophobia (a prejudice against Islam that has deep roots in Christian culture, transmitted to secular modernity: see Runnymeade 1997; and Said 1995, the classic on the transmission of this prejudice) from religious and non-religious commentators, as well as forms of what I have called ideological and principled secularism. It is time to flush out these two latter terms.

Principled secularism

The philosophical names behind these two currents of secularism run through Descartes, Locke, Hume, Rousseau, Kant, Marx, and Comte: establishing the domain of the secular, a political space that is autonomous from religion, and present for the service and betterment of man (and eventually women). The actual word "secularism" emerged in 1846 according to the *Oxford English Dictionary*, with the Birmingham-born agnostic George Jacob Holyoake (1817–1906), who was not anti-religion, but pro-natural reason and humanity. Holyoake argued:

> Secularism is that which seeks the development of the physical, moral, and intellectual nature of man to the highest possible point, as the immediate duty of life – which inculcates the practical sufficiency of natural morality apart from Atheism, Theism, or the Bible – which selects as its methods of procedure the promotion of human improvement by material means, and proposes these positive agreements as the common bond of union, to all who would regulate life by reason and ennoble it by service. (Holyoake 1870, 17)

I would suggest, based on various empirical surveys regarding organized religion in Europe, that Holyoake's basic philosophy underpins most civilized Europeans who seek material prosperity within the European Union. Recall Holyoake finding this aspect, "the promotion of human improvement by material means," the "common bond" of people. This does not preclude care for the poor and downtrodden, through what Holyoake calls "service." Apart from the material improvement, the only other "common bond," at least procedurally, is the use of "natural morality" and "reason," which must thus avoid theism and the Bible (and to bring this up to date, one can add the Quran). Holyoake's inclusion of atheism along with theism and the Bible is interesting, for it indicates his concern to avoid all "ideologies" in his promotion of a free society. This can be done only through the promotion of his own agnosticism that he believed to be neutral, although of course it is not. In another publication Holyoake explicitly says that "Secularism is a code of duty pertaining to this life, founded on considerations purely human, and intended mainly for those who find theology indefinite or inadequate, unreliable or unbelievable" (1896, 35). Holyoake campaigned vigorously for the secularization of education in all public schools, a key, he thought, to producing a new culture of pluralism, of religions and non-religions. Holyoake's principled secularism is a proposal for furthering public debate, which is allegedly neutral to the veracity of religious forms of discourse, but confident that public debate can only be productive when shorn of religious moorings, as these are not commonly shared. Instead, public debate should be based on reason and our common nature, allegedly shared by all.

There are elements of principled secularism running through most European countries, the United States, and also non-Western countries like India, and each instantiation brings out very variable dynamics, so no easy generalizations are possible. In Europe, for example, those countries that have retained a "state religion" like England, Greece, and Denmark have differing characteristics to those that have not, like Austria, Belgium, Italy, Spain, and Germany. The United States' separation of religion and state is very religion-friendly and encourages civic religion, quite unlike France, whose separation of religion and state is constitutionally not dissimilar to that of the United States but has developed in a very different direction due to the strong anti-Catholic tendency in French history. India, with a majority Hindu population and the third biggest Muslim population in the world, adopted a British model of legal and constitutional separation between religion and state, which was seen to be the only way to deal with religious "factionalism," but has been subject to rigorous criticisms from some Hindu and Muslim groups.

Holyoake's most sophisticated heir is to be found in John Rawls (1993), who is representative of the best traditions of what has come to be called political liberalism. The early Rawls excludes what he calls "comprehensive doctrines" (religions and ideologies) from the public square for they are incapable of forming the basis of consensus, except in drawing together those that agree with those particular comprehensive doctrines. Rawls is aiming to include in the process all reasonable people, which can also include those who hold comprehensive doctrines, but their doctrines cannot be the basis of defining and enfranchising "reasonable people." Rather, since public policy requires coercion and force to keep it in place, it must be developed through a properly public procedure that is neutral to comprehensive doctrines, but the good so defined must obviously be capable of winning assent from comprehensive doctrinal positions. Hence, the procedural process requires giving what Rawls calls "public reasons" for any proposals regarding the common good. Rawls sees this process as the only way to secure the common good in pluralist democracies. This procedural argument, with significant variations, is to be found in the influential works of political and social theorists such as Ronald Dworkin and Jürgen Habermas.

Rawls, in his later work (2001), is particularly sensitive to the problems raised by religious groups critical of his ideas and he specifies a number of points to clarify and develop his earlier thesis. First, he distances himself from what I shall be calling ideological secularism and what he calls anti-Christian "Enlightenment liberalism," because it is a comprehensive doctrine posing as a neutral process. This is to be applauded. Second, Rawls does not want to exclude religions from the public square, but rather requires that they should translate their public policy, so that "public reasons" can be given for their goals. For example, rather than opposing abortion on the grounds that the Bible is against murder, or that Aquinas' natural-law reasoning leads to such a conclusion, or that the Catholic magisterium says it is wrong (to choose limited examples), it is better to advance the case based on "public reason" grounds, which make the arguments accessible and debatable by all, such as opposition based on scientific evidence about the possible "human life" enjoyed by embryos aged under 20 weeks, or the general principle that it is always wrong to kill an innocent life, and so on. The latter general principle conforms to the norms of equality and justice applicable in all cases, and is thus acceptable as a public good. The former constitutes scientific evidence that the principle that it is wrong to kill innocent life is rightly applied to the case of abortion prior to twenty weeks. Only then can there be reasoned debate. In effect Rawls requires that religions translate their thick description reasoning (based on the Bible, tradition, canon law, magisterial teachings, and so on) into thin description or public reasoning which allows any person to follow the force of the argument. Rawls claims that in these two moves he is not anti-religious.

From my theological perspective, principled secularism is problematic on three counts. This is not to deny that it has supporters among both Christian and Muslim communities (see Insole 2004 for Christianity; Soroush 2000 for Islam), but I would argue that usually its religious supporters are to be found from within those whose concept of "religion" has been shaped by modernity in the manner outlined in the previous chapter. Admittedly, my objections are not decisive, but part of a cumulative argument as to whether principled secularism can deliver on its goals. First, Rawls excludes religions from public discourse in quite explicit terms in his earlier works, where he will not accept religious arguments in the public square. The later Rawls, who seems to move away from this exclusion, actually wants them translated into "public speak" so that they can enter the public square. But is such translation possible or desirable? And whose language should be the preferred one for universal discourse? Such translation is clearly possible, as in the example on abortion given above, but the example also clearly indicates one of the problems: the idiomatic translation must take place from one language (thick religious description) into another language (thin public reasons). One must ask, to whom does this latter language naturally belong, and on what grounds can it claim to be the common language? The obvious answer is that "public speak" is the language that eschews all and any religious discourse at all. As with Holyoake, it is the natural language of the agnostic secular person. It is at this point that political liberalism can be challenged as generating an irresolvable lacuna. It excludes in a principled manner comprehensive doctrines as a solution to the problem of conflicting comprehensive doctrines; but then smuggles in a normative comprehensive doctrine (secular agnosticism with its concomitant "neutral" proceduralism) to stand in as arbitrator in disputes, the force to be applied if such disputes cannot be resolved and, even more problematically, as the only means by which public debate can be conducted. It is fair to conclude that Rawls enforces a mode of secular discourse with an implicit comprehensive doctrinal worldview, despite his claiming otherwise, as the only means of peaceful coexistence in a pluralist society. He fails because he cannot achieve his stated goal of eschewing comprehensive doctrines in providing a solution to the clash of comprehensive doctrines; and he fails because he privileges one mode of public discourse (the principled secular modern), when the public square, properly understood, is actually made up of many varying forms of discourse. In practical politics and public discussion, Rawls' approach would have to exclude Martin Luther King and Gandhi. Indeed, Tony Blair, once he had retired from three terms of office as prime minister of the UK, told the BBC that, while it was commonplace in the US for politicians to talk about their religious convictions, "you talk about it in our system and, frankly, people do think you're a nutter." Why? Because British voters imagined that leaders who were informed by religion would "commune with the man upstairs and then come back and say 'Right, I've been told the answer and that's it" (see http://news.bbc.co.uk/1/hi/uk_politics/7111620.stm). The presumption is that religious persons cannot argue for their positions. Some cannot, but as a generalization this is inadequate.

This leads to a second objection. In the process of translation Rawls innocently presumes that religions are not transformed or damaged by this process of translation. But is that the case? Nicholas Wolterstorff (1996, 149) argues that Rawls' position makes any form of religious argument a political heresy. The wider point here is that Rawls' position actually makes any religion that refuses to translate itself into secular terms religiously fundamentalist, and thus incapable of reasoned discourse. I am not supporting religious or secular fundamentalism, but the role of reason within the given of revelation. Remove reason in relation to revelation, and fideism and voluntarism are the outcome. One can see these two ends of the spectrum in both Christianity and Islam, in such a way that reason and faith can operate together – a position advanced by Aquinas and opposed in the voluntarism of Duns Scotus, which parallels Averroes as opposed to Ibn Hazzm, or Nasir al-Din Tusi compared to Ghazali in Islamic thought. In Rawls, however, we find what appears to be the founding role of reason as the arbiter of revelation. Since everything can be translated into secular public discourse, which is seen as exclusively reasonable, it means that anything that cannot be so translated is unreasonable. If the authorities within a tradition (the Bible, Aquinas, and the Catholic magisterium, to keep with the earlier example) and the specific types of argument within a tradition (analogy from biblical precedence, typological readings of the Bible, reason explicating these findings) are not allowed to operate when those giving reasons are giving their "public" reasons, then the authority of religious argument is being subtly transferred to the authority of "reason alone," which is quite different from a religious tradition being able to mount reasonable arguments on its own behalf. I am charging Rawls with two unintended outcomes: first, only allowing certain types of liberal modernizing religions to participate in public discourse; and, second, actually intruding upon both the accepted authorities and the manners of argumentation within historical religions that rationally claim to have a right to participate in formulating the common good. Both of these outcomes go against Rawls' stated aims in his later writings, but both of these outcomes show the problematic basis of procedural liberalism to deal with contemporary pluralist societies, for the die is cast on behalf of one group while claiming to be neutral to all groups.

My final criticism of Rawls is an elaboration of a point raised already regarding Rawls' restriction on forms of public argument. The point is nicely put by Iris Marion Young, who argues that "when political dialogue aims at solving collective problems, it justly requires a plurality of perspectives, speaking styles and ways of expressing the particularity of social situations" (Young 1996, 132; and see also Stout 2004, 67–75). Besides reason, which is faintly reminiscent of Enlightenment liberalism, public discourse is saturated with jokes, rhetoric, stories, laments, immanent criticism (criticizing an opponent based on the supposed internal incoherence of their position – as I have been doing with Rawls above), religious discourse, and confusion. The point Young makes about the plurality of thick discourses with all their attendant difficulties is germane, for I am contending that Rawls' solution actually bypasses the very problem it sets out to deal with: real religious diversity having to engage with difference. Rawls fails in his goal as he fails to see himself as belonging to a "religious" group within the fray. He projects his proceduralism beyond the fray by creating the hybrid of "public reason," which turns out to be a cloak under which secular contractualism manages the public square. Very similar criticisms can be mounted against Habermas. Rawls is sometimes seen as epitomizing the US public square and Habermas, the European. I will return to Habermas in chapter 6. If principled secularism is part of the problem, rather than the solution, let us briefly turn to ideological secularism, which is more self-aware of its "religious" nature, of its having a comprehensive doctrine. However, ideological secularism is equally, if not more, problematic in resolving the problem of living together in a religious pluralist society.

Ideological secularism

In 1870, Holyoake publicly debated with Charles Bradlaugh (1883–91), a renowned atheist who succeeded Holyoake as president of the London Secular Society in 1858. Bradlaugh nicely indicates the *telos* of ideological secularism in his argument against Holyoake:

> Although at present it may be perfectly true that all men who are Secularists are not Atheists, I put it that in my opinion the logical consequences of the acceptance of Secularism must be that man gets to Atheism if he has brains enough to comprehend. . . . You cannot have a scheme of morality without Atheism. The Utilitarian scheme is a defiance of the doctrine of Providence and a protest against God. (Bonner 1895, 334, citing Bradlaugh)

Pope John Paul II would have agreed with Bradlaugh's claim regarding utilitarianism; that it is finally incompatible with Christian ethics. However, the pope actually turned on its head Bradlaugh's initial premise, for

John Paul argued that atheism cannot sustain ethics, as it is reductionist regarding the dimensions of the human person as well as not able to ontologically ground the "good" (Pope John Paul II 1993). Bradlaugh was adamant that secularism could only be established with the disproof of religion. This is the second current of modernity: ideological secularism, rooted in atheism.

Most civilized Europeans are not intellectually rigorous enough (in Bradlaugh's terms) to be classified as hard atheists. I say this with the important exception of Marx and Marxists – who constitute a very important part of recent European history, although now struggling to breathe due to the debris of the Berlin wall. If Rawls represents the major social thinker of principled secularism, Marx is the major social thinker representing ideological secularism in terms of his committed atheism and dialectical materialism. His lack of commitment to democratic pluralism and his avowed concern to liberate the masses from their tutelage to religion, a certain form of Christianity to be sure, perhaps indicate one *telos* of atheistic materialism. From a theological viewpoint, Marx's solution also ignores the problem entirely, and indeed seeks to impose a single ideology, which is the condition upon which freedom and justice are said to be established. The supersession of difference as a way of solving the problems arising from difference is a sleight of hand similar in structure to the way principled secularism employs a single ideology upon all to resolve the clash of differing ideologies. Nevertheless, Marx's concerns for social justice and the material conditions of the poor are important legacies from his Jewish–Christian influences, and Christian, Jewish, and Muslim thinkers have been rightly occupied in retrieving these themes and concerns, although wrongly believing Marx's social science is key to this recovery (see Boff 1985; Ellis 1989; and Esack 1997, respectively; and for criticism of this turn to social science, see Ratzinger 1988b, 152–64, 255–76; and Milbank 1990, 206–58).

In Europe there are no governments that can be called Marxist, although one might locate this type of aggressive atheist secularism in the French Republic's popular understanding of *laïcité*, which excludes all public signs of religion and thus, as a nation, promotes irreligion. Admittedly, this is a result of both Marxist socialism and France's imperialist conquests of North Africa, from where its major Muslim population derives, and French public reaction to this immigration. In the old Soviet Union and in China there is active religious repression (see Christian Persecution Info website: www.christianpersecution.info/) deriving from ideological atheism. I tentatively conclude that ideological atheism has very little resource to engage with the problems of a religiously pluralist society as, like its cousin, principled secularism, it only attempts a solution by reduction or repression, which is no solution at all.

Postmodern pragmatic secularism

Alasdair MacIntyre (1990) has argued that postmodernity is the parasitic afterbirth of modernity, for it is premised on a thoroughgoing critique of liberal modernity but not able to provide a constructive alternative. In its refusal of the universality of reason (thereby undercutting the entire modernist project), in its claim that all discourse is a will to power (thereby transforming the ontological into the political), and in its promotion of non-foundationalism as a basic methodology for all disciplines (thereby calling for a new paradigm in knowledge following Foucault), postmodern philosophy has been deeply successful in questioning modernity's religious pretensions to binding universal discourse, but it has found it difficult to provide the resources to move forward. In my own immanent critique above, I have echoed many of these postmodern criticisms. Theologians should be grateful for allies in the arguments against secular modernity. However, this alliance with postmodernism is of limited use, as many postmodern theoreticians are equally suspicious of religious discourse, seeing the same problematic foundationalism present, which on the social level often spawns a disregard for religious culture analogous to disregard shown by the modern. Indeed, MacIntyre notes that what is left after postmodernity is the irresolvable conflict of cultures and discourses, without any possibility of mediation, for there is (rightly) no neutral point from which to mediate. Nietzsche saw this with remarkable clarity, for once God is dead, only culture wars survive – in effect, the struggle for supremacy.

Terry Eagleton (2000) makes a similar point in his review of Stanley Fish's postmodern critique of liberalism, *The Trouble with Principle* (1999), where Fish advances similar arguments to the ones I have made regarding liberalism. However, Eagleton identifies Fish's inability to do anything other than rhetorically defend late capitalist hedonism, for this is the particularity within which Fish is ensconced. Stanley Hauerwas suggests this is an "overly harsh" judgment, but then goes on to concede the point (Hauerwas 2007, 88). Eagleton criticizes Fish for doing

> what so much Post-Modern thought does when confronted with a "bad" universality – which is to say, set up a "bad" particularism in its place.

> [Postmodernists] fail to grasp that such militant particularism is just the flipside of the vacuous universalism it deplores, rather than a genuine alternative to it. (Eagleton 2000)

Eagleton adds, and this is germane to my argument,

> Stanley Fish is the flipside to John Rawls rather as tribalism is the terrible twin of globalism, or the view from nowhere is inevitably countered by the view from us alone. (2000)

Fish, like his influential postmodern pragmatist counterpart, Richard Rorty, is committed to democratic conversation but, like the procedural moderns they criticize, they have no conception of the common good, except in maintaining conversation.

This interesting trajectory is seen in Rorty's work. In his classic *Philosophy and the Mirror of Nature* (1979), Rorty argued for the importance of "conversation" precisely in those areas where "normal" discourse is unable to advance, given the lack of commonly accepted standards. In this type of exercise societies are able to move from attaining consensus on mutually agreed grounds to discerning the "relation between alternative standards of justification, and from there to the actual changes in those standards which make up intellectual history" (1979, 398). This appears to be a plea for genealogy. But even in this openness to conversation, which perhaps stems more from late capitalist delight with consumer choice, in this instance in the intellectual supermarket, Rorty's openness seems oriented toward the exercise of genealogy, which in itself does not show how such conversations might proceed. Admittedly, such conversations may not proceed and this is not Rorty's wish or fault, but in Rorty's later work we find a curious embargo on such conversations that mirrors Rawls but derives from Rorty's pragmatism, not dissimilar to Bradlaugh's utilitarianism, which is quite different from Rawls' liberalism.

In his telling essay entitled "Religion as a Conversation-Stopper" (1999), Rorty suggests a pragmatic "restraint" upon religious discourse is required in public discourse. This is for the simple reason that recourse to religious reasons in such arguments is inclined to generate the unspoken reaction: "So what? We weren't discussing your private life; we were discussing public policy. Don't bother us with matters that are not our concern" (1999, 171). Rorty, like Fish, is critical of liberalism (and lumps together what I have distinguished as principled and ideological liberalism) and even grants that it is

> hypocrisy [to say] that believers somehow have no right to base their political views on their religious faith, whereas we atheists have every right to base ours on Enlightenment philosophy. The claim that in doing so we are appealing to reason, whereas the religious are being irrational, is hokum. (1999, 172)

However, this very admission simply enshrines the prejudice of Rorty's caste group, and is subject to Eagleton's scathing criticisms of Fish: postmodernism is bankrupt as it is an inversion of modernity, simply exchanging the "universal" for a "particular," a "particular" that is finally based on enjoyment and aesthetic criteria, which Eagleton unmasks as late capitalism.

In his critical discussion of Rorty, Jeffrey Stout makes a very pertinent point about religion being a conversation-stopper by helpfully distinguishing between two aspects of religion in such public discourse:

> we need to distinguish between discursive problems that arise because religious premises are not widely shared and those that arise because the people who avow such premises are not prepared to argue for them.

The latter is certainly not the preserve of religions, for Stout adds, "Everyone holds some beliefs on nonreligious topics without claiming to know that they are true" (2004, 87). But the distinction is helpful in clarifying where the problem lies: clearly in religious and non-religious people not being able to "argue" in support of their basic commitments and claims. It would seem that the objection here might be shared by religionists following Aquinas, Tusi, or Averroes on the one hand and following Scotus, Ghazali, and Ibn Hazm on the other, an argument about the primary role of reason over voluntarism. I will return to this point in chapter 6.

Beyond the secular – religion in the public square according to Jeffrey Stout and Alasdair MacIntyre

Stout (2004) and MacIntyre (1990) have been seminal contributors to this debate. In their most recent work both are critical of the exclusion of religious voices from the public square. Both are critical of modernity's alleged neutrality and disembodied reason, although MacIntyre more trenchantly so. Both write out of a Christian orientation: Stout as a Protestant shaped by Hegel, Whitman, Emerson, and pragmatism in the form of Robert Brandom, and MacIntyre as a Catholic, shaped by Aristotle and Aquinas. Both privilege civic society and local community over the nation state. However, Stout is deeply critical of MacIntyre, which makes a comparison of their positions all the more helpful in developing a model to understand our question.

Stout moves one step forward from John Rawls, in arguing that the public square is constituted by different religious voices, and by silencing them Rawls encourages a public square that will eventually destroy democracy as is not concerned with the voices of all its citizens. Stout then makes three decisive moves in his argument. First, all groups engaged in conversation must believe in the importance of the open conversation that democracy and civil society promote. They need to be committed to this forum, or else conversation ends (or does not even begin). Second, all diverse groups, religious or otherwise, must have a confidence that it is in such conversations that resolutions can be arrived at, even on issues that MacIntyre presents as intractable and incommensurable. While MacIntyre holds that it is impossible for moral discussion to achieve resolution without agreement over comprehensive doctrines, Stout finds this despair to be misplaced. Stout notes that interminable arguments over votes for women, slavery, and smoking in public places do eventually result in agreement, consensus, and effective democratic political decision-making. And Stout, like MacIntyre, believes thick description emerges in local communities and discussion is vital at that level. But Stout is deeply critical of MacIntyre's skepticism about democracy, which MacIntyre asserts is a charade, where money and forms of established power are far more decisive than detailed argument. Third, Stout's own position is dependent on a form of Hegelian pragmatism, which encourages conversation and *ad hoc* resolutions that reflect what can be achieved from conversation.

I want to highlight two points to show what is problematic in Stout's thesis, without denying its marked sensitivity to the religious question and his penetrating criticisms of the liberal tradition. First, Stout makes democracy the sacred cow at center stage, a sacred cow that is not necessarily valued *per se* by different religious communities, and is admittedly underdefined in Stout's own thesis (see Hauerwas 2007, 147–51). This does not mean that some religious communities have not developed complex theologies to engage with and support democracy. They have, as we have already seen. However, it does mean that once again a Trojan horse is slipped into the religious citadel, such that there is an *a priori* requirement to accept a key element of secular modernity's trajectory before participation at the public table is permitted. As Coles pertinently argues (2005, 316), Stout acknowledges that democracy disrupts traditions that legitimate the reproduction of hierarchical power based on elites' claims to possess a privileged exclusive interpretative relationship to an inherited legacy of truth. Stout instead promotes self-reliant democratic selves who select the sources on which they depend, who use them and adjust them according to local questions and rework the past for our needs. But this type of prioritizing of the democratic structure and process, which collapses back into Rawlsianism, has the effect of encouraging only liberal religious traditions (that accept modernity) to the public square, silencing the disruptive and differently structured past, and denigrates as archaic voices that emerge from a hierarchical forum. Stout sometimes recognizes this (e.g., 1981, 201–2), but he does not address the concerns, just acknowledges they exist. Coles shows how this compromises the Barthian emphasis on Christ's primacy in worldly engagement. It equally compromises the Catholic emphasis on the primacy of the church in shaping primary loyalty in Christ. This is why Stout is so critical of MacIntyre, whose primary loyalty lies in protecting traditions of inquiry, not the democratic process *per se.* In Luke Bretherton's words:

> For Stout the threat to justice takes the form of a threat to the democratic tradition whereas for MacIntyre it takes the form of a threat to the process of tradition constituted rationality. (2008)

Second, Stout's dependence on conversation as the path to light is a version of Hegelian optimism, rooted in a low estimation of sin. While not wishing to denigrate democracy, it does not help to ignore the totalitarian dangers present within democracy as noted by John Paul II above. MacIntyre's criticisms are not without force, and Stout even seems to concede that in America it is difficult to call government democratic due to the powerful corporate pressures on legislation (2004, 305). However, Stout is correct that MacIntyre owes us a greater explication of his disdain for the democratic principle (even if the practice is so often corrupt and shallow). Democratic forums cannot be a guarantee of truth, and conversation, while deeply important if it serves human dignity, might equally lead one deeper into congealed darkness rather than resolved light as Stout so optimistically believes. Coles gives this particular point a theological underpinning:

> Stout's moderate rhetoric is entwined with a relatively diminished sense of the extent of the damages wrought by the present order of things and the depth of transformations necessary to repair our world. (2005, 320)

Starkly put, Stout seems to seek salvation through conversation. While there is much that is attractive about Stout's proposal, he fails to take seriously the difference of voices constituting the public square, and fails to give appropriate space to hierarchical traditions of reasoned argument. For a fuller accounting we turn to MacIntyre.

MacIntyre's position robustly places tradition-specific reasoning and practice as the means of the pursuit of justice, not democracy, as does Stout. This well serves the Catholic position I will shortly develop, for it starts with a self-conscious tradition-specific notion of justice and the good, granted in principle to all those involved in the public square, rather than assuming an overarching commonly acceptable procedure (Rawls), or adopting an ideology committed to excluding alternative conceptions of the good from the public square (Marx), or apparently claiming that anything goes, yet finally enforcing a particular upon all in a manner that cannot be adequately justified (Fish and Rorty), except through majority rule or philosophical pragmatism (Stout, Rorty, and Fish). MacIntyre is serious about the authority of tradition and the complex and differing manner in which traditions operate. Contrary to Stout's criticisms (2004, 118–39), MacIntyre is well aware of both the internal plurality of a single tradition (1990, 58–81 is one of many examples), and the manner in which "tradition" is often *ad hoc*, ill-formed, and very fluid (62–78). MacIntyre is also sensitive to how non-foundational reasoned debate takes place successfully, or fails to, within a single tradition and, importantly, between differing traditions. He thus navigates a path between modernity's universalism and postmodernity's particularism. Further, and most importantly, MacIntyre is aware that he is advancing a particular comprehensive doctrinal viewpoint, which nevertheless facilitates real openness to critical discussion and exchange, because it is grounded in both reason and faith, MacIntyre's Aristotelian-Thomism. MacIntyre is clear that he is not a theologian, nor doing theology, but a philosopher. My use of him is as a theologian who requires philosophy and reason to explicate the theological task.

Elsewhere I have looked at the development of MacIntyre's thought (2005, 25–37). I will summarize the end result of his project (especially in MacIntyre 1990). MacIntyre argues that Western European society is confronted by three rival traditions of intellectual and moral inquiry, each with its own epistemological, ontological, ethical, and methodological assumptions. While they may seem incommensurable, in the sense that they do not have agreed criteria by which to establish the truth of their positions, MacIntyre also seeks to show that there may be the possibility of a historically narrated rational debate between them, such that one might emerge as superior. What are the three rival versions? First, there is the Enlightenment project, which I have been calling secular modernity. Second, there is the postmodern, which is both parasitic upon the Enlightenment and utterly related to it. MacIntyre explains this by showing that the key to the modern was its abandonment of its Aristotelian heritage, and with this they thereby rejected a syllogistic way of justifying the rules of morality on the basis of a properly defined human *telos*. Both the modern and the postmodern rejected the only way of coherently moving from an apprehension of what is to an apprehension of what ought to be. The Enlightenment's rejection of teleology resulted in their interminable disagreement about how the rules of morality might be justified. Eventually all that could be agreed was that people ought to be free to agree or disagree, and the birth of the modern nation state and liberal democracy was its social and political counterpart.

However, with no common *telos*, even this minimal consensus would eventually come into question. Nietzsche for MacIntyre was inevitable, given the irresolvable lacunae within the Enlightenment project that replaced the *telos* of the common good with the formal requirement of human freedom. Nietzsche saw that there could be no real foundation for ethics in this stance and consequently celebrated the will to power, which was always the repressed truth within the Enlightenment. MacIntyre carries out immanent criticism of both these traditions, and provides a reading of their history from his Aristotelian-Thomist tradition. Here, we glimpse his and my own suggested path for argument between rival traditions.

The third position from which MacIntyre can reveal and narrate the shortcomings of the modern and postmodern is Aristotelian-Thomism, mediated by Pope Leo XIII's *Aeterni Patris*. He shows how this tradition actually emerged out of a debate between rival traditions at the University of Paris, out of the arguments between the Augustinian and Aristotelian visions, embodying a synthesis of both. This historical narration is part of Leo XIII's argument, for he argues that the manner in which each tradition is able to narrate the other in a way that shows the genesis of its weaknesses and the manner in which the rival tradition can actually more successfully attend to that weakness, allows for the possibility of victory in such debates.

One might formalize this into rules of engagement. First, there is the need to understand another tradition from the "inside," by learning its language. (See also the discussion on Lindbeck in chapter 2.) Second, only then is it possible to locate the internal weaknesses and unresolved lacunae within that tradition. Third, one must then explain how and why those weaknesses arose and how they might be better attended to from within an alternative tradition of inquiry. Clearly, "better" here requires qualification, because this "alternative" resolution removes the problem only by changing the grounds upon which it is resolved. For example, I have been arguing above that it is better to be a principled secularist than an ideological one regarding the problem of different voices in the public square. But I have then argued that principled secularism also fails and that there is a "better" answer to the problem found in Catholic thought. The principled secularist will rightly complain that they want to resolve the problem while remaining a principled secularist, and here is the challenge. I argue (with MacIntyre) that this is impossible to do with the terms of principled secularism, so the principled secularist committed to attending to this problem is faced with four alternatives: give up, convert, advance a better solution within her own tradition, or resort to force. Many will of course go for the third option, and MacIntyre does not suggest that these issues resolve themselves quickly. MacIntyre believes that this type of rational dialectics really takes seriously intellectual differences and attends to them. If MacIntyre's position is projected into the public square, be it in local communities and small-scale practices, I think we have a genuine advance in the discussion.

MacIntyre takes so seriously the importance of different traditions and the conditions for their intellectual growth that he rightly suggests the establishment of rival universities,

> each modelled on, but improving upon, its own best predecessors, the Thomist perhaps upon Paris in 1272, the genealogist [postmodern] upon Vincennes in 1968 [and I would add, the modern, upon Berlin in 1810]. And thus the wider society would be confronted with the claims of rival universities, each advancing its own enquiries in its own terms and each securing the type of agreement necessary to ensure the progress and flourishing of its enquiries by its own set of exclusions and prohibitions, formal and informal. But then also required would be a set of institutionalized forums in which the debate between rival types of enquiry was afforded rhetorical expression. (1990, 234, my brackets)

Readers will have noted that there is not a single gesture toward democracy as the condition for the flourishing of public debate. This is both an enormous strength and a limited weakness. It is a strength because MacIntyre's position recognizes that some traditions have internal reasons for engaging in such debate and others do not. The three traditions he is discussing all want to argue with their rivals.

Further, and this is my extrapolation of MacIntyre, some traditions will wish to engage in critical debate but not on the condition that they must subscribe to democracy first. If that tradition exists within a democracy as do Christianity and Islam in Europe, it *might* have to account for its attitude to democracy. I say might, rather than must, as the force or necessity of this "accounting" will be different. For example, the Amish communities who withdraw from society in North America and do not vote, but live in a democracy, "account" in one manner; and the Catholic church's conditional approval and critique of democracy in the voice of John Paul II is another manner of relating to democracy. There is a broad spectrum of views on democracy among Catholics: some who argue a divine sanction to democracy like Richard John Neuhaus; and others, like MacIntyre, who have little respect for its practices.

The strength of not placing democracy before tradition (exemplified in the title of Stout's book) is the wide-ranging inclusion of different voices. The weakness is evinced in the final phrase cited in the quote just given: "But then also required would be a set of institutionalized forums in which the debate between rival types of enquiry was afforded rhetorical expression." Who provides these institutionalized forums to advance the public good? Without democratic institutions, there is a danger (and that is as strongly put as is necessary) that MacIntyre's proposals for in-depth public debate might be a forum for only the rich and powerful elites in society. MacIntyre would rightly counter that this is just as likely in American democracy. In England, however, there has been a tradition, for example, of government funding for religious schools in primary and secondary education (up to the age of 18), which has meant Catholic, Church of England, Jewish, and more recently Muslim schools that allow for the cultivation of tradition-specific interests but are "balanced" by two things. First, the need to allow non-Christians (or whatever the school might be) to attend Christian schools and, second, government inspectorate visits to ensure that a proper level of education is taking place. Likewise, in legislature, the House of Lords has reserved seats for a limited number of bishops from the Church of England and, more recently, this has been extended to include representatives from Judaism and Islam. Catholic bishops cannot hold such political office, so declined the invitation. With the separation of church/religion and state in the United States, MacIntyre's judgment about democracy may be more appropriate, but it is certainly not the case in England and in some other European countries (see Cesari 2004, 65–88).

There is a serious problem with MacIntyre's position, requiring adaptation, not abandonment. MacIntyre's public square is ominously missing the plural voices from other religions, especially Islam, an omission highlighted by the Muslim convert and philosopher Muhammad Legenhausen. He rightly highlights Islam's relationship to the Aristotelian tradition upon which MacIntyre is so dependent, and therefore criticizes MacIntyre's inexplicable omission of Islam in his consideration. Legenhausen also suggests that Islam could equally address the aporia within MacIntyre's argument against modernity in *After Virtue*, just as later Catholicism would resolve that aporia in MacIntyre's position. Islam fulfills the condition of providing a community of practice that might resist modernity, and offers an account of the virtues and morality based on its inclusion of Aristotle in various elements of its philosophical–theological tradition in, for example, the work of Ibn Sina (Avicenna) and Ibn Rushd (Averroes) during the eleventh and twelfth centuries and Mulla Sad'ra during the seventeenth. Legenhausen goes further in suggesting that Islam is able to offer a theocratic solution, avoiding both "nationalism and liberalism," an alternative that is "not taken seriously by Western theorists" (1997, 169). In the next chapter I will return to this challenging point. To account for MacIntyre's lack, one must simply extend the range of voices engaged with. To be fair to MacIntyre, a single human can only do so much, and MacIntyre has in fact engaged with Confucian moral thought (1991). It is up to others to extend this conversation according to varying expertise.

Conclusion

It would be facile and inaccurate to conclude this section on postmodernity claiming that Rorty and Fish are exhaustive exemplars of the phenomenon; likewise with modernity and its exemplars. A careful, lengthier, study is required to look at important differences between moderns and between postmoderns and between both groups, such as MacIntyre has already begun to provide. Nevertheless, my argument in this chapter has been that secular attempts to address religious plurality in the public square tend to be in danger of stifling religious discourse in the public square. "Tend to" is the strongest claim that I can make on the basis of the limited but important thinkers I have looked at. I have made an argument that the issue of the role of religion in the public square is premised upon the following question: whose public square are we referring to? If we refer to the public square in Europe, I have argued that religion is in danger of public extinction because of the logic of secular modernity's and postmodernity's public square. But is there a comprehensive doctrine that will facilitate the free exchange in the public square that I have been presuming possible in my immanent critiques of these three versions of liberalism? I think the answer is yes, and it is to be found within the two main alternative traditions in Europe: Islam and Christianity. Let us turn to these two traditions of reasoned debate to see if they can facilitate greater freedoms than modernity and postmodernity.

6

Christian and Muslim Public Squares

Roman Catholicism, Modernity, and Religious Plurality

It is arguable that the Roman Catholic church went through – and is still going through – two stages in its relationship to modernity. The first stage, still intact at the beginning of the nineteenth century, was marked by a deep suspicion of the emerging secular modern states and also of the attendant "religious indifferentism" that was seen as its corollary. Technically, "indifferentism" is the position that all religions are (more or less) equal paths to the one God. It is important to see the connection between these two issues. The link between secular modern states and indifferentism was regarded as a logical rather than contingent one. Insomuch as the secular state granted equal civic status and rights to all religions, it offended against the rule that error has no rights. In granting all religion equal rights, the state thereby promoted indifferentism. John Courtney Murray, an American Jesuit central to pushing the shift to a new position, nicely summarizes the first phase:

> First, the state is bound not only on the natural law but also on the positive divine law whereby the Church was established. Therefore the state has the duty, per se and in principle, to recognize by constitutional law that the Church is a perfect society *sue iuris* and that it is the only religious society which has a right *iure divino* to public existence and action. (Murray 1965, 10)

As the church lost its following in Europe, the context changed regarding the relation of church to state, so that this teaching was contextualized. Thus, the link would increasingly be seen as contingent, and thereby a shift slowly occurred, both in terms of the church's attitude to other religions and in terms of the secular state.

This first stage is historically exemplified by Gregory XVI in 1832, followed by Pope Pius IX's encyclical *Quanta Cura* (1864), to which the "Syllabus of Condemned Errors" was attached. Error 16 reads: "Men can find the way of eternal salvation and attain eternal salvation by the practice of any religion whatever." This is anathema. Error 79, also condemned, is the claim that civic liberties for all religions do not lead to indifferentism. This teaching continues up until 1953, when Pius XII reiterates the principle upon which toleration of other religions is founded, for it cannot be founded on rights:

> Thus the two principles are clarified to which recourse must be had in concrete cases for the answer to the serious question concerning the attitude which the jurist, the statesman and the sovereign Catholic state is to adopt in consideration of the community of nations in regard to a formula of religious and moral toleration. . . . First: that which does not correspond to truth or to the norm of morality objectively has no right to exist, to be spread or to be activated. Secondly: failure to impede this with civil laws and coercive measures can nevertheless be justified in the interests of a higher and more general good. (*Ci riesce*, 6)

Taken today without further contextualization, this would require Catholics to oppose the freedom of religions in the public square!

Vatican II, 100 years later, exemplifies the second stage. The important changes of circumstance that facilitated this development were: the collapse of Catholic states that undergirded much of the papal teachings from 1832 on; the acceptance that many from other religions were not willfully erroneous in holding to the truth of their own religions; the acceptance that on natural law grounds, other religions (with careful qualification) should be granted equal civic rights to the Catholic church regarding the free practice of their religion; the recognition that in a non-Catholic world the arguments for religious freedoms for Catholics alone would not be plausible; the acceptance that other religions had elements of truth, goodness, beauty, and morality within them; and the American experience whereby a constitutional split between state and religion did not lead to indifferentism or the suppression of Catholicism. Together, these factors generated a remarkable development in doctrine or, in the eyes of its critics, an unacceptable U-turn. At the council, the Catholic church actually welcomed various aspects of modernity but reinterpreted and developed these aspects within an ecclesial and Christological approach. I think this is decisive for a proper understanding of the council, which is often accused of capitulating too much to the modern world.

Four documents from Vatican II are particularly important for our purpose. First, *Dignitatis Humanae* (*Declaration on Religious Liberty* 1965, 2; all Vatican II documetns cited are from Tanner 1990) affirms that:

> [the] human person has a right to religious freedom. This freedom means that all men are to be immune from coercion on the part of individuals or of social groups and of any human power, in such wise that in matters religious no one is to be forced to act in a manner contrary to his own beliefs. Nor is anyone to be restrained from acting in accordance with his own beliefs, whether privately or publicly, whether alone or in association, within due limits.

To some this heretically overturned the previous magisterial teaching on the matter (see Davies 1992). However, the following sentence in the *Declaration* indicates that this was not really the case, for the affirmation rests on very different considerations to that of secularism (contractual obligation, state power, natural universal rights of man – all, in one sense, human constructions without being subject to revelation or natural law), and can thus be understood as an unfolding of the doctrine regarding the dignity of the human person made in the image of God:

> the right to religious freedom has its foundation in the very dignity of the human person, as this dignity is known through the revealed Word of God and by reason itself. This right of the human person to religious freedom is to be recognized in the constitutional law whereby society is governed. Thus it is to become a civil right. (2)

Because these rights are applicable to the human person, they are then equally applicable to the religion to which a person belongs. Given that both sets of rights are based on God, as proclaimed by the church, it is still a requirement that civil law be influenced by the truth proclaimed by the Catholic church. Insomuch as there is a coincidence of outcome of "rights" based on differing grounds, religious freedoms within "due limits" have been the mark of modern European and American societies.

Paragraph 2 of the *Declaration* is well worth pondering, for it is clearly a development in social doctrine of some importance. First, we see that "rights language" is grounded in Christian revelation and reason together, and therefore very different from secular modernity's grounding of rights language in contractual or universal rights. The contents of rights deriving from revelation may well be different from the contents of rights deriving from contractual or universal rights. Rights language in Christianity also indicates an intrinsic link between natural law and God, reason within faith, which both calls into question an ethics that is not finally grounded in God, and ensures that this ethical approach can be argued for from revelation by means of reason. This latter point is vital given our earlier discussion about the importance of religion being able to defend itself and explicate its claims in the public square. Second, it affirms the civic basis of religious pluralism, making it clear that such pluralism does not in any way logically lead to indifferentism. Thus, proper legal and civic tolerance is based not on an indifference to the question of truth, nor upon the suspension of comprehensive doctrines, but, conversely, on truth and a comprehensive doctrine that facilitates real space for difference and diversity, "within due limits" as is necessary. It is not appropriate to provide constitutional and legal detail to "due limits," but the council is only concerned to provide a general principle. Governments and religious and non-religious bodies in each situation will have to attend to what constitutes "due limits." As we will see with Islam in the next section, the danger of indifferentism is an important stumbling point for some Islamic theologians for, if granting equal civic rights leads to indifferentism regarding religious truth, than such a step is unacceptable.

Third, it shows that various ethical truths regarding the dignity of the human person must be embedded in civic society if the "common good" is to be maintained; purely procedural processes cannot safeguard truth, however important such processes are. This is an important point for our discussion because we come to a serious clash regarding the *telos* of two different visions: secular modernity's prizing of "democracy" as a central value constituting the greatest good; and the Catholic church's prizing of "God" as the greatest good. Of course there is no straightforward clash between democracy and Catholicism, but a theological understanding of democracy places it in a very different light. Pope John Paul II expressed the complex relationship thus, 26 years after *Dignitatis Humanae*:

> Nowadays there is a tendency to claim that agnosticism and sceptical relativism are the philosophy and the basic attitude which correspond to democratic forms of political life. Those who are convinced that they know the truth and firmly adhere to it are considered unreliable from a democratic point of view, since they do not accept that truth is determined by

> the majority, or that it is subject to variation according to different political trends. It must be observed in this regard that if there is no ultimate truth to guide and direct political action, then ideas and convictions can easily be manipulated for reasons of power. As history demonstrates, a democracy without values easily turns into open or thinly disguised totalitarianism. (1991, 46)

This analysis is akin to my argument in the previous chapter, showing how modernity can lead to thinly disguised totalitarianism and how postmodernity is finally incapable of resisting this drift. The value of democracy as a means for encouraging public debate, accountability, and civic participation is to be understood as a contingent and possible means, not a necessary and indispensable means (as is the case in Rawls' political liberalism). Four years later, John Paul II would write that democracy is fundamentally

> "a system" and as such is a means and not an end. Its "moral" value is not automatic, but depends on conformity to the moral law to which it, like every other form of human behaviour, must be subject. (1995, 70)

Fourth, this stake in the common good requires that the church has a right and duty to campaign for civic law on certain issues, without requiring a Christendom model to underpin this intervention as is often feared or falsely portrayed by sections of the European press. As a transnational body, the church has a role in national and international politics through the work of the Vatican, through non-governmental bodies, and through the nation states within which the church exists, from its clerical and lay circles in manners appropriate to each group. To require the Church to remove itself from the debate in the public square is to drift into totalitarianism.

The second important document for our purpose is *Nostra Aetate* (*Declaration on the Relation of the Church to non-Christian Religions* 1965). The document focuses exclusively on what is held in common among religions, and what brings people together. It is a pastoral, not a dogmatic, document as the title, "Declaration," indicates. It deals with Judaism, Islam, Buddhism, Hinduism, and African tribal religions – ordering them respectively in terms of their closeness and commonness with the Christian faith. Reading it together with the *Declaration on Religious Liberty*, one can actually begin to see how the situation of religious plurality might be fruitful in promoting the "common good" and need not be the cause of tension and strife – despite the significant differences between the religions. In Islam, for example, the council fathers affirm that Muslims worship a transcendent creator God, strive to follow the "hidden decrees of God, just as Abraham submitted himself to God's plan," have a high regard for Jesus and for his virgin Mother, and strive to live an upright life through prayer, almsdeeds and fasting (3). Islam significantly calls for a move out of the past rut where "many quarrels and dissensions" have marked the relationship, and calls for "mutual understanding; for the benefit of all men, let them together preserve and promote peace, liberty, social justice and moral values" (3). The key to this passage lies in the close commonality of moral beliefs and ritual practices (without assuming any doctrinal agreement), and the consequent concern for social justice, peace, and freedom to be found in both religions. This alleged common social concern requires testing and explication, but the council fathers are indicating key areas where common social action might be possible. There is a recognition that the "common good" envisaged by the church may well overlap with that sought after in other religions. This is what should be pursued for the good of society.

An explication of this social cooperation might be found, for example, in the Vatican's close working together with Muslims at the United Nations' Conference Population Summit in Cairo in 1998 to promote social justice and common moral values. Or earlier, in 1986, at the Day of Prayer for Peace in Assisi, convened by John Paul II, where each religion witnessed to the others' prayer for peace in a divided world. A strong Muslim witness from many different branches of Islam was present. The prayer traditions of Islam were seen operating together with the Christian for the common goal of peace. Such cooperation can also be seen in the Vatican's fierce resistance to the invasion of Iraq and its repeated criticisms of Islamophobia during that conflict. There are many such examples, none of which should dilute the contestation of truth claims between the two religions, but such contentions should not hinder public conversation and debate. The point is that there is a real attempt to overcome years of mutual hostility and forge a working alliance based on what is held in common. The process is going to be long and complex, and each side is right to perceive problems and occasional hypocrisy. I have been underlining how none of this desire for close cooperation with Islam requires the adoption of indifferentism.

Indifferentism is rejected without reserve in *Lumen Gentium* (*The Dogmatic Constitution on the Church* 1964). This text states that:

> Basing itself on scripture and tradition, [this council] teaches that the Church, a pilgrim now on earth, is necessary for salvation: the one Christ is the mediator and the way of salvation. (14)

Here, we are dealing with dogmatic issues, as the title of the document indicates. It goes on to show (see parts I and IV of this book) that these "exclusivist" claims, which fully accord with the traditional *extra ecclesia nulla salus* teaching, do not amount to the damnation of all non-Catholic humankind as is so often assumed. It is perfectly in keeping with what is said about Islam in *Nostra Aetate*. Mahmoud Ayoub, a Muslim scholar in the United States, wrongly criticized John Paul II's outlook as inconsistent in promoting dialogue and cooperation with Islam on the one hand, and on the other hand still promoting mission and Christ's salvific uniqueness (Ayoub 1999, 171–86). Ayoub is not alone is so doing and this same criticism has been made by many Jewish scholars ever since Vatican II. I have been trying to show that these two stances are not mutually incompatible: indifferentism is not a condition of civic toleration and respect for other religions. This nicely leads us to our final Vatican document to complete our inspection of the context of this shift in the church's attitude to modernity and other religions.

In *Ad Gentes* (*Decree on the Church's Missionary Activity* 1965), we find the continuation of this theme: that other religions and cultures have much that is good, true, and beautiful, and in conversion to Christ, none of this is ever lost, but

> whatever goodness is found in the minds and hearts of men, or in the particular customs and cultures of peoples, far from being lost is purified, raised to a higher level and reaches its perfection, for the glory of God, the confusion of the demon, and the happiness of men. (9)

In case this sounds as though the church only teaches others and brings them to their final goal, which may sound patronizing and inattentive to the history of interreligious engagements, two balancing statements should be cited, so that the full organic picture of the council's teachings emerges. First, the church fully acknowledges how it learns from "the history and development of mankind," "from the riches hidden in various cultures, through which greater light is thrown on the nature of man and new avenues to truth are opened up" (*Gaudium et Spes, Pastoral Constitution on the Church in the Modern World*, 44). This specifically relates to intercultural and interreligious history.

There is a real possibility of mutual learning and growth in the process of dialogue and mission between religions. Second, in *Dignitatis Humanae* (12), there is a clear acknowledgment that the church's own behavior has at times been "hardly in keeping with the spirit of the Gospel and was even opposed to it." This acknowledgment was explicated more richly and controversially at the turn of the millennium in what was called the "Day of Forgiveness" by John Paul II, who called for repentance of the past sins of the church against Christian unity, intolerance, and violence in the service of truth. Mission is in humble service to the Lord's message, not a false confidence in the church's own life and history, which requires scrutiny, repentance, and, of course, celebration and gratitude.

Conclusions

First, the Catholic church is still working through its encounter with modernity, a relatively "new" event, with some important themes unfolding. In post-Christian pluralist Europe, a "secular" form of government that is not inimical to religion, and indeed helps and promotes religions, is clearly acceptable to Vatican II. However, as voiced by the two most recent popes, John Paul II and Benedict XVI, this relationship is not without tensions for, in allying democracy to secular modernity and its atheist, agnostic, and relativist sacred canopies, there is a danger of totalitarianism where the public voice of religion will be silenced. The need for some shared conception of the common good is required for healthy democracy, and the attainment of some shared conception requires religion to have its voice in the public square, or the common good will be diminished.

Second, it is clear that the church is concerned to protect religious freedoms for itself, as well as for all religions, "within limits," in the new world order. This freedom is based on revelation and reason, not contractual human-rights talk or universal declarations by joint committees. Again, this brings the church into conflict with modernity on an ideological rather than practical level, but interestingly brings it into deep harmony with Judaism and Islam, insomuch as they too utilize "revelation" and "reason" to propound their cosmological–social vision. This commonality suggests the need for serious conversations between the Abrahamic faiths, which have already begun bilaterally and trilaterally, although this should not obscure very real differences that emerge between Islam, Judaism, and Christianity, especially regarding each religion's propensity to fideism and voluntarism, undercutting the sapiential role of reason.

Third, the Catholic church operates with a radically open attitude toward other religions on the pastoral and social level, but not on the dogmatic level. The new post-1965 openness encourages interreligious cooperation at every level for the attainment of the common good, for justice, peace, and equality, to the greater glory of God. In this sense the Catholic position is an important force for cohesion and harmony. Huntington's thesis is squarely called into question. Indeed, with religion in the driving seat, the inverse *may* be possible: not a clash, but fecund conversations and cooperation. The Catholic church's dogmatic position on Christology, trinity, and church that hold to the exclusive salvific power of the trinitarian God made known in Christ, mediated by his church, is a stumbling block to some Muslims (as we have seen) but I have tried to defend its internal consistency in parts I and IV of this book, and in this chapter shown its social implications in favor of religious freedom in the public square and of the common good. Further, I have argued earlier that this Catholic position does not involve the damnation of all non-Christians, nor does it involve the rejection of the profound cultural and spiritual heritage of the great world religions, nor does it mean that the mystery of God is exhausted in Catholic Christianity. Hence, I consider it a matter of apologetics, not logic, to explain how dialogue and mission are held together and promoted with equal vigor, never to the exclusion of either.

Fourth, if it is argued that the Christian missionary imperative will lead to a clash of civilizations, as Islam, like Christianity, contains a universal missionary dynamic, two responses might be made. The manner in which each religion understands and practices its universal mission is a matter to be evaluated. From the Catholic position, it is clear in theory that mission without regard to religious freedom, freedom of conscience, and freedom from all coercion is a contradiction in terms and unacceptable. In the next section we will see how there is an Islamic parallel to this position. The second response to this challenge is to note that modernity's missionary drive has led to great bloodshed and violence (see chapter 4) so no group should claim the high ground, but Catholic teaching emphasizes that the common good, as opposed to a clash of civilization, is the social priority for the church.

Islam, Reasoned Debate, and Religious Plurality

Armando Salvatore (2007) has made out a strong case challenging the definition of the "public square" in contemporary European discussion in a way that further develops my own argument. He is not alone in this. From a Muslim perspective see Asad (2003, 181–204) and Zaman (2002). Salvatore argues that Habermas, the key European theoretician of the "public square," is already open to four cumulative criticisms within European-American discussion: a lack of attention to class- and gender-based alternative publics, resulting in the perpetuation of a male bourgeois ideal type; a minimization of national and historical differences among various instances of modern public spheres; a lack of regard for the complex intertwining between local, national, and transnational public spheres; and the overly normative tenor of the characterization of the public sphere as singularly modern and Western (2007, 8). Salvatore trenchantly adds to these four a fifth criticism that is particularly germane: that Habermas falsely attributes the formation of the public square to Kant and the European Enlightenment, failing to trace its genealogy further back to the Christian and Muslim traditions that developed out of the Greek, generating overlapping and differing forms of public reasoning, without which the Enlightenment could not have been born. Christianity and Islam universalize and develop the localized Greek Aristotelian inheritance into a form of universal public reasoning and debate, through the practical reasoning of Latin Christendom (in Thomas Aquinas' fusion of Augustine and Aristotle in the thirteenth century), and in the jurisprudential traditions of what Salvatore calls "Sunni Islamdom" (in the writings of Abu Ishaq al-Shatibi, the Andalusian jurist of the fourteenth century). Of course, it was not just the Sunni tradition that developed this pre-Enlightenment legacy:

> Immanuel Kant was not born in Iraq; public reasoning has, however, a long tradition in Islamic jurisprudence, both Sunni and Shi'a, that flourished in that country and inspired Islamic reform. (Salvatore and Eickelman 2006, xv)

The importance of Salvatore's work is to show the resourcefulness of Islam in addressing the question of "religion in the public square" and its challenge to modernity's way of construing the question. First, I will look at two examples of public reasoning and discussion within a public square *formed* by Islam. Admittedly, these are outside the European context, but are important in offering alternative models of public reasoning and, given Islam's transnational nature, such models are worth examining. I do this to show that "democracy" can be shaped on a Muslim, rather than secular, constitutional basis (in the case of the Iranian revolution of 1979); and, second, to show that even in what is considered to be one of the most repressive non-democratic Muslim societies in the world, Saudi Arabia, "public reasoning" and "debate" are active and at times vibrant, always operating within a particular set of parameters, but parameters drawn differently from those of the European model. Both cases require us to rethink the nature of public debate and, in Iran's case, democracy. I do not want to valorize either society, but to highlight the intra-traditional sense in which my questions might be addressed within Islam. Second, I will return back to Europe and the United States to explore whether Islam is growing actively vibrant within existing democratic structures or, like much of Christianity, assimilating to modernity in this process – or, as is often feared, developing non-democratic clusters of culture. In this very brief survey of the tip of a complex iceberg, I hope to indicate that the conversation about the common good has only just started and, while it is fraught and complex, there are grounds for much hope in reasoned conversations. A clash of civilizations might happen if either tradition loses its theological relationship to reason.

The Islamic Republic of Iran and the revolutionary experiment in democratic Islam

The Islamic Republic of Iran, founded in 1979, provides an interesting set of questions about the assumptions regarding democracy and the public square that have emerged in secular traditions. It undercuts three basic assumptions and suggests an entirely different model from the one we saw emerging from within the Catholic church. First, Iran shows an alternative to the Habermasian model that requires the equality of all participants and unrestricted discussion as the forum whereby truth and justice can be determined. Instead, we find a mixture of universal suffrage (for those aged 16 and above, both male and female) and religious authority, which is both elected and unelected, but whose power is seen as determinative in judging what elected bodies are legislating. "Religious authority can be an essential part of the construction of public religious discourse in many different ways" (Salvatore and Eickelman 2006, xxi). Iran is one instance, but Mali, India, Indonesia, and Syria all provide very different instances of this principle (see the essays by Brian Didier, Paulo G. Pinto, and Benjamin F. Soares in Salvatore and Eickelman 2006). Second, Iran shows the possibility of a democracy undergirded by an Islamic constitution, rather than the secular constitution that is thought to be intrinsic to democracy by the major theoreticians examined in chapter 5. In this sense, Iran is a remarkable and even utterly novel example of a Muslim form of democracy, not withstanding many of its problems and shortcomings. Third, Iran indicates one way in which Islam and modernity creatively meet, whereby there are changes to both traditions but changes determined at least in part through a prior fidelity to religious norms, not the simple accommodation of religion to modernity, as has happened in much of Christianity's recent history. Fred Halliday rightly alerts us to the complex causal forces shaping Iranian Islam, especially the revolution's dependence on the modernizing of educational elements introduced by the Shah, as well as on economic and internal and external political factors during that period (Halliday 1996, 42–75). However, this does not undermine the genuine and peculiar Islamic Shiite contribution to this experiment in Islamic democracy, as even Halliday acknowledges (1996, 57–63).

The Islamic Republic's constitution (1979) was revised in 1989 and contains within it a source of constant discussion requiring public debate. It is based on two potentially conflicting principles, the absolute sovereignty of God (principles 2 and 56) and the people's right to determine their own destiny (principle 3:8), thus opening the door to religious and rational debate over issues of government and society. This structural tension is also embodied in the constitution's three executive branches: in the chief of state – the Supreme Religious Leader; the head of government – the president; and the cabinet – the Council of Ministers. Further, it is embodied in three overseeing bodies: the Assembly of Experts, the Expediency Council, and the Council of Guardians of the Constitution. The chief of state, the Supreme Religious Leader (*Rahbar*), is currently Ayatollah Ali Hoseini-Khamenei (who succeeded Ayatollah Ruhollah Khomeini after his death in 1989). The CIA veteran Graham Fuller provides an interesting description of this office:

> a major innovation, designed in principle to embody the highest level of religious qualification and moral leadership to stand above and oversee the general political process. He represents the highest power in the state. The Supreme Leader is not elected but rather selected by a clerical commission of senior ayatollahs who are charged with selecting the cleric with the highest moral and juridical qualifications to ensure the ultimate Islamic correctness of state policies. (Fuller 2003, 102)

The "clerical commission" is the Assembly of Experts, all of whose members are directly elected by the people, but who must be qualified *mujtahids* (experts in Islamic law).

Two interesting points are worth noting about the "highest power in the state." First, the popularly elected overseeing body of the Assembly of Experts, which contains 86 religious scholars of high standing (in 2008), has the constitutional power to elect a successor after the death of the Supreme Leader and to depose the Supreme Leader if deemed necessary. Hence, the unelected but selected Supreme Leader is always constitutionally deselectable by an elected group of religious authorities. To critics who argue that the Iranian model has a final lack of real democratic freedom in having a religious Supreme Leader who can overrule democratically elected politicians, it can be argued back that elected groups do hold supreme constitutional power even if this particular group is basically constituted by religious scholars. Second, Fuller notes the parallel of this position within the United States:

> The position of the Supreme Leader of course structurally weakens the functioning of the democratic process since he can legally overrule democratically-based decision-making processes of government and is not answerable to the general public since he is not popularly elected. This position perhaps also partially resembles the members of the U.S. Supreme Court who are not elected but selected for life by the president on the basis of their jurisprudential capabilities in protection of the Constitution – in principle over and above politics. (2003, 103)

The analogy is a helpful one as it brings out the importance of jurisprudence in the matter of establishing the common good, even if, here, it is the *sharia* in Iran. In England it is common law (which has its roots in Christian culture); in the United States it is the constitution and the laws of the Supreme Court. It must be recalled that the constitution of Iran was democratically accepted by 98 percent of eligible voters in 1979. It is a democratic constitution.

The head of government at the time of writing (2008) is Mahmoud Ahmadinejad (elected in 2005). He has constitutional powers to select his cabinet, the Council of Ministers, who are formed out of the elected representatives of the provinces. Ahmadinejad, a radical conservative and former agent of the Revolutionary Guard (a body created by Ayatollah Khomeini and with a very mixed track record due to its sometimes brutal repression), replaced two modernizers, Ali Akbar Hashemi Rafsanjani, who won a landslide victory in August 1989, and Mohammad Khatami, who won in 1997. It is possible that Rafsanjani's future was sealed by the Council of Guardians, made up of six clerics chosen by the Supreme Leader and six jurists recommended by the judiciary, who have the constitutional power to vet political candidates for suitability, to supervise national elections, and to determine whether proposed legislation is constitutional and faithful to Islamic law. In October 2004 the Council of Guardians vetoed more than 2,500 candidates for parliamentary elections, most of them reformers and Khatamites; for the 2008 elections 1,700 candidates were likewise vetoed. The removal of candidates has led to a drop in the numbers of voters participating in elections (independent estimates state 47 percent, the lowest of the eight parliamentary elections held in Iran). Nevertheless, in the 2008 elections, despite such a large removal of candidates, the reformers increased their power to 46 seats compared to Ahmadinejad's 117. Conservative critics of Ahmadinejad won 53 seats. While the Council of Guardians has a restricting effect on the candidates in Iran's general election, it is worth noting that there are different restricting effects on candidates running for election in European countries and the US. In the US, the self-proclaimed leader of the "free world," money has a major restricting effect. As I write prior to the 2008 US elections, the May 20 edition of the *Los Angeles Times* reports that Hillary Clinton is now $20.88m in debt in running her campaign, while Barack Obama has $46.5m left in the bank compared to John McCain's $21.7m reserve. In every democracy, there are restricting effects of various kinds, which reflect the major concerns of the population – Islamic unity in Iran, for instance, and money in the United States, although that is probably too gross a simplification.

It is far too early to make judgments about the complex constitutional checks and balances that steer the Islamic Republic of Iran into its thirtieth year but, as Fuller notes, it has generated intense public debate, which must play the democratic game on "Islamic turf":

> Conservative, liberal, right or left, clerical rule versus secularism, democracy versus authoritarian institutions, socially restrictive or permissive, statist or civil libertarian, free market or centralized economy – the entire debate is encompassed within the vocabulary, frame of reference, and coinage of Islam. (2003, 105; for a thorough survey of the variety of religious differences within Islam up to the late 1970s, see Akhavi 1980)

This has also meant that probably

> nowhere else in the world has Islamic thinking been "force-marched" at such a speed in the field of political and social theory – opening new ranges of argumentation on all sides about the nature of politics and its relationship to Islamic thought. (Fuller 2003, 106)

None of this should obscure the often justified criticisms that the practice of the government and the clerics is not always in keeping with the spirit and aims of the constitution and sometimes amounts to intimidation, politically unjustified exclusion, and repression. All these charges are possible against Western democratic countries during their turbulent histories.

Let me briefly look at one particular issue within Iranian Islamic society: religious pluralism. The constitution clearly marks the establishment of an Islamic religious state, with the Shiite Twelver Ja'fari School at center stage, but it makes constitutional room for other Muslim traditions and, most importantly, for named non-Muslim religions. Article 12 states:

> The official religion of Iran is Islam and the Twelver Ja'fari school [in *usul al-Din* and *fiqh*], and this principle will remain eternally immutable. Other Islamic schools, including the Hanafi, Shafi'i, Maliki, Hanbali, and Zaydi, are to be accorded full respect, and their followers are free to act in accordance with their own jurisprudence in performing their religious rites. These schools enjoy official status in matters pertaining to religious education, affairs of personal status (marriage, divorce, inheritance, and wills) and related litigation in courts of law. In regions of the country where Muslims following any one of these schools of fiqh constitute the majority, local regulations, within the bounds of the jurisdiction of local councils, are to be in accordance with the respective school of fiqh, without infringing upon the rights of the followers of other schools.

This acceptance of internal Muslim diversity is typical of the earlier traditions in Iran during the Safavid period (see Petrushevsky 1985), in Muslim Spain, and in parts of the Ottoman Empire. However, what is remarkably novel about the Islamic Republic of Iran is its constitutional provision in article 13:

> Zoroastrian, Jewish, and Christian Iranians are the only recognized religious minorities, who, within the limits of the law, are free to perform their religious rites and ceremonies, and to act according to their own canon in matters of personal affairs and religious education.

Furthermore, there are five out of a total of 270 seats reserved for religious minorities in the legislative body, which is a high ratio given that the Baha'i, Christian, Zoroastrian, Mandean (who are counted as Christians but do not see themselves as such), and Jewish religious minorities constitute less that 2 percent of the population. If one excludes the Baha'is, which is what is done in practice, as they are deemed an anti-Iranian group, then no more than 1 percent of the population have five seats reserved for them. This constitutes an extension of the traditional allowance for the "people of the book," the *dhimmis*, Jews and Christians, who have received valid but partial revelations that have now been superseded by Islam. So much for the theory; working out the practice has been complex.

The Baha'is have been systematically persecuted, although Iran argued at the United Nations in the mid-1980s that this group was an anti-Iranian political, not religious, group. The UN was unconvinced and Iran was convicted of failing to abide by the Universal Declaration of Human Rights, to which it is a signatory. In 2006 the Iranian Ministry of the Interior declared that the Baha'is were a misguided and wayward sect. The persecution of Baha'is cannot be lightly dismissed or ignored, and many have died under persecution. There have been reports of harassment and intimidation from Jewish groups, but given the anti-Zionism in the Middle East, Iran's record is quite remarkable in allowing Hebrew and religious teaching institutions and freedom of passage for Jews, including to Israel. Evangelical Christians have also faced some pressures, in part because apostasy is punishable by death, and such Christians welcome converts. The continued reports of the US Department of State on the restrictions of religious freedoms in Iran do not make for comfortable reading (see www.state.gov), but the constitutional demands have been carried out in the political decision-making process, as well as in matters of personal affairs and religious education, in a way that is still trail-blazing.

Does this type of religious tolerance, such as it is, require indifferentism in relation to Islam? Constitutionally, clearly not, as it is deemed in article 2 that:

> The Islamic Republic is a system based on belief in: 1. the One God (as stated in the phrase "There is no god except Allah"), His exclusive sovereignty and the right to legislate, and the necessity of submission to His commands; 2. Divine revelation and its fundamental role in setting forth the laws; 3. the return to God in the Hereafter, and the constructive role of this belief in the course of man's ascent towards God; 4. the justice of God in creation and legislation; 5. continuous leadership (*imamah*) and perpetual guidance, and its fundamental role in ensuring the uninterrupted process of the revolution of Islam; 6. the exalted dignity and value of man, and his freedom coupled with responsibility before God; in which equity, justice, political, economic, social, and cultural independence, and national solidarity are secured.

The American philosopher and convert to Islam, Muhammad Legenhausen, provides a theological rationale to this approach. It is interesting because of its analogical parallels with the Catholic position we have seen above and because Legenhausen left the United States after his conversion to reside in Iran.

Legenhausen seeks to establish the uniqueness of the Islamic position in contrast to the reductive pluralism of John Hick (in which believers are unable to say what they believe to be ultimate), the inclusivism of Karl Rahner (in which non-Christians are patronizingly said to have implicit beliefs), and the exclusivism of traditional Christianity, which, according to Legenhausen, consigns the majority of humanity to damnation (2006, 102; see also his wider treatment of related issues in 1999) Legenhausen argues that in Islam

> the two issues of correct faith and salvation need to be clearly distinguished. According to Islam, the correct religion ordained by God is that revealed to the last of His chosen prophets, Muhammad (s); this and no other religion is required by Allah of all mankind. In this sense, Islam is exclusivist. However, at various times prior to His final revelation, God ordained other religions by means of His prophets. So, the reason why the religion brought by Moses ('a) is not acceptable today is not that what Moses taught was wrong or incompatible with the teachings brought by Muhammad (s), for they taught basically the same things, but because God has ordained the latter teachings for this era.[1] (2006, 68)

Legenhausen's point is that Islam is exclusivist in "the claim of the sole superiority of Islam among the religions of the world," that is, in matters of "correct faith" (2006, 95). In contrast, Islam is

> pluralistic insofar as it admits that a plurality of religious traditions contain divine light and truth, that it is the responsibility of true believers to treat the followers of other traditions with acceptance and respect, and that the followers of other traditions may find the way to salvation through their own faiths by the grace of God. (2006, 95)

While Legenhausen does not treat the question of the Baha'is and only explicitly addresses the traditional *dhimmis*, Jews and Christians, the logic of the position he advances is not dissimilar to that of Karl Rahner in Legenhausen's provisional "salvific" legitimation of non-Muslim religions within the economy of salvation, prior to the decisive event of Muhammad.

After this event, all religions are superseded by the one true religion, Islam (both in its generic general sense of submission to God, and in its particular cultic and legal sense, embodied within Shiite Islam). Islam's "abrogation" (2006, 89) of these religions takes place through the full truth of Muhammad's revealed religion, not through a nullification of Moses' religion *per se*, even though it must be admitted that both Judaism and Christianity have "become corrupted" in their transmission of the true revelation given to them (2006, 93). The difference between Rahner and Legenhausen is that Legenhausen does not want to speak about implicit belief, but only what is actually present in the prophetic traditions of Judaism and Islam, following the traditional Quranic teachings that there have been many prophets of God, and Muhammad is the last and the greatest, the seal of the prophets. Legenhausen provides resources to address other religions in his drawing upon the *hadith*, where Abu Dharr reports that the Prophet "told him there were one hundred and twenty four thousand prophets" before himself and that the "identities of all the prophets are not known" (2006, 102).

Four points can be usefully made about Legenhausen's argument. First, it provides a theologically and philosophically sophisticated defense of one possible traditional Quranic position on the matter, such that the truth of Islam is maintained against all other religions, which are seen as imperfect, but nevertheless capable of providing contact with the true God (in a provisional and qualified manner). Second, it is this divine relationship that provides the grounds for "acceptance and respect" at a social and civic level, not a contractual or universalized form of "human rights" that is not grounded in Islam. Third, it demonstrates an interesting analogical parallel to the Catholic move in relation to modernity, but in this particular maneuver, showing Islam's resourcefulness to address the questions of modernity without having to accept modernity's terms. It is thus spurious, if not a typically "secular liberal" trope, to argue that claiming one's religion to be true is "in direct contradiction of the principle of equality among religions as it exists in the human rights model" (Cesari 2004, 168). Equality of rights does not grant any truth status to the beliefs held by citizens. Fourth, Legenhausen's arguments are not of course solely representative of the complex spectrum of views within what I am calling non-liberal forms of Islam. Among liberal forms of Islam, there is Hick-like pluralism (Askari 1985), and Knitter-like liberationist pluralism (Esack 1997), and the very interesting Sufi perennialist approach that is critical of Hick, but ends up replicating his position (Shah-Kazemi 2006). Among non-liberal forms of Islam, on the "right" of Legenhausen so to speak, there are gradations of views regarding the status of non-Muslim religions (salvifically and in terms of civil and social rights, with both necessary and contingent relationships between these two issues being argued for), and on the "far right," the declared invalidity of even Muslim traditions that differ from itself (classically the position of Wahabism). Clearly, there is a range of complex debates to be had intra-traditionally within Islam. I find views like Legenhausen's the most attractive, both for intra- and for extra-traditional reasons. Intra-traditionally, because they do not capitulate to modernity, and extra-traditionally, because they secure what is most important in the Christian vision at a pragmatic level: the right to religious freedom at the civic level. Practically, the way this is implemented in Iran is open to criticism, but it is also open to criticism from within Iran's own public square on Islamic grounds.

Saudi Arabia and public reasoning

Let me briefly turn to Saudi Arabia and Talal Asad's illuminating argument that among Saudi Wahabi theologians and preachers there is serious public debate on matters regarding the state and religion, conducted entirely in Arabic and by properly trained scholars in public mosques and through electronic circulation of their sermons and talks. Asad also seeks to contrast two forms of public discourse: the Kantian Enlightenment model, and the Saudi one, showing that their real differences lie not in the extent of "freedoms," but in utterly different concepts of "freedom" due to deeply contrasting notions of "autonomy." What both have in common is the need for discipline and power, such that for Kant the limits of freedom come to an end when obeying political authority is concerned. This is not just related to Kant's living under the monarchical rule of Frederick II, as Foucault argues, but rather it indicates the necessary limits of freedom, contingently and sometimes arbitrarily set, that presuppose the possibilities of freedom. Violent coercion as a means of persuasion is not the exclusive pattern of pre-modern religions, for "it should not be forgotten that we owe the most terrible examples of coercion in modern times to secular totalitarian regimes – Nazism and Stalinism" (Asad 1993, 236).

Asad narrates how the kingdom of Saudi Arabia was built in 1932 on the historical alliance of two families: the House of ash-Shaikh (descendants of the eighteenth-century Najdi religious reformer Muhammad bin 'Abdul-Wahhāb) and the House of Sa'ud (now the royal clan, descendants of a Najdi tribal chief). The religious establishment, no longer primarily from the House of ash-Shaikh, is basic to the structure of Saudi society and informs the Islam that the state upholds. Hence, while oil revenue has raised huge wealth and brought about rapid change including profound modernizing influences, the state, despite contrary predictions, has remained resolutely Islamic. Nevertheless, the tensions between modernity and Wahabism constantly burst out. The seizing of the *Haram* (the most sacred sanctuary) in Mecca in 1979 by Madhist insurgents, and their religious condemnation of the regime for housing US troops on Muslim soil, is an example of these tensions. But Asad wants to challenge what is taken as

> a self-evident general thesis; the Saudi *'ulamā* [earlier translated by Asad as "divines"] (sing., *'ālim*), being traditional, reject any change in the status quo, because refusal to change is the essence of tradition. (1993, 209)

Rather, Asad argues that change and debate are central to this tradition, while remaining faithful to a particular form of Islam that seeks to live by the practices of the first three generations of Muslims (see also the seasoned academic political writer, Piscatori 1983, in support of this reading).

Asad counters this "self-evident general thesis" by arguing four points. First, the *'ulamā* accepted many elements of modernization with little or no question: "new forms of transport including paved roads, new modes of building and printing, electricity, new medicines and types of medical treatment, and so forth." Second, the *'ulamā* carry out the same

> process by which the *long–established indigenous practices* (such as veneration of saints' tombs) were judged to be un-Islamic by the Wahhabi reformers of Arabia . . . and then forcibly eliminated. That is, like all practical criticism, orthodox criticism seeks to construct a relation of discursive dominance. (1993, 210)

Hence, Asad argues, with copious illustration, that

> the critical discourses of Saudi's *'ulamā* (like those of Muhammad 'Abdul-Wahhāb before them) presuppose the concept of an orthodox Islam. Muslims in Saudi Arabia (as elsewhere) disagree profoundly over what orthodox Islam is, but as *Muslims* their differences are fought out on the ground of that concept. (1993, 210)

Elsewhere Asad counters the thesis that it is better to speak of "Islams" on the basis that the various traditions are related formally through common founding texts and, temporally, through diverging authoritative interpreters (Asad 1986). Asad shows how this process of change has been well documented in regard to *sharia* rules (religious laws). Echoing MacIntyre, whom he does not explicitly cite, Asad writes:

> What is involved in such changes is not a simple ad hoc acceptance of new arrangements but the attempt to redescribe norms and concepts with the aid of tradition-guided reasoning. The authority of that redescription, among those familiar with and committed to that tradition, has depended historically on how successful the underlying reasoning was judged to be. This is not to say that the *implementation* of those changes has depended entirely on that authority. (1986, 211)

In Saudi the *'ulamā* provide "advice" (*nasīha*), something called for by the *sharia* as a precondition of moral rectitude (*istiqāma*), not "criticism" (*naqd*), with its adversarial overtones (1986, 212). Asad contrasts this process with the "closed position" of Sayyid Qutb who argued that, because Egypt was a society of heathens (*jāhiliyya*), which meant that the practice of a Muslim's religion (*dīn*) became impossible, there could be no discussion in Egypt about the truth that Qutb put forward. Qutb's position conforms better to the "self-evident general thesis."

Asad traces the "Islamic tradition of public criticism" in Saudi through the process of the Friday sermon (*khutbā*) and theological lectures (often recorded and circulated widely, increasingly through the internet). Most of the preachers are graduates of the new Islamic universities in Saudi Arabia, and Asad shows how *nasīha* can be understood as moral–political criticism. He looks at the discussion regarding a Muslim aggressor being confronted with the aid of a force of unbelievers. He notes important differences of opinion with, for example, Āl Za'ayr's argument that it is the *duty* of Muslims to criticize political authority if they are endangering the *umma* or being unjust, in contrast to the European model, which sees political criticism as a *right* whose exercise is therefore optional. The central difference between the two models of political criticism is that the first requires various conditions regarding "knowledge of the rules and models of virtuous living, and of the most effective way of conveying these to others" through "kindness and gentleness in performing the act of *nasīha*" (1986, 218). Asad argues that this virtue-based tradition differs considerably from the polity of the Enlightenment:

> The virtuous Muslim is thus seen not as an autonomous individual who assents to a set of universalizable maxims but as an individual inhabiting the moral space shared by all who are together bound to God (the *umma*). (1986, 219)

Compare this to Kant's

> individuals aspiring to self-determination and dispassionate judgement, whose moral foundation is universal reason, not disciplined virtues. . . . Thus, in the world assumed by Zaʿayr, particular personal virtues must already be in place before practical reasoning can be properly carried out; in the Enlightenment world, practical reasoning yields an ethical maxim only where it is universalizable as a general law. (1986, 220)

Therefore the *umma* "is the concept of a religious-political space – divinely sanctioned and eternally valid – within which rational discussion, debate, and criticisms can be conducted," operating with the common assumption that dependence upon God (rather than Kantian individual autonomy) constitutes genuine autonomy (1986, 223). The most important conclusion to Asad's study is his successful analysis of easy condemnations of different forms of public reasoning by applying standards alien to that form of reasoning. Hence, *nasīha* can be viewed from two very different perspectives:

> Since the objective of *nasīha* is the person who has transgressed God's eternal commands, its normative reason can be regarded as a repressive technique for securing social conformity to divinely ordained norms, which many people today are unwilling to tolerate silently. But there is also another way of understanding *nasīha*. It reflects the principle that a well-regulated polity depends on its members being virtuous individuals who are partly responsible for one another's moral condition – and therefore in part on continuous moral criticism. (1986, 233)

I am trying to highlight the profound differences of understanding of the "public square" (clearly conceived differently according to one's religion, be it Catholic, Muslim, or secular) and, thus, the highly complex discussion that must be had about the relation of "religion" and the "public square." To paraphrase MacIntyre: "whose religion and which public square" are at stake? In political terms, Europe's public square belongs to the citizens who shape it and thus within three generations might in principle be a

Muslim public square. Iran shows how a democratic country can operate with a different constitutional basis from any present Western country. Saudi Arabia displays another point entirely: that public reasoning does not require democracy, but those who are able and qualified to participate in such reasoning. In both countries, what is utterly important, in differing degrees, is the manner in which public reasoning still operates.

From a Catholic perspective, differing arguments are to be employed in differing situations. I have already shown how this might be done in terms of secularism, but it would require an immanent critique of these differing forms of Islam to address the internal lacunae and unresolved tensions. The internal critique is already being performed within Iran and Saudi Arabia. External critiques would then, following MacIntyre, amount to showing, through a genealogical narration of that form of Islam, how its unresolved lacunae are better addressed by a rival tradition, in this case Christianity. This kind of debate has hardly started. Let me illustrate this. When Christian leaders demand the same rights for Christians in, say Saudi Arabia, as granted to Muslims in Europe (as has been consistently done by Roman Catholics since Pope John Paul II's latter pontificate), this simply translates as "be like us." There are no reasons given for this request, except that: "this is what we do." I think it would be more plausible to argue that Saudi Arabia is inadequately engaging with the Quran's teachings on other religions, on justice, and on the common good. One should draw heavily on alternative orthodox Muslim interpreters to engage in immanent criticism. If in the end "we" just do not like the Quran's teachings, that is another matter entirely. If we think the teachings are contrary to the truth, as a Catholic Christian is bound to think, then extra-traditional criticism must still be allied to intra-traditional criticism. Just political pressure is a legitimate means to attaining such political goals as freedom for Christians to practice their faith, but I am focusing on public reasoning and discussion in this chapter, not statecraft. To conclude this chapter, let me return to the public squares in Europe and the United States, and ask the question: what of Islam in these contexts?

Islam and Euro-American democracies

One of the best recent socio-political surveys of this question is Jocelyne Cesari's *When Islam and Democracy Meet: Muslims in Europe and in the United States* (2004; see also Fuller 2003; and Jenkins 2007, who covers only Europe). Cesari argues that Muslims in both continents, and especially in the US, have acclimatized to democratic structures and, in some ways, Islam has undergone a reform through the process. The reform is in term of the secularizing of its practices and institutions in a manner analogous to that undergone by Christianity in Europe. In fact, in Europe, Islam has been structured along the lines of the church–state relationship that exists in the particular country where Muslims reside. These relationships exist as three principal "types," although the latter type can be subdivided: "the cooperation between Church and State, the existence of a State-sponsored religion, or the total separation of religion and politics" (2004, 65). In the latter, total separation, there are two branches: the French "ideological" model, which is anti-religion, and the US model, which is pro-civic religion. Cesari examines the ways these models work in the first group, in Austria, Belgium, Italy, Spain, and Germany, and highlights the radical progression in Spain as most interesting, and possibly related to the strong Muslim roots in Spain in the Middle Ages. In the second group we find the UK, Denmark, and Greece, and, in the third group, France, with Comte's secular ideological underpinning.

Cesari also explores the difference between American and European Muslims. In the US, Asian and Arab Muslims are more highly educated, with large numbers within the university system, which spawns a greater intellectual leadership and more focused structural amalgamations. The US also has a less educated Muslim stratum, but this is to be found mainly within the large number of black American converts, and only a very tiny minority are anti-democratic. Fuller charts a similar process whereby politically active Muslim groups across the globe

> increasingly accept the "universality" of democracy, seek to become part of the democratic order, and believe that they will benefit from this kind of political order. As they become integrated into the system, they lose much of their ideological fervour and take on the characteristics of "normal" political parties. (2003, xix)

Both Cesari and Fuller are sanguine about small-minority anti-democratic elements that get far more publicity than their size warrants, and, along with Jenkins, all identify England and France as the two major places for Muslim anti-democratic elements, due to high unemployment, low education, and cultural alienation experienced by young Muslim men.

Clearly, each situation is complex and the brush strokes above are far too broad to form a precise picture, except to indicate that the general pattern is one of active involvement within the democratic structures, with varying degrees of "secularizing" setting in through this process. To focus on the issues a little, it is worth examining the important work of Tariq Ramadan, who proposes the development of a specific "European Muslim" identity, as his book titles indicate: *To Be A European Muslim* (1999) and *Western Muslims and the Future of Islam* (2004). Ramadan's father was the pupil and son-in-law of the founder of the Muslim Brotherhood, Hasan al-Banna. His father, Said Ramadan, took over the leadership of the Brotherhood after al-Banna's assassination in 1949, but eventually left Egypt for Switzerland in 1953, when the Brotherhood was banned and some members arrested and tortured by President Nasser. Ramadan, born in Switzerland, has a remarkable fluency in two cultures: the *salafi* traditions of his family (with a training in Arabic and Islam at the University of Al Azhar, Cairo) and a European cultural education with three degrees from the University of Geneva, including philosophy, French literature, Arabic and Islamic studies, and a doctorate on Nietzsche. Ramadan has drawn considerable press attention: due to his Brotherhood background there is continuing debate about whether he is a "fundamentalist" in disguise (see Fourest 2008), while more attentive readers have seen him as a Muslim Rawlsian (March 2007); and there was much controversy in 2004 over the US government's revocation of a visa for him to take up a Chair at Notre Dame University due to donations of $940 to two charities that were discovered to have provided funds to Hamas (unknown to Ramadan); and earlier, in 2003, he was charged with anti-Semitism because of his criticism of the Jewish bias of certain French intellectuals and of Paul Wolfowitz. In my view, Ramadan has argued a very cogent position that does not make him a fundamentalist, nor a terrorist, nor a racial anti-Semite.

Ramadan argues for a new conceptuality regarding Islam in the West, as the European context breaks through the traditional boundaries of *dar al-Islam* (the abode of Islam – as in a fully Muslim country) and *dar al-harb* (abode of war – living where one cannot be a full Muslim). Instead, Muslims live in a new and promising context: *dar al-shahada* (the abode of witness), whereby they can bear witness to their faith in a self-critical manner, striving to serve the "common good" (*al-maslaha*). Europe is a missionary field, neither a place of war nor a Muslim country, and this mission is carried out without coercion or force, but through the self-critical practice of the Muslim faith and through public argument. Ramadan cites the Quran: "If your Lord had so willed, everyone on earth would have believed. Is it for you to compel people to be believers?" (10.99). According to Ramadan this new situation also calls for special hermeneutical attention regarding the reading of the Quran and Sunna, the normative texts that should be interpreted in context (regarding their historical background) and carefully applied to each new situation, such as the European, through *fatwas* (legal judgments) based on the jurisprudential traditions and reasoning (*ijtihad*).

Ramadan locates his own position in relation to five other interpretative strategies within the Muslim tradition (2004, 24–8). I outline these, as they allow us to see a range of relations between political debates and differing forms of scriptural exegesis, and I offer examples that are not necessarily found in Ramadan's text. First, there is Scholastic traditionalism where the Quran or Sunna (the actions of the Prophet) or *hadith* (traditions regarding the prophet; and the overlap with Sunna is debated) are interpreted through exclusive reference to one or other school of jurisprudence (mainly the Hanafi, Maliki, Shafii, Hanbali, Zaydi, Jafari). This tradition is present in the US and UK through Indo-Pakistani groups and in Germany among the Turks. They are mostly concerned with religious practices and are "uninterested in and even rejecting of any connection with the Western social milieu, in which they simply cannot conceive that they have any way of participating" (2004, 25). This is a form of apolitical Islam concerned to maintain its own practices without a sense of social engagement. Second, there is *Salafi* literalism, which is the rejection of the mediation of jurisprudential schools. The Quran and the Sunna are "interpreted in an immediate way, without scholarly conclaves" (2004, 25); the text cannot be subject to interpretation, which by definition contains error or innovation (*bida*). This tradition is found in Saudi Arabia, Jordan, Egypt, and Syria. Asad's discussion of Wahabism above calls into question this slightly one-dimensional picture presented by Ramadan. Even allegedly uninterpreted texts must be explicated. Third comes Ramadan's own postion: *Salafi* reformism, which reads texts in context, based on the purposes and intentions of the law and jurisprudence (*fiqh*), and through reasoning (*ijtihad*). This tradition has a wide audience in the modern Muslim world and Ramadan cites major thinkers like the Turkish reformer Said al-Nursi, the Egyptians Hasan al-Banna and Sayyid Qutb, the Pakistani Muhammad Iqbal and Sayyid Abul A'la Mawdudi, the Iranian Ali Shariati, the Algerian and Tunisian Nahda reformist movement, and the al-Adl wal-Ishan of Morocco. This tradition aims to be faithful to Muslim identity and religious practice and recognizes the Western constitutional structure encouraging citizenship and national loyalty (within reasonable bounds). This is in part why March sees Ramadan as compatible with Rawls' proceduralism, as Ramadan criticizes *ideological* democracy, but seems to have faith in democracy itself. While March is insufficiently critical of Rawls, his judgment on Ramadan is accurate. Fourth, there is political literalist *Salafism*, which is concerned to establish an Islamic caliphate state as the basis of social and political action, is deeply anti-Western, and promotes *jihad*. In the West Hizb al-Tahrir and Al-Muhajirun movements are the best known and are found within various factional networks. Fifth, there is the Liberal or Rationalist Reformist exegetical tradition born out of Western influences in the colonial period. It supports a division between state and religion. Hence, on the one hand, we might get a Mustafa Kemal Ataturk and the modern Turkish state project, which imposes an almost French model; and, on the other hand, there are forms of liberal Islam not unlike liberal Protestantism (in the work of Sachedina 2001; and see Legenhausen's very incisive criticism of Sachedina: 2002). Finally, there is Sufism, with diverse groups (Naqshbandis, Qadiris, and Shadhillis, the largest) arguing that the scriptural texts have deep meaning that require time, meditation, and the cultivation of the inner life. Some Sufis are socially active within this remit, others not so.

What is helpful about Ramadan's typology is not its utter accuracy, but its patterning, which allows us to realize the complexity of intra-traditional debate across and between differing schools. But as Asad argues, there is still room for speaking of "Islam," not "Islams," as all these differing versions still have in common the authority of the Quran and the *hadith*. Through *fiqh* and *ijtihad* Ramadan carefully thinks through a range of issues regarding European Muslims in their new context. For example, on the social, political, and economic front, Ramadan challenges Muslims to move forward and develop an engagement not built on the legal fallbacks of necessity and need, nor on defending Muslim interests alone (as is the pattern of the Jewish lobby in the US), but founded on Muslims' practicing responsibility for the common good. This is based on the

> universal principles of Islam concerning the brotherhood of mankind, the necessity for justice and equality before the law, the need for involvement, and, last, service to others that requires that attention be given constantly in society to the evaluation of the moral quality of actions, the motivations and abilities of the significant actors, and the ultimate nature of the dynamics that are set in motion. (2004, 168)

This is what constitutes Muslim citizenship. Ramadan calls into question the claim that:

> the democratic system ([which is] not a Qur'anic concept) does not respect Islamic criteria (the criteria of *shura*), and a Muslim in the United States or Europe, outside his natural home (*dar al-islam*), must distance himself from any support for a system opposed to Islamic values. (2004, 159; and see especially 2000, part II: "Shura or Democracy?" where Ramadan shows, not entirely convincingly, confidence in procedural democracy that does not impose moral or religious values upon its citizens)

Ramadan calls for a radical economic approach to society based on the interpretation of *zakat* (a socially purifying tax) and *riba* (prohibition against usury), which leads him to an unqualified condemnation of neo-liberalism (characterized by interest and financial speculation):

> We know that these practices are in total material contradiction to Islamic principles on which the Qur'anic revelation is explicit: whoever engages in speculation or the practice of usury is at war with the Transcendent. (2004, 176, citing Quran 2:278–9)

How is it possible for Muslims to live within neo-liberal economic society? Ramadan answers that this is possible only by involvement in the system with the exclusive aim of moving out of it (after housing and family have been secured, which is a basic necessity). He wants to see *zakat* employed through national and international groups with a long-range intention of removing poverty and inequality, nothing less, and *riba* as working toward the same ends, developing fair trade, grass-root exchange, without aim of profit other than toward social betterment.

Regarding other religions, Ramadan argues that the outcome of reading the Quran on this matter will depend on which school of exegesis one belongs to. For example, he notes how literalists cite various Quranic texts to show that there should be no civic rights or value attributed to the people of the book: "Religion in the sight of God is Islam" (Quran 3.19), and "He who desires religion other than Islam will not find himself accepted and in the hereafter he will be among the losers" (Quran 3.85). Like Legenhausen, Ramadan argues that in the Quran there are two meanings to the word "*Islam*" (to submit): first, a universal and generic (submission to the creator God to be found in all theistic religions and natural religions); and, second, the specific and particular form of religion whose final prophet is Muhammad. Literalists have employed only the "restricted meaning of the second definition, while the generic definition makes better sense of the Islamic message as a whole" (2004, 206).

Of Christians, literalists cite: "They are certainly in a state of denial [*kafara*], those who have said that God was the Messiah the son of Mary" (Quran 5.17). Ramadan makes a number of points in response. *Kuffar* (plural) is translated "infidels" and "miscreants," but Ramadan argues that this Arabic term has "a neutral sense in the Islamic sciences, and it is clearly perceived at various levels" (2004, 205). It can mean someone who properly knows the truth and rejects it, such as the satanic figure of Iblis in the Quran, or it can mean someone who has not accepted a lesser truth (the nature of a particular commandment), or someone who has not accepted a truth because they have not properly understood it. The Jews and Christians have accepted a truth (belief in God) and thus cannot be called "miscreants" or non-believers, even though they deny (*yakfuru*) the truth of the message and its Prophet. Second, Ramadan cites an important *sura* that must be read together with 5.17:

> Certainly, those who have believed, the Jews, the Christians, and the Sabaens, all those who have believed in God and in the last day of judgement and who have done good – they will have their reward from God. They will not be afraid and they will not grieve. (Quran 2.62; there is some dispute as to who the Sabaens were and whether they continue today)

This facilitates the type of interpretation that Legenhausen advances, but Ramadan must first address the argument that 2.62 is abrogated (*mansukh*) by 3.85 and 5.17 cited above, on the basis of an opinion attributed to Ibn Abbas reported in Tabari's commentary. Ramadan says this interpretation pays

> no regard to the rule of abrogation, which specifies that only verses stipulating obligations or prohibitions (which many change in the course of revelation) can be abrogated but not information, which cannot be true one day and untrue the next. This verse [2.62] is clearly giving information. (206–7)

Ramadan also cites:

> If God had willed, he would have made you one community but things are as they are to test you in what He has given you. So compete with each other in doing good. (Quran 5.48)

From this he develops the position that religious diversity is a good thing, for it encourages each religion to strive in moral goodness in the light of the other, thus also helping one know one's own religion better.

I have only touched on Ramadan's very helpful discussion of the Quran, and there are certain aspects that require further clarification: what of non-theistic religions? What of the claim that a religious law cannot be enforced upon those who do not hold that religion, even if that law arising from a particular tradition requires universal applications (as the abortion debate is construed by some, in contrast to a law that requires fasting by Muslims during Ramadan)? And what of apostasy from Islam (in relation to conversion being possible through interreligious dialogue)? Nevertheless, most importantly, Ramadan is able to theologically validate religious plurality in the European context, without either negating the finality and completeness of particular (rather than generic) Islam, or accepting the truth claims of other religions. Like Legenhausen, Ramadan is also able to underwrite civic religious pluralism and civic religious freedoms, one within a Muslim constitution, one within European constitutions; one from within the "Scholastic tradition" and Ramadan from within the *salafi* reform tradition. Neither of them compromise on the truth of the Quran or the finality of Islam. These are serious achievements whereby questions generated by modernity are dealt with very thoughtfully without adopting modernity's solutions and by retaining orthodox strategies of public reasoning from religious resources.

Conclusions

What conclusions can be drawn from Part III? First, I have sought to question the assumption that religions must take their place within the public square as allocated them through modernity's discourse. Second, I have tried to show that religions are in serious danger of being made to conform to modernity if they take up this challenge without questioning various operative assumptions within it. Third, I have called into question the nature of the European Enlightenment "public square," suggesting that genealogically it is profoundly dependent on the Greek, Christian, and Muslim heritage. Fourth, I have shown how Catholicism and certain forms of Islam in the modern period can construe "freedom," "tolerance," "public reasoning," "civic religious liberties and pluralism" in ways that further call into question modernity's assumptions that it is the sole purveyor of such sacred goods. Fifth, I have suggested that rather than a clash of civilizations resulting from a clash of religious cultures (Huntington), the contrary is very possible because both traditions are capable of placing a high value on reasoned debate. Both traditions also have problematic strands that do not locate reason within the divine, which was one of the real concerns of Pope Benedict's ill-fated Regensburg lecture in 2006, whereby the resource of religion to engage rationally can be questionably subordinated to pure obedience to God's will, even if this will is irrational. This is why Benedict cited Manuel II Paleologus' dialogues and compared Ibn Hazm's voluntarism with Duns Scotus' voluntarism, which leads toward a God who is not "even bound to truth and goodness" so that

> God's transcendence and otherness are so exalted that our reason, our sense of the true and good, are no longer an authentic mirror to God, whose deepest possibilities remain eternally unattainable and hidden behind his actual decisions. (Benedict XVI 2006)

Sixth, even if some or most of my argument is accepted, the dialogue of religions in the public square has hardly begun in Europe. Fostering a dialogue that takes differences of starting point seriously promises to be more fruitful. If we want to respect the civic rights of religious communities, rather than curtail them prior to committed public conversation, there needs to finally be a real engagement with the difficulties before us.

Note

1. ('a) stands for " 'alayhi al-salam," "peace be with him," which is used for prophets and Imams, and (s) stands for "salAllahu alayhi wa alihi wa salam," which means "may Allah bless him and his progeny and grant them peace" (literally "God's blessings upon him and his progeny and peace"), which is only used for the Prophet Muhammad.

PART IV

Christ's Descent into Hell

7

Old Doctrines for New Jobs

Introduction

In chapter 1 I argued that the universal-access exclusivist position is one of the most plausible of theological options in holding together three important points: (1) the necessity of Christ, the trinity, and the church for salvation; (2) that holding this first point does not result in a denigration of non-Christian religions (but rather, the openness to recognize their profound differences and possible similarities), nor does it result in a pessimistic attitude regarding the salvation of non-Christians (as it is entirely compatible with a hopeful universalism); and (3) that the salvation of non-Christians is resolved post-mortem (after death). This answer is most important as it relieves the pastoral pressure on Christians who cannot imagine that a good and just God could countenance the damnation of so many unevangelized, who may seek the good and follow their conscience at great personal cost. The pastoral pressure regarding this matter can only be plausibly resolved if this third point is rooted in solid doctrinal resources. This is what I hope to do in this part of the book.

The descent into hell is affirmed in the Apostles' Creed, although it is sometimes professed with little sense of what is being said or its significance both for daily Christian living and for the eschatological vision entailed in this creedal profession. In entering into hell to further our exploration, we will find a rich and complex tradition, which might leave some readers shocked and surprised, but hopefully challenged as well. I ask such readers to stick with the argument and judge it on its biblical, traditional, and rational merits because this teaching has been held for so long. In part I of this book I noted that Protestant thinkers like George Lindbeck, Donald Lake, and Origen Jathanna had employed differing types of post-mortem resolution to the question of how non-Christians might be saved, but the first two do not give much detail to this claim and Jathanna explicates it in terms of reincarnation, which contains no basis in the Bible and very little in the tradition. I think the post-mortem solution is actually implied in my own tradition, Roman Catholicism, so I would like to show this before proceeding to the actual contents of the doctrine. It is implied in two ways. First, because there has been no developed answer as to how the good non-Christian is actually saved. Second, because the "descent into hell" teaching provides resources to answer this question in terms of a post-mortem solution. Let us look at both these ways.

The Catholic church teaches explicitly that a non-Christian can be saved with the following qualifications, which I shall take as granted from now on. First, it is assumed that Jane (to give her a name) has not known the gospel; it is assumed that she cannot make new decisions after death, for death represents the final summation and end of the person's life; it is assumed that baptism is required both to bring about and signify Jane's regeneration – the church is a necessity of means and precept; it is assumed that Jane has lived a good life, following the truth to the best of her ability, in the light of her conscience; it is assumed that possibilities of the good, true, and beautiful life might be found in positive elements within her religion (let us say Buddhism as it is not theistic), and in this way Jane is acting in response to the promptings of the Holy Spirit who is the foundation of our freedom and search for truth; and, finally, it is assumed, thankfully, that we have no way of actually making any clear judgments about who Jane might be in history; she is a *type* to highlight what is at stake.

The Catholic church teaches explicitly that Jane might be saved. Vatican II's *Lumen Gentium* (16; subsequently *LG*) outlines the different ways non-Catholic Christians, those from other religions, and even atheists, are related to the church. It concludes:

> Nor does divine Providence deny the helps that are necessary for salvation to those who, through no fault of their own, have not yet attained to the express recognition of God yet who strive, not without divine grace, to lead an upright life.

Hence, explicit recognition of God is not required in this life ("not yet attained") for the possibility of salvation. The church is also explicit about the problems thus left unresolved. In *Dominus Iesus* (subsequently *DI*), a teaching document issued by the Congregation for the Doctrine of the Faith, the matter is stated thus:

> With respect to the *way* in which the salvific grace of God – which is always given by means of Christ in the Spirit and has a mysterious relationship to the Church – comes to individual non-Christians, the Second Vatican Council limited itself to the statement that God bestows it "in ways known to himself" [citing *Decree on the Church's Missionary Activity* 1965, *Ad Gentes*, 7]. (2000, 21)

Does this latter mean that we should desist from inquiry? Fortunately, it is immediately added:

> Theologians are seeking to understand this question more fully. Their work is to be encouraged, since it is certainly useful for understanding better God's salvific plan and the ways in which it is accomplished.

DI is not referring to the unquestioned reality of Christ's grace in the non-Christian's life through conscience and elements within their religions. The question is: how can original and personal sins be forgiven, how can persons consciously share in the beatific vision, how can they participate in the joy and glory of the risen Lord, without knowing Christ and his church in any possible way when they die as non-Christians?

The usual answer is that they can *implicitly* know Christ and his church through an implicit or unconscious desire (*votum ecclesiae*). Faith in God and doing good works was the minimal requirement for salvation, deriving from Hebrews 11:6: "Now it is impossible to please God without faith, since anyone who comes to him must believe that he exists and rewards those who try to find him." This position is found in Aquinas and then actually applied to non-Christians from the sixteenth century on (see Sullivan 1992, 63–161). By the late nineteenth century, Catholic theologians began to develop this minimal requirement in the light of non-theistic religions that had impressive moral codes and developed ascetical and spiritual practices to allow for the concept of "implicit theism" (Lombardi 1956, 54–65). The rise of secularism also required a reconsideration. Rahner, for example, classically argued that the inner *telos* of every genuinely good and charitable act is oriented toward and presupposes God, regardless of whether the person is a theist (1969). In this way, good works dependent on grace became the minimal requirement for salvation in the absence of evangelization. As noted in chapter 1, this still failed to explain how such people become explicitly aware of the Blessed Trinity when they die unaware of the Blessed Trinity and are not allowed to make any more free decisions after death. Ontologically, they have become "related" to the reality of God through grace, but epistemologically do not know God in the way God has revealed himself so that the lack of unity between the epistemological and ontological is deeply unsatisfactory, for the beatific vision requires both. This is precisely why the Lutheran Lindbeck posits the necessity of a *fides ex auditu* after death, so that a proper conformation to the gospel might be fulfilled, a proper relationship to the living and true triune God, before Jane, who chooses the gospel in this post-mortem scenario, comes to the fullness of redemption. But Lindbeck's solution falls foul of the Augustinian prohibition against such changes and freedom after death (see below for more on this). I want to argue that this complex nest of questions falls away and is resolved in looking more closely at the descent into hell, which allows us to take up solutions offered by Lindbeck and Lake and others, and integrate them into this doctrinal tenet: *Christus descendit ad infernos*, "he descended into hell." I shall also look at some ways in which this teaching does not help to address our question, despite very strong claims to the contrary.

One final point needs to be clarified. The descent into hell is only mentioned in the Apostles' Creed and, because of this and on biblical grounds, the evangelical scholar Wayne Grudem argues that the "descent" is a "late intruder into the Apostles' Creed that really never belonged there in the first place. On historical and Scriptural grounds, it deserves to be removed" (1991, 103). After surveying five key New Testament "descent" passages (Acts 2:7, Romans 10:6–7, Ephesians 4:8–9; 1 Peter 3:18–20; and 1 Peter 4:6), Grudem concludes "this idea is not taught in Scripture at all." Thus, "there would be all gain and no loss if it were dropped from the Creed once for all" (1991, 113). The Reformed theologian David Lauber rightly criticizes Grudem's conclusion. Lauber argues that the descent "is the logical consequence of a synthetic reading of Scripture, and rigorous reflection on the implications of the *pro nobis* character of Jesus Christ's life and passion" (2004, 111). There are many important doctrines that evolve out of a synthetic reading of scripture, and certain doctrines are not to be found in scripture in the words and conceptualities used by the church. This would apply to the hypostatic union, the assumption and Immaculate Conception of Mary, the Mother of God, and also to purgatory. Further, Grudem's claim that there would be no loss if this claim were dropped from the Creed is open to serious objections, as we will be seeing that the descent actually does an awful lot of theological work, which would be lost were the teaching to be excommunicated by Grudem. It would also overturn the continuous teachings of the Roman Catholic and Orthodox churches. These gains will be explicated in what follows; the reader can be the judge.

"The Descent": Introduction to the "Circles of Hell"

In Roman Catholic theology, the "descent into hell" is a complex and shifting picture, but it bears important marks of continuity to establish certain doctrinal points. It is fair to say that the main map through the tradition has displayed the following four points.

First, the world was divided into three parts: heaven, earth, and "hell," the "netherworld," sometimes portrayed as being below the surface of the earth. Hell, like heaven, does not properly speaking have any time and space location but both affirm ontological realities. In what follows we must avoid imagining literal states, although the wonderful and sometimes garish details given to these states in art, liturgy, and literature are well worth attending to for the truths they wish to depict. The ultimate destiny of all humans is either heaven in eternal adoration of the Blessed Trinity, in union with the entire church and the angels, or hell, variously conceived in terms of pain, torment, suffering, and graded regarding the extent of sin, but, fundamentally, without God, in a state of privation. The one exception to this either/or scenario, according to an established but not expressly authorized tradition, is the case of unbaptized infants – see below.

Second, hell (singular: the *infernum*; plural: the *inferna*) has four different aspects, which are given differing spatial and geographical tropes, but contain fundamentally ontological and epistemological claims, which will be the subject of my focus. Again, the tropes should not be taken literally, but they do relate to unseen realities, not just subjective inner states of individuals or communities. The first of these states is hell, the place of damnation (*damnatorum*). This is traditionally thought of as "hell" in modern popular Christian imagination, and is a perduring reality. Whether it is empty or overflowing is a subject for much debate, although until the seventeenth century, with a few exceptions, it was thought to be very well populated. Moderns prefer it to be empty. From now on I shall call this "hell." Then there is the *limbus puerorum* (the limbo of unbaptized infants), a state that has always been disputed, and still is today. This, if it exists, is a perduring reality in which unbaptized infants reside. God's mercy forbids their damnation and God's justice forbids their salvation, as they are not free of original sin, for they are without baptism into the church. I shall call this the "children's limbo." Then there is the limbo of the just (*limbus patrum* – the limbo of the fathers), where the just who lived before Christ await their redemption. The limbo of the just is thought of as empty after Christ's descent to the just. This state is not a perduring reality. I shall call it the "limbo of the just." Finally, there is *purgatorium*, purgatory. This is a place of purification, where those who die in a state of grace and without mortal sin, but with venial sin, undergo purification and expiate their sins (*poenae peccatorum*). After this purification they are able to enjoy the Blessed Trinity, face to face, which would not be possible were they still tainted by sin. There is considerable controversy about every aspect of these four states, and they have been understood and depicted in very different ways during the history of the church. I shall attend to some of this detail below, but for now, I hope my map will guide the reader on our journey.

Third, after an extensive survey of the Bible, tradition, magisterial teachings, art, and popular literature, Alyssa Lyra Pitstick in her exhaustive and seminal study *Light in Darkness: Hans Urs von Balthasar and the Catholic Doctrine of Christ's Descent into Hell* summarizes her findings in four theses regarding Christ's relation to these four states in his descent:

> First, Christ descended in His soul united to His divine Person only to the limbo of the Fathers. Second, His power and authority were made known throughout all of hell, taken generically. Third, He thereby accomplished the two purposes of the Descent, which were to "liberate the just" by conferring on them the glory of heaven and "to proclaim His power". Finally, His descent was glorious, and Christ did not suffer the pain proper to any of the abodes of hell. (2007, 342)

Aspects of Pitstick's depiction will be clarified as we proceed, but I accept her well proven four contentions. Her succinct summary of the materials is very helpful, especially in highlighting Christ's descent in his soul to the limbo of the just and not in this manner to the other regions, although his power and authority are known in all four regions through his descent. The other extensive treatment of this topic is Strynkowski (1971), upon whom Pitstick draws. She indicates very minor differences of judgment (for example, Pitstick 2007, 382, note 100).

Fourth, "salvation" is to be understood as relating to statements in three time tenses: in the reality of the cross that took place in a specific time and place, the cause of salvation (past); in the reality of the present, by which we share in Christ's cross in the new life of discipleship (present); and in the reality of the future participation in the beatific vision, which is the summation and fulfillment of our present journey (future). For Jesus, Mary, and the saints in heaven, there is a perfect unity between all three tenses, although different in Jesus of course who is divine, who is eternal life. The future tense has often been encoded by theologians in the past century within the frameworks of existentialism and then Marxism, rightly stressing that Christian claims about the future are also about the nature of the now within history, in both its individual dimension (existentialism) and its social and political dimension (Marxism), but they have falsely restricted the full nature of these Christian claims by limiting their full range of reference to this life. Eschatology is also about post-mortem reality. Because Christ is God, speaking of his action always requires this threefold reference, enfolded within a fourth, eternity. This will be important to recall during some of my speculations below.

The remaining part of the book will be divided into four sections, dealing individually with the limbo of the just, purgatory, the children's limbo, and hell proper – in the order of their descent into the place from which there is no return. I will argue that the solution to our problem lies in the resources offered in these four doctrinal areas for, given the various dogmatic parameters stipulated above, only in the event of the "descent" does the unity of the epistemological and ontological take place to answer satisfactorily the question about Jane.

The Limbo of the Just and the Unevangelized

The early church faced a very familiar problem to that faced by people today: what happened to their non-Christian relatives, their Jewish ancestors who had followed God, and those remarkable, wise, and upright figures such as Plato and Virgil? Could all these unevangelized be lost? The modern question can be analogically transposed by a Hindu convert, without suggesting Judaism and Hinduism are alike in revelatory features: what happens to all my Hindu relatives whom I know, in the light of Christ, to have led good and sometimes holy lives and sought to follow their conscience? And what happens to all those wise and upright teachers like Sankara and Ramanuja? The *preparatio evangelica* (preparation for the gospel), the *Logos spermatikos* (the activity of the Logos prior to the incarnation), and the *prisca theologia* (the knowledge of revelation derived from the Old Testament) were conceptually employed by early Christians to acknowledge the great learning, wisdom, and profound teachings of the ancients. This was not a unanimous opinion (see Saldanha 1984; Hacker 1980). But what of the *actual salvation* of these ancients, the holy men and women, who had existed before Christ? The ancient answer is most instructive.

From the second century it was held by some that Christ's "descent into hell" was to the limbo of the just, to preach the gospel to those who had died before the incarnation and to guide them into heaven. The wide array of textual, liturgical, and artistic sources for this teaching are comprehensively outlined in Pitstick (2007, 7–84). This teaching was grounded on a number of biblical texts, the most important being Luke 16:22 – the parable of Dives and Lazarus at "Abraham's bosom"; Luke 23:43 – where Jesus on the cross tells the penitent thief that "today you shall be with me in paradise"; Ephesians 4:9 – where Paul says that before Jesus ascended he "also descended first into the lower parts of the earth"; and 1 Peter 3:18–4:6, which I shall quote in full, as it is probably the most pivotal:

> Christ himself died once and for all for sins, the upright for the sake of the guilty, to lead us to God. In the body he was put to death, in the spirit he was raised to life, and, in the spirit, he went to preach to the spirits in prison. They refused to believe long ago, while God patiently waited to receive them, in Noah's time when the ark was being built. In it only a few, that is eight souls, were saved through water. It is the baptism corresponding to this water which saves you now – not the washing off of physical dirt but the pledge of a good conscience given to God through the resurrection of Jesus Christ, who has entered heaven and is at God's right hand, with angels, ruling forces and powers subject to him. [4:1–6] As Christ has undergone bodily suffering, you too should arm yourselves with the same conviction, that anyone who has undergone bodily suffering has broken with sin, because for the rest of life on earth that person is ruled not by human passions but only by the will of God. You spent quite long enough in the past living the sort of life that gentiles choose to live, behaving in a debauched way, giving way to your passions, drinking to excess, having wild parties and drunken orgies and sacrilegiously worshipping false gods. So people are taken aback that you no longer hurry off with them to join this flood which is rushing down to ruin, and then abuse you for it. They will have to answer for it before the judge who is to judge the living and the dead. And this was why the gospel was brought to the dead as well, so that, though in their bodies they had undergone the judgement that faces all humanity, in their spirit they might enjoy the life of God.

There are different strands of interpretation. First, some of the earliest commentaries on this text saw it as implying that Christ preaches to the dead in the underworld, to all those who came before him and had not heard the gospel ("For Christ also died for sins once for all, the righteous for the unrighteous"), including sinners. Second, some of the commentaries saw this as referring only to the just who had died before the time of Christ. Third, some of the commentaries importantly included among the just both Jews and pagans. Fourth, some of the commentaries also indicate that, insomuch as Christ descends to the just, so does the church, thereby making sense of the requirement for inclusion into the church as a condition of salvation. These are disparate and overlapping traditions and, by the fifth century, they had become more consolidated into a single teaching that remained unquestioned with staggering continuity until the time of the Reformation. What we see, and will examine in a little more depth now, is that the early Christians were most concerned about the equivalent to them of my person Jane, the good non-Christian. The descent into the limbo of the just provides us with analogical conceptual resources to address the question of Jane with some precision and with attention to a number of the problems that I am seeking to address.

To examine the exegesis of all these scriptural passages is beyond my scope, but I will track some interesting readings of 1 Peter 3–4 to move forward. Clement of Alexandria (ca 150–215), in *The Stromata* 6.6, was the first to employ 1 Peter 3–4 to address the question of the salvation of the ancients, although before him the other texts were already employed for this purpose. Clement was no universalist. He argues that Christ came to preach to both the righteous Jews and those who were punished by the flood, as the latter may have learnt from their punishments. This is because

> God's punishments are saving and disciplinary, leading to conversion . . . and especially since souls, although darkened by passions, when released from their bodies, are able to perceive more clearly, because of their being no longer obstructed by the paltry flesh. (*The Stromata* 6.6)

Clement's notion of a second chance, a conversion after death, was to become unacceptable in the Latin Western tradition after Augustine's emphatic denial of such a possibility, and it disappears from the commentary tradition after the fourth century. Clement also extends the scope of Christ's preaching activity beyond the Jews, to the gentiles:

> If, then, He preached only to the Jews, who wanted the knowledge and faith of the Saviour, it is plain that, since God is no respecter of persons,

> the apostles also, as here, so there, preached the Gospel to those of the heathen who were ready for conversion. (See also *The Stromata* 2.43, 5.)

This part of his commentary forms a long tradition that includes both Jews and pagans in the limbo of the just.

Clement uses the *Shepherd of Hermas* (IX, 16:5–7) to establish the authority of his reading and to show that in the descent, the church as the body to Christ's head is also present in the limbo of the just. I shall cite the entire remarkable passage from the *Shepherd*, as it will support a key part of my later argument:

> the apostles and the teachers who preached the name of the Son of God, after they had fallen asleep in the power and faith of the Son of God, preached also . . . to them that had fallen asleep before them, and themselves gave unto them the seal of the preaching. Therefore they went down with them into the water, and came up again. . . . So by their means they were quickened into life, and came to the full knowledge of the name of the Son of God. (IX, 16:5–7; see Daniélou's commentary, 1964, 233–48.)

Clement suggests that the apostles, mimicking the gospel pattern of Christ preaching to the Jews and the apostles extending the gospel to the gentiles, also therefore descended into Hades to preach to the gentiles after Christ had preached to the righteous Jews. The biblical pattern is repeated *after* their death, which indicates how, after the resurrection, the church is seen as Christ's body with Christ as the head. It also means that, where Christ is, there is his church. In Clement we see that Christ's descent is shared by all who die with, in, and for him. They are united to his passion and descent, as much as to his ascension. Thus, the entire church shares in the reality of the "body of Christ," which would mean, to use later terminology, that in the descent into the limbo of the just we see the instrumental causality of both Christ and his church as the means to salvation.

It is worth noting an alternative tradition that does not require the disciples to enter into the limbo of the just, but nevertheless sees Christ baptizing in this limbo, thereby making the same point. This baptizing of all is attributed to Christ in the second century non-canonical *Epistle of the Apostles* 27:

> For to that end went I down unto the place of Lazarus, and preached unto the righteous and the prophets, that they might come out of the rest which is below and come up into that which is above; and I poured out upon them

> with my right hand the water of life and forgiveness and salvation from all evil, as I have done unto you and unto them that believe on me. (James 1924, 495)

This baptismal action by Christ is an incorporation of the just into his church, into his risen body. Both these texts thereby hold to the instrumental causality of the church for the salvation of the unevangelized in the time of Christ's descent.

Clement does not explain how the apostles can preach in the limbo of the just when Christ's resurrection has not happened when the preaching takes place. Neither does he explain why the apostles enter into limbo to preach since the just enter into heaven with Christ's resurrection. These questions are framed from the context of the later consolidated tradition, so they are not a weakness or problem in Clement. It is clear, despite these issues, what Clement's concerns are. They are to explain, at a minimum, how those before Christ enter the gates of heaven so that after death they receive Christ and are baptized into his body, and enter into heaven. At a maximum, Clement also seems to teach that the descent extends a second chance to the unrighteous who have received their due punishment, but this part of Clement does not find support in the later tradition. In a single stroke Clement solves many of the problems I want to address: the necessity of Christ and his church as a means of salvation and the explicit relationship of the unevangelized to the Blessed Trinity that is a precondition of salvation are both addressed through the descent into the limbo of the just. Analogically, this is a very promising avenue for our problematic.

This manner of interpreting 1 Peter 3–4 is continued by Origen (*De Principiis* 2.5). Origen defends the position that God is both merciful and just and that the great punishments inflicted by God in the Old Testament must be understood as corrective punishment and not necessarily as definitive damnation. Indeed, 1 Peter 3–4 indicates the very point that there will be a further opportunity to follow Christ after death, after just punishment has been applied for sins on earth. There is a similar theme to Clement in emphasizing the educative nature of punishment. To support his argument Origen turns to scripture, citing Ezekiel 16:53:

> I will restore their fortunes, both the fortunes of Sodom and her daughters, and the fortunes of Samaria and her daughters, and I will restore your own fortunes in the midst of them.

This passage is taken by Origen to indicate that, after punishment of those who have sinned, there is the possibility of a restoration of relationship back with God. However, it should be noted that, in his response to Celsus (*Against Celsus* 2.43), Origen says Christ converted only those "who were suitable and were willing to hear him" (30), which runs counter to any easy universalism. This latter emphasis on Christ's preaching to those who would accept him was to become the major interpretation of 1 Peter 3–4 in the later tradition, mainly to address Augustine's strongly authoritative opposition to after-death conversion. It meant that Christ preached to those who would have followed him had they heard the gospel, the just, and so did not require a total change of heart and a full conversion, so to speak, but rather a fulfillment of what was already present in that person at the time of death coming to its full maturation. Augustine's concern was thus met because someone who is destined for damnation at death cannot be saved by an event that takes place after death. It would be right to say that the person is destined for salvation and the descent employs Christological resources to throw light upon how that might be envisaged. Again, we see a way of answering our question coming into focus.

Cyril of Alexandria follows Origen's line, and his optimistic reading of 1 Peter 3–4 continues for some time in the Greek church. John Damascene, in his *The Orthodox Faith* 4:29, argues a similar case, although John is very clear that Christ saves only the righteous who deserve salvation. However, the liberation of souls from the prison of death before Christ, including some of the wicked, is a favorite theme in early Syriac literature according to Dalton (1989, 31). Here again, outside the Latin Western tradition was a clear answer to the problem of those good (and bad) Jews and pagans prior to the time of Christ, although it must be emphasized that, apart from Origen, none of the above sources approach any sort of universalism. I will not be arguing for universalism because it is disallowed by the church and, at best, may be a hope, nothing more.

Augustine's alternative interpretations of the 1 Peter 3–4 passage centered on the problematic implication of some sort of change in those to whom Christ preached ("who formerly did not obey" – v.20). Augustine, without denying Christ's "descent," established, for him, by Psalms 15 (16):10 and Acts 2:24, 27, suggests 1 Peter 3–4 be understood as Christ's pre-existent nature preaching to Noah's sinful contemporaries during their lifetime, through the person of Noah. Thus the passage refers to those who responded positively to Noah's/Christ's teachings just before the flood. Augustine's argument continues that since some of these sinful contemporaries had repented but were drowned in the flood and died without being on the ark, this means that Christ descends only to those who are already "saved," like those who responded to Noah, but who had appeared to be damned in the flood narrative. This is an ingenious argument that attends to the difficult references to Noah. According to Augustine all such people must await Christ for the completion of the process that started in their positive response to Noah/Christ. Without necessarily following Augustine's interpretation of the pre-existent Christ operating in Noah, the descent was increasingly understood as Christ's coming to set the just free, rather than his preaching the gospel to those who had earlier rejected God. Preaching comes to be understood as an announcement of Christ's lordship, his proclaiming that what they have secretly desired is now here: the entry into heaven has finally come. This Augustinian reading explains how Christ is involved in the explicit redemption of those who would in fact accept him when they meet him in the limbo of the just. This also means that it is possible to see the limbo of the just as providing a solution that overcomes the prohibition on "conversion," a new decision in the next life, for in one sense no conversion is required but a completion of the person's life and their destiny. There must be adequate continuity in the person's life for them to "qualify" for being present in the limbo of the just. Allied with Clement's insight that the church is co-present with Christ, we have an answer to the question of Jane coming clearly into focus.

Admittedly, an entirely different interpretation developed in the Reformation. Martin Luther views the descent purely as Christ's proclamation of damnation to the many souls who deserve such a fate! This view dominated the Lutheran tradition up to the eighteenth century, but was also known in Aquinas' time – and resisted by Aquinas. Aquinas is found dismissing it in *ST*, 3, 52, a. 2, ad. 3, to follow the consolidated tradition. In *ST*, III, q. 52, a. 5, Aquinas argues that:

> the Holy Fathers were detained in hell [the limbo of the just] for the reason, that, owing to our first parent's sin, the approach to the life of glory was not opened. And so when Christ descended into hell He delivered the holy Fathers from thence.

For Aquinas and many others before him, it is only the holy and righteous Jews and gentiles that are saved through this descent into the limbo of the just, not the unrighteous and the wicked. At least in the Western Latin tradition there is a strong line of continuity of interpretation that provides us with a possible solution to our question.

For the moment, it only seems to provide an answer related to those who died before Christ, but need it be so restricted? Can we analogically argue that the limbo of the just must conceptually exist in relation to non-Christians like Jane who are in a similar situation to the pre-Christian just? The answer I think is a yes and a no, and both sides of this answer are important to keep in tension. Remember, we must not imagine this solution as a celestial waiting room under the earth, but a conceptual theological datum based on the tradition that provides an answer uniting the ontological and epistemological to explain the case of Jane's salvation, as it did for the just before the time of Christ. If we pursue this avenue with these qualifications in mind, there are some interesting lessons to be learnt regarding our present view of non-Christian religions.

Overcoming objections to the use of the limbo of the just in addressing the question

There are obvious objections that must be answered before we can proceed. First, are other religions to be equated with Israel, whose just are the main inhabitants of the limbo of the just? Surely this minimizes the unique nature of Israel's covenant which is the basis and presupposition for Christ's new covenant? Second, if the limbo of the just is empty, as Christ opens the doors to heaven in his resurrection, then the analogy breaks down, as no one need be awaiting heaven in the same way as those persons did before Christ. Third, is the limbo of the just a liturgical and living reality in the life of the church or simply a relic from antiquity, which might have been true and relevant for what it addressed but is no longer helpful after the resurrection? I think all these three objections can be addressed, at least enough to employ this resource to address our question about Jane, and to acknowledge the limitations of such an application.

To deal with the first objection: we cannot conflate the status of the pre-messianic Jews with post-messianic non-Christians. I do not want to mitigate the *sui generis* nature of Judaism, both after and before the time of Christ. Nevertheless, Clement was not the only father to see that what can be applied to the pre-messianic Jews might be analogically applied to the gentiles, and we today can analogically relate both categories to the world religions. Clement has already insisted that the law (for the Jews) and philosophy (for the Greeks) had provided bridges to the gospel, and God would not fail those who sincerely walked these precarious paths. Hence, if the righteous Jew is not said to "convert," but rather to come to fulfillment, it is fair to conclude that this is also possibly true, with a very different sense of fulfillment, in the case of the righteous pagan. The "different sense" relates to the reality of the covenant embedded within Israel, which is not embedded in other religions, not to the righteousness that might be present within Israel and other religions. Furthermore, as we saw in chapter 6, Vatican II provided sufficient grounds for developing this analogy, whereby other religions are capable of mediating the good, true, and beautiful, reflecting the Light that is a Light to all nations. Developing this answer does not therefore eradicate the *sui generis* nature of Israel.

It is worth noting the limbo of the just contains such righteous people that it calls into question any notion of superior righteousness among Christians, compared to non-Christian religions. The limbo of the just reflects upon the present world order in an unsettling and helpful manner, requiring a great humility when dealing with non-Christians. This point is startlingly made by Albertus Magnus, Aquinas' teacher, who wrote much on our topic. For Albertus, the limbo of the just is *closer* to heaven than either purgatory or the children's limbo. In what follows I am using Christopher Beiting's lucid study of Albertus (2004). The startling righteousness of some non-Christians should not come as a surprise to us as the tradition of the holy pagans of the Old Testament and of the noble Greek philosophers and sages indicates that not only Jews, but also pagans, followed the truth in differing and very impressive ways (see Daniélou 1957 for an explication of this tradition). It is most significant to see this recognition of non-Christian righteousness embedded within mainstream Western orthodoxy in the tradition of the descent into hell. Indeed, Albertus argues that while suffrages (indulgences, prayers to aid those in purgatory) are required for those in purgatory, they are not required for the fathers in the limbo of the just, not because they have already moved on, but because

> they did not need them, they were rather so excellent that "they were able to aid those others who were in purgatory more fully than they were able to be aided by [suffrages]." (Beiting 2004 , 507–8; citing Albertus *In IV Sent.*, d. 45, article 5)

This is because the just have inherited bad personal merit due to the stain of original sin, compared to those in purgatory, who have bad personal merit through their own faults, since the stain of original sin was cleansed in baptism. If original sin could not be cleansed until the coming of Christ, Albertus is giving due honor to the remarkable righteousness attained despite this in comparison to those in purgatory who are still being cleansed for their bad personal merit. This difference is symbolized in the quality of punishments in each realm: purgatory is injurious (the fires) and a little dark, rather than primarily dark, the latter being reserved to hell. The limbo of the just is not injurious and also a little dark. Albertus' gradations are obviously important in telling us about the perceived status of the non-Christian, rather than the quality of lighting in these realms. The most important implication to take from this is that non-Christian religions and cultures may produce and cultivate great goodness, truth, and righteousness. Clearly, for Albertus, this only applies to the saints of Israel and possibly a handful of pagans. Numbers are not what is important, but the principles and conceptual theological datum established in the doctrine of the limbo of the just.

Before returning to the second objection concerning my use of the limbo of the just, let me look at one more question raised by Albertus. Albertus' geography does raise a very interesting question that is worth lingering over as it helps relate the limbo of the just to purgatory in a rich Christological fashion. Is it entirely credible that the "just" will be utterly pure, ready for the beatific vision, without any further journey of purification? Some medieval theologians argued that the just had been through the fires of purgatory prior to entering the limbo of the just so that they can enter into heaven immediately after Christ's resurrection, but this option is not really lucid, as it makes purgatory entirely un-Christological. This is because, prior to Christ, purgatory could not be regarded as a cleansing process directly related to Christ, but only indirectly, as Christ had not come. Admittedly, purgatory has sometimes lost its Christological character in the work of some scholars, but the best arguments about its nature require these Christological features that can properly be said to be "indispensable" (see below). Admittedly, there is no question that the just should not be able to enter heaven immediately consequent to the resurrection, as this is what the tradition implies. But it does still raise an interesting problem: will none of the just require any purification?

For example, if we take the good thief in Luke 23:43, most of the fathers have it that Dismas (the name given to him by the majority) is found in the limbo of the just, not in heaven (for no one could enter, until Christ's resurrection). But surely Dismas would require something like purgatory to complete his journey of purification? He makes a confession of faith, but the accumulated venial sin of a lifetime would still require purgation. And the same could be said of the righteous recently converted, in Augustine's reading of 1 Peter 3–4, who then immediately drowned in the flood. Would not those who had responded positively to Noah's teaching still require "time" to mature into the new life of faith that they had begun? Might they not be like most humans, "on the way," but not fully purified? The point here is not that God is unable to bear sin and imperfection in us, but that we are unable to bear the fullness of glory without purification. I am not arguing that Christ is unable to transform the individual instantaneously. Rather, from the human point of view, if one inhabitant of the limbo of the just, Dismas for example, might still require purification, why not others? There was speculation in the tradition that Dismas already knew Jesus in Galilee, but his having been a thief, not an innocent wrongly convicted, is the clear implication of Luke's narrative (Luke 23:39–43). The answer to this question about the purification of the "just," after Augustine's proper prohibition on "conversion" after death, inevitably played down the possibility of any impurity, even venial sin, such that Albertus can suggest the ineffectiveness of the suffrages for those in the limbo of the just compared to those in purgatory. However, if both the limbo of the just and purgatory are Christologically understood, there is something to be said for an argument that integrates the two, rather than insisting on a strict separation, or a sequence that logically places purgatory prior to the limbo of the just.

I would tentatively suggest the following conclusions so far. First, the limbo of the just conceptually explains the entry of non-Christians into a relationship with Christ and his church, and their subsequent enjoyment of the beatific vision. Second, the limbo of the just illuminates the necessity of Christ and the church as a means of salvation and unites the ontological (which has already begun in this life, in ways that have already been articulated in part – through conscience, through noble and good elements within a person's religion, through the activity of grace and the Holy Spirit in both these modes) with the epistemological, thus allowing the fulfillment of salvation to come about and addressing the entire cluster of problems related to Jane. Third, conceptually, it is very likely that some of the just, after their encounter with Christ and his church in the analogical space of the limbo of the just, will require purification, and then they, like their Christian brothers and sisters, may enter the Christological fires of purgatory. I will elaborate on this purgatorial point below. This does not detract from the possibility that some will enter heaven immediately without this purgatorial cleansing, however difficult that might be to imagine. However, since Mary, Jesus' mother, has done this and is the first fruit of her Son's salvation, this is not only possible, but also imaginable. We can now turn to the second objection: the limbo of the just is empty after the descent, because Christ is now raised from the dead. At first sight this seems a decisive objection. But is it?

The limbo of the just is thought to be empty by theologians for the obvious reason that, after Christ's descent, the righteous who awaited him are redeemed. Interestingly, Albertus thinks it still continues to exist, "so far as substance is concerned, but not so far as reason." By this he means the conceptual space is still there, but there is no reason for any to enter there as Christ has now opened the doors to heaven to all the just unevangelized. Albertus does not expect this space to continue into eternity, so it is interesting that he keeps it in place even after the just have entered into heaven. Beiting speculates that, for Albertus, it may serve as "an extra buffer zone between hell and the *limbus puerorum*" (Beiting 2004, 502), but it is difficult to see how it can act thus, as there is no chance of escape from the children's limbo in Albertus' view. The buffer is redundant. The key to understanding the emptiness of the limbo of the just is that, from the time of the earliest Christians to Albertus and a little later, certainly no later than the sixteenth century, most Christians assumed that, after Christ's resurrection, all peoples choose between the acceptance or rejection of the gospel – there are no longer any other options. The assumption is that the entire world is confronted with the gospel and must accept or reject it, or twist it into heresy, which is to reject it, or to fall into schism and/or heresy, as did the Jews and Muslims and other schismatic groups.

This ancient assumption is no longer tenable as we now know that, throughout Christian history, there have been billions of people and cultures who have not heard the gospel. Historical consciousness, travel, communication, geographic discoveries, and so on allow us to see the contextuality of this early assumption. Further, this assumption does not have any dogmatic truths attached to it except the one that no one can hear the gospel and reject it, and be in a state of grace. That dogmatic assumption is kept intact in my proposal. There are epistemologically and ontologically possibly millions of unevangelized who are in the same state as those in the limbo of the just, and not until all have heard the gospel can the limbo of the just play the analogical explanatory role to explain their fate such as I have outlined above. Clearly, the limbo of the just will not persist and is temporary, but it will continue to analogically operate in teaching that the just are never lost and await the Lord's coming after their death, just as do Christians. There are many like Jane who have not heard the gospel and who follow the good, true, and beautiful, whose religion may have many elements perhaps (akin to law and philosophy) that encourage them to walk the precarious bridge toward a merciful God who would not exclude them.

Just as the early church sought to address this problem by positing the limbo of the just and preaching the descent into hell, so, I suggest, can Christians today confess this same descent, as they do in the Apostles' Creed in the liturgy. At the level of subjective truth the events of the descent cannot be denied, although, objectively speaking, Christ's resurrection means that the gates of heaven are now open and one objective sense of the descent doctrine has now objectively changed the nature of reality. If we understand this solution to operate between the objective reality that the limbo of the just is empty now and the subjective reality that there are many who subjectively still exist in the state of those who entered the limbo of the just, this doctrine provides a sound solution to the problem we have been investigating: it does not require "conversion," but a coming to maturation and completion, or, in exceptional cases, the immediate enjoyment of God's vision when confronted by Christ in his descent into the limbo of the just. It does not require unconscious desire, but a response to the good news preached by Christ and his church, thereby explaining the epistemological, Christological, and ecclesiological elements that were problematic until this solution is employed. It does not negate or downplay the historical lives lived by people and communities as building God's kingdom in "inchoate" ways, in seeking goodness, truth, and beauty, as best they can. It is precisely in these ways that such peoples already begin to participate in the life of the triune God. Indeed, this solution actually makes proper sense of those many positive elements singled out by Vatican II and later magisterial statements. It does not negate the teaching that there are only two final destinations that await us all (with the exception of children's limbo, yet to be examined). Finally, it keeps within the parameters I have sketched above, especially in remaining deeply Christological and ecclesiological.

There is one final objection to be faced. In positing this solution, am I minimizing the glory of the resurrection by emphasizing the subjective context of the descent doctrine? This would be an acceptable criticism if only the subjective context is emphasized, but I have tried to be more nuanced and relate this doctrine to purgatory (an argument yet to be developed) and emphasized that it does not override the objective truth that the gates of heaven are now open after the descent and resurrection, whereas they were not open prior to this. Rather, the descent explains, now as it did then, how the fruits of the cross are applied to those before Christ and can continue to explain how the fruits of the cross are applied to those analogically living before Christ, even if they are chronologically living after Christ. I think a liturgical practice will help secure my argument against this serious objection. My contention is that in the Eucharist, the site of the crucified and risen Christ on earth, we find this movement between the subjective and objective orders without compromising either.

Eucharistic mediation

It is worth attending to an interesting discussion on this precise matter in the work of the Catholic Jesuit Francis A. Sullivan. Sullivan argues that the church "must in some way be actively involved in the accomplishment of God's plan to reconcile the world to himself" (1992, 157). How can this instrumental causality be understood if many die without ever knowing the church? Sullivan gives the interesting answer that it is understood through the prayers of the church. He argues, drawing upon Pius XII's *Mystici Corporis*, that the prayers of the church for the salvation of the world are actually instrumental in the salvation of all. *Mystici* says:

> Dying on the Cross He left to His Church the immense treasury of the Redemption, towards which she contributed nothing. But when those graces come to be distributed, not only does He share this work of sanctification with His Church, but He wills that in some way it be due to her action. This is a deep mystery, and an inexhaustible subject of meditation, that the salvation of many depends on the prayers and voluntary penances which the members of the Mystical Body of Jesus Christ offer for this intention. (1943, 44)

Based on this, Sullivan argues that the instrumental causality of the church in the salvation of all is through her prayers and penance for all peoples. Sullivan does not take the context of Pius' passage fully into consideration, which actually relates the argument to indulgences and purgatory, based, as it is, on the "treasury of the Redemption" and the "power of the keys" granted to the church. This terminology expresses the church's powers to dispose of the fruits of redemption, the treasury, won by Christ, primarily through the sacrament of forgiveness, but also through the practices of indulgences in relation to purgatory (see further on this: Rahner 1973, 166–98; and Schmaus 1975, 241–52). As we shall see later, this purgatorial context might actually help Sullivan's arguments, in a way that he does not himself intend, but that I would intend.

Sullivan points to Eucharistic Prayers Three and Four to illustrate his contention. In Four, for example, the Eucharist is offered with the prayer: "Remember those who take part in this offering, those here present, and all your people, and all who seek you with a sincere heart." Sullivan argues that the "seekers" are non-Christians for whom this sacrifice is offered. And the prayer that follows is also relevant: "Remember those who have died in the peace of Christ, and all the dead whose faith is known to you alone." Sullivan comments on this latter group:

> These last are the ones who never had the opportunity to profess their faith with the Christian community, and yet who arrived at saving faith through the grace which the Holy Spirit offered to them "in a manner known only to God." (1992, 160)

Thus, Sullivan concludes: "the church plays an instrumental role in the hidden work of the Holy Spirit for the salvation of those 'whose faith is known to God alone'" (1992, 160). I find Sullivan's solution tenable and attractive, and will attempt to develop it further. However, it faces an objection from Jacques Dupuis regarding the implication of the instrumental causality of the church that must be addressed before I can proceed.

Dupuis argues that Sullivan's answer "is not of the order of efficiency but of the moral order and of finality" (1997, 350; a point that Sullivan seems to concede in 2002, 50–1, especially note 8). Dupuis gives a very precise and possibly too constricting sense to the meaning of the instrumental causality of the church, which must require *fides ex auditu*, the proclamation and preaching activity of the church (1997, 350). This allows Dupuis to discount the prayers of the church for the salvation of all as being instrumentally causal, arguing instead that the church has only a final causality in relation to non-Christians. This makes room for "substitutive mediations" (1997, 351) in Dupuis' alternative approach, such that other religions might be viewed as instruments of salvation, but with Christ as the efficient and final cause of this grace, not the church. Dupuis is keen to remove the church and replace it with Christ in terms of instrumental causality, but this is questionable in positing a separation between Christ and his body.

The Congregation for the Doctrine of the Faith's (subsequently CDF) *Notification on the Book Toward a Christian Theology of Religious Pluralism* (2001) is critical of Dupuis on this very point. In the *Notification* there is a clear insistence on both aspects of the church's saving operation: as both sign and instrumental cause. In speaking of possible erroneous interpretations or ambiguities in Dupuis' text regarding the church's status, the *Notification* notes a number of problems, only the sixth and seventh of which are relevant to this discussion. The CDF states what is required for orthodox faith and questions whether this element is present in Dupuis' position:

> 6. It must be firmly believed that the Church is sign and instrument of salvation for all people. It is contrary to the Catholic faith to consider the different religions of the world as ways of salvation complementary to the Church. 7. According to Catholic doctrine, the followers of other religions are oriented to the Church and are all called to become part of her. (2001, IV)

If the instrumental causality of the church is denied, as it is by Dupuis, it follows for Dupuis that other religions can be viewed as instruments of salvation, for how else do people in these religions otherwise gain salvation? But his solution is not considered admissible by the teaching authority of his church.

The *Notification* is underlining two points relevant to my discussion. First, that the instrumental causality of the church must be maintained, even though is not yet clear how this should be done. Second, it suggests that in Dupuis' work the denial of the instrumental causality of the church in relation to non-Christian religions leads to affirming other religions as instruments of salvation, which is incompatible with Catholic doctrine. Citing the *Notification* here is not a closure to further discussion, but a way of stressing that the instrumental causality of the church is seen as vital to a proper understanding of the church's nature. In proposition 6, the *Notification* cites *DI* 16. Clearly what is at stake in this entire discussion is the relation of Christ to his church. Dupuis, calling upon Rahner, prizes the two apart, even if with extreme sophistication and delicacy:

> Rahner has stressed the perduring role of mediation by the humanity of Jesus Christ, even in the beatific vision (Rahner 1967). As for the Church, it exercises its derived mediation in the strict sense through the proclamation of the word and the sacred economy celebrated in and by the Church communities. (1997, 350)

It should be noted that, in the last part of the sentence, Dupuis seems to concede the point he is arguing against Sullivan, for it is precisely the "sacred economy," the liturgy, and specifically the Eucharist, to which Sullivan's argument attributes the church's mediation as efficient causality. However, while the church's mediatory role is always a "derived mediation," it cannot be bypassed without bypassing Christ, precisely for the reason given by the *Notification* in *DI* 16:

> just as the head and members of a living body, though not identical, are inseparable, so too Christ and the Church can neither be confused nor separated, and constitute a single "whole Christ".

This same inseparability is also expressed in the New Testament by the analogy of the church as the "Bride of Christ" and one that we saw at the outset of this investigation in Clement and the early fathers. Sullivan's argument seems to address the signifying and instrumental nature of the church by seeing the body of Christ's prayer as having an instrumental causal nature in applying its fruits to the just unevangelized.

With Sullivan's helpful contribution in mind, let me pursue this point to fully respond to the third objection. When Catholics speak of Christ's death "once and for all," this does not mean that the Eucharist is not a sacrifice in the proper Christological sense. The Eucharist in the present tense actually participates in the event of the cross, an event in the past tense, to apply the fruits of the cross to the church (in the future tense). The Eucharist is the eternal sacrifice of God's self-giving love. If the Eucharist enacts the cross in this ontological and participatory sense, it must also be the case with the "descent into hell," as it is with the resurrection. Clearly a lot more argument is required to establish this point, but to claim this movement between the subjective and objective elements of the atonement in the Eucharist is not to detract an iota from the once-and-for-all nature of the atoning death and resurrection. Rather, it is to iterate that its superabundant merits require mediation, to both the church and the world, and the Eucharist embodies this mediation both retrospectively, in the now, and in the future. I want to suggest that the descent takes place not only at every holy mass said, where the sacrifice of the cross *is* present, but also and especially during the Easter *triduum*, at that solemn and dark liturgical moment at the time of Jesus' death on Good Friday and his descent into hell on Holy Saturday.

First, consider the special prayers for the Good Friday liturgy and how, after the revisions following Vatican II, these prayers are structured according to *Lumen Gentium* 16, but still have the same concern as prior to Vatican II: to hold the hope of salvation for all before us, those with us, and those to come, while always recognizing the necessity of Christ for the fullness of salvation. It is worth citing these prayers in detail, for I am arguing that they are a liturgical correlation to the limbo of the just. This is central to my argument. Prior to Vatican II, the bidding prayers for the Good Friday service were as follows (my italics and added square brackets for explanation):

> 1 For the unity of the Church. Let us pray also for heretics and schismatics, that our Lord and God may save them from their errors and be pleased to recall them to our holy Mother the Catholic and Apostolic Church.
>
> *Let us pray*: Almighty and everlasting God, You save all men and will that *none should be lost*; look down on those who are deceived by the wiles of the devil, that with the evil of heresy removed from their hearts, the erring may repent and return to the unity of Your truth. Through our Lord . . .
>
> 2 For the conversion of the Jews. Let us pray also for the Jews that the Lord our God may take the veil from their hearts and that they also may acknowledge our Lord Jesus Christ.
>
> *Let us pray*: Almighty and everlasting God, You do not refuse Your mercy even to the Jews; hear the prayers which we offer for the blindness of that people so that they may acknowledge the light of Your truth, which is Christ, and be delivered from their darkness. [The notorious phrase "the perfidious Jews" was removed by Pope John XXIII in 1959.] Through our Lord . . .
>
> 3 For the conversion of pagans [Latin: *infidelium*]: Let us pray also for the pagans, that almighty God may take away iniquity from their hearts, so that they may forsake their idols and be converted to the living and true God and His only Son, Jesus Christ, our God and Lord.
>
> *Let us pray*: Almighty and everlasting God, *You always demand not the death but the life of sinners*; in Your goodness hear our prayer; free them from the worship of idols and unite them to Your holy Church for the praise and glory of Your name. Through our Lord . . .

Note how this liturgical text is changed after Vatican II, breaking these three groups into four following the structuring of *Lumen Gentium* 16, and excising what might be considered as "offensive" statements (presumably if overheard by those about whom they speak, but also in part reflecting a real shift of emphasis). Note in what follows how the revisions maintain the same thematic concerns at the liturgical point in the year marking the descent into hell, where the church, through Christ, becomes instrumental in the salvation of non-Christians (my emphases in italics and added square brackets in what follows):

> 1 For the unity of Christians: Let us pray for all our brothers and sisters who share our faith in Jesus Christ, that God may gather and keep together *in one Church* all those who seek the truth with sincerity. . . .

2 For the Jewish people: Let us pray for the Jewish people, the first to hear the word of God, that they *may continue to grow in love of his name and in faithfulness to his covenant.*

Let us pray: Almighty and eternal God, long ago you gave your promise to Abraham and his posterity. Listen to your Church as we pray that the people you first made your own *may arrive at the fullness of redemption*. We ask this through Christ our Lord.

3 For those who do not believe in Christ [*all the theistic religions and non-religious*]: Let us pray for those who do not believe in Christ, that the *light of the Holy Spirit may show them the way to salvation.*

Let us pray: Almighty and eternal God, enable those who do not acknowledge Christ *to find the truth as they walk before you in sincerity of heart*. Help us . . . to become more perfect witnesses of your love in the sight of men.

4 For those who do not believe in God [*some religions and non-religious*]: Let us pray for those who do not believe in God, that they may find him by sincerely following all that is right.

Let us pray: Almighty and eternal God, you created mankind so that all might *long to find you* and have peace when *you are found*. Grant that, in spite of the hurtful things [*no longer* "idols"] that stand in their way, they *may all recognise in the lives of Christians the tokens of your love and mercy*, and gladly acknowledge you as the one true God and Father of us all.

While the pre-Conciliar prayers are tough, clear, and uncompromising, but lack the nuance of the modern, they too, as with the modern prayers, desire that all enter into the church to gain salvation so that "none may be lost." The prayers distinguish different categories of nearness and farness (echoing the categories established in saying that the true church "subsists in," rather than "is," the Catholic church, and the subsequent order of different groups' relation to the Catholic church – *Lumen Gentium* 16). The prayers *mimic* an action taking place in the descent of Christ into the limbo of the just, with the different types of just peoples (not individuals), such that the life of the church may be the means whereby those outside it recognize the "love and mercy" of God and come to fully enjoy the fruits of Christ's resurrection and participate in this beatific new life. The reality of the descent that took place after Christ died is present in the now of the life of the church, as a future *hope* that all may be saved.

It is important to stress the three different tenses (past, present, future) through which these prayers operate, for they are the prayers of the church (past, present, and future) and the prayers that actually instrumentally bring about a reality (following Sullivan's argument); these prayers have an efficacious power because they are the prayers of the church, not those of a private individual. The liturgical reality, like the Eucharistic sign, affects the grace it signifies, so that these prayers bring about an instrumental relation of efficacy to the unevangelized non-Christians, like Jane and her entire community (past, present, and future).

A dispute continues about Pope Benedict's February 2008 decision to amend the Good Friday prayer for the Jews from 2 above, to a version as follows:

> Let us also pray for the Jews: That our God and Lord may illuminate their hearts, that they acknowledge Jesus Christ is the Saviour of all men. (Let us pray. Kneel. Rise.)
>
> Almighty and eternal God, who want that all men be saved and come to the recognition of the truth, propitiously grant that even as the fullness of the peoples enters Thy Church, all Israel be saved. Through Christ Our Lord. Amen.

This rendition is in keeping with the theology being advanced in this book. I cannot see how this prayer can be charged with either changing the teachings of Vatican II or with targeting Jews for missionary activity as has been claimed by some Jews and Christians who are critical of the new prayer. Rather, I would argue that it recognizes the hope that all may enter into the church; it draws on Paul's teaching in Romans 9–11; and it affirms the salvific instrumentality of both Christ and his church.

Conclusions

Let me summarize my tentative argument related to the descent into the limbo of the just. First, the descent into the limbo of the just has a liturgical correlation in the Eucharist for, in the Eucharist, the once-and-for-all sacrifice of Calvary is present, in a dramatic and particular manner during the Easter liturgy. This means that the Eucharist enacts, celebrates, and makes present the cross, the descent into hell, and the resurrection, so that the fruits of this sacrifice may become available to all. This means that the descent is a liturgical reality present in the life of the church, not an arcane and embarrassing doctrine. How might this doctrine then apply to our problem? Second, in response to this question, the limbo of the just should be used to theologically address the problem of Jane, to explain how, after death, Jane and her people might arrive at salvation and enjoyment of the beatific vision, to unite the ontological relation with Christ that she might enjoy on earth with the epistemological relation required for the beatific vision. Third, this solution preserves the teachings of the church that the gates of heaven are open with the resurrection (the objective truth of the descent teaching) while retaining the subjective element of that teaching, given that Jane shares the same logical space as the righteous pre-messianic Jew or pagan. Fourth, it explains through a traditional creedal doctrine the necessity of Christ and his church for salvation. Fifth, it keeps entirely open the question of the nature and extent of the *preparatio evangelica* that non-Christian religions might provide, for it keeps open the question regarding the truth, goodness, and beauty to be found in non-Christians and their religions. This is precisely the type of task that a historically oriented comparative theology might address, without stepping back from difficult and informed judgments that both affirm and challenge various teachings and practices in other religions. Sixth, drawing on this resource does not require a post-mortem conversion. This doctrine allows for proper continuity as well as for the newness of the relationship with Christ. Such newness will also be analogically present in the Christian experience of purgation after death, to which we will turn shortly. Seventh, the limbo of the just is seen as provisional and not perduring, and thus is a temporary stage on the path toward the beatific vision and cannot in any way contradict the final two ends that are possible: heaven or hell. Eighth, if the limbo of the just is integrated into the doctrine of purgatory in the way I have presented it, it makes it especially attractive in developing a fuller explanation of this solution, and it is to this fuller explanation that I now turn. Ninth, I have not tried to rehabilitate the limbo of the just in any literal sense suggesting a pre-heavenly waiting room, but have tried to recover the theological datum contained in this teaching to establish that a post-mortem solution regarding the final destiny of non-Christians has important and long-standing precedence in the history of the church. I would suggest that Lindbeck's and Lake's positions are best integrated into this solution to defend them more robustly from critics. This would of course take more argument. In this way Reform and Catholic intentions can be harmonized.

In the next chapter I enter the final three circles of hell to further elaborate upon the answer that has become crystallized in this chapter.

8

Further into the Inferno

Purgatory and the Non-Christian

I shall not address the many debated questions about purgatory, regarding its duration, location, nature of fire and punishments, biblical basis, dogmatic history, and so on, but refer the reader to two recent convincing rehabilitations of the doctrine (Rahner 1984 and Ratzinger 1988a; for a good theological history, Bastian 1981). In Ratzinger's case, we also have a bold ecumenical proposal that he thinks may be acceptable to the Orthodox and East, which again underlines the ecumenical intention of my solution, even if it operates within the Western Latin tradition. The fact that purgatory does not become crystallized until the twelfth century as Le Goff argues (1990) is ontologically irrelevant. Le Goff falsely isolates the term "purgatory" in the literature, rather than recognizing clusters of concepts that pre-existed the twelfth century and implied what became later formulated in the term. Hence, we cannot say with Le Goff that purgatory is the "invention" of the twelfth century, but rather a period in which the doctrine becomes formalized in a certain manner. This is not to detract from Le Goff's valuable social history of the doctrine. Finally, Fenn's remarkable study (1995) allows us, not him, to use his arguments as Gregory suggests in a review (1998) "to fund an important theological critique of modernity and its religious origins." Fenn shows the bankruptcy of purgatory's legal and penal legacy if shorn of its orientation toward the fullness of redemption and entirely secularized. In this truncated form it signifies despair at lack of perfection, rather than a hope and structured movement toward perfection. As Skotnicki shows, it ties modernity into despair through the loss of the full sense of "restorative justice" (2006, 104) intrinsic to the doctrine's theological context.

DiNoia (1992) is alone among recent Catholic theologians in employing purgatory to complement Protestant prospective (future) salvation solutions regarding the non-Christian. Let me briefly repeat his basic argument, especially the features that bear upon my concerns. DiNoia argues that, at best, other religions may be *preparatio evangelica*, in keeping with Vatican II. This will mean that there are elements, not structures, of grace within them. However, for DiNoia, other religions must be taken at face value, respecting what they say about their ultimate ends (*nirvana*, *moksha*, and so on) and the means to these ends (following the Noble Eightfold Path, following our caste and status in life, and so on). Hence, DiNoia emphasizes rightly the profound differences in vision and practice that make up different religious paths. He is careful not to conflate these varied ends with the end of the beatific vision. Nevertheless, it is possible at death that non-Christians may be "justified or in a state of grace, but unprepared for the full enjoyment of bliss" (1992, 105). DiNoia argues that, because purgatory provides the context whereby those who are not ready for the immediate enjoyment of beatitude might be "integrated" and transformed (Rahner 1984) and conformed by Christ's judging fire (Ratzinger 1988a), and because such non-Christians are justified or in a state of grace, "then surely there is no reason in principle to rule [purgatory] out for non-Christians" (1992, 105). DiNoia accepts that, cognitively, there may be deep discontinuity for such non-Christians, but there are also and always "continuities" (1992, 106). He rightly points out that discontinuities and disruptive re-education will also occur for many Christians in the process of purgation. This solution is akin to the one I am advancing, but obviously different in two respects. I suggest the limbo of the just as the presupposition of purgatory for the non-Christian, and I question whether purgatory can be assimilated to the non-Christian without further argument, as it has traditionally been understood as the process for those who are already epistemologically "in Christ," which is not the case for Jane. Before seeing if DiNoia's solution and my own can be coherently related, let me turn to an interesting criticism of DiNoia's solution from the Catholic Jesuit Edward Oakes.

Oakes raises three objections against DiNoia, only the third of which I think has real force. He argues that the salvation of non-Christians is to be found in Balthasar's Holy Saturday theology that teaches that Christ descends into hell proper, not to the limbo of the just and other circles of hell. I shall return to his positive proposals below, but here focus on his three criticisms of DiNoia. First, purgatory "hardly commands the assent of the whole spectrum of Christianity, with Protestants especially wary of this allegedly non-biblical and extraneous teaching" (Oakes 2007, 188). It is strange that Oakes raises this objection, as his own solution, Christ's descent into hell proper, is decidedly problematic for the same reasons, and has even been criticized as heretical – insomuch as Pitstick criticizes Balthasar, whom Oakes follows, of serious unorthodoxy. Second, Oakes argues that:

> a whole set of problems has never been resolved by Catholic theologians who subscribe to the existence and reality of purgatory; the questions of temporality, place, duration, imagery, and the like. (2007, 188)

Again, this applies to his own Balthasarian solution, as well as being an issue fully acknowledged by DiNoia (1992, 104). What of Oakes' third objection?

> Admittedly, [DiNoia] holds that nothing "in principle" would exclude non-Christians from [purgatory], provided they die justified or in a state of grace. But that seems to beg the question that he was trying to solve: how can a specifically Christian grace be said to operate among adherents of other religions *before* death? To grant to nonbelievers a Christian grace that gives access to a Christian purgatory seems to veer already toward the pluralist position. (2007, 188)

This is the position that DiNoia criticizes so effectively. Oakes' objection is an important one, as it draws attention to an internal tension within DiNoia's own position. DiNoia holds two tenets: other religions should be seen as professing different means and ends to that of Christianity while at the same time, he argues, non-Christians in these religions may be justified or in a state of grace. The basic problem is Christological and ecclesial here for, by arguing for the genuine varieties of ends within the different religions, DiNoia rightly says their ends are not Christological and their means are not ecclesiological. He remains close to Lindbeck in this respect. Oakes, by contrast, pushes his own criticism too hard, for even Balthasar, whom he is commending as an alternative, acknowledges that grace exists outside the visible church and, indeed, Balthasar allows for continuities between Christianity and other religions, but only within an always greater discontinuity. This is a proper use of analogy and this is the position I would advocate, which steers a middle path between incommensurability (Lindbeck and DiNoia) and easy assimilation (Rahner and pluralists). Hence, the tension is one that must be kept open and alive and not resolved, as it would collapse into either claiming other religions as salvific mediations, or claiming them to be worthless human grasping toward the mystery. Holding the two tenets in tension indicates an attempt to steer through an admittedly difficult middle ground.

My own analogical conceptual use of the limbo of the just better addresses Oakes' objections, resolves DiNoia's internal tensions, and provides a plausible solution that keeps purgatory Christian (so to speak), in allowing that those who require further purification after hearing the gospel preached to them in the limbo of the just may enter purgatory to complete their pilgrimage into the community of saints and the blessed. This particular solution has additional benefits. First, it allows for the Christological centrality of the limbo of the just to continue through into purgatory. The Vatican II document *Gaudium et spes* (*GS*) 22 maintains that "in some way" (*quodammodo*) Christ is related to every human being. This clearly requires the Christological focus of purgatory to be foregrounded, which also addresses the critique sometimes aimed at purgatory, by both Catholics and non-Catholics, that it lacks a proper Christological focus. Here I am happy to follow Ratzinger (1988a) and Pope Benedict XVI (Ratzinger as Pope) in his encyclical *Spe Salvi* (2007), where the purgatorial "fires" are Christologically understood, and aligned with God's justice and mercy. Benedict writes:

> Some recent theologians are of the opinion that the fire which both burns and saves is Christ himself, the Judge and Saviour. The encounter with him is the decisive act of judgement. Before his gaze all falsehood melts away. This encounter with him, as it burns us, transforms and frees us, allows us to become truly ourselves. All that we build during our lives can prove to be mere straw, pure bluster, and it collapses. Yet in the pain of this encounter, when the impurity and sickness of our lives become evident to us, there lies salvation. His gaze, the touch of his heart heals us through an undeniably painful transformation "as through fire." But it is a blessed pain, in which the holy power of his love sears through us like a flame, enabling us to become totally ourselves and thus totally of God. In this way the inter-relation between justice and grace also becomes clear: the way we live our lives is not immaterial, but our defilement does not stain us for ever if we have at least continued to reach out towards Christ, towards truth and towards love. (2007, 47)

While it is not made explicit that the last clause of this sentence refers to non-Christians, its inclusion allows for that possibility.

If this Christological focus is important, it also leads to a serious communitarian dimension, which highlights the instrumental causality of

Christ and his church as the means to salvation. We have already seen in chapter 7 the church's presence in the limbo of the just through the apostles' work of baptizing there following Christ, and thus the indwelling of the church in Christ (in Clement and *The Shepherd*). This instrumental causality is highlighted again in purgatory, reminding us of Sullivan's important arguments regarding the prayers of the church. Ratzinger points to the roots of the doctrine of purgatory in the prayers for the dead found in the early Christian church and, prior to that, in Jewish prayers for the deceased who had sinned (2 Maccabees 12:38–45). This prayerful practice indicates the church's instrumental role, through the solidarity of love, incarnate in Jesus:

> The belief that love can reach into the afterlife, that reciprocal giving and receiving is possible, in which our affection for one another continues beyond the limits of death – this has been a fundamental conviction of Christianity throughout the ages. (2007, 48)

The reciprocal nature of giving and receiving is found in the heart of the divine life, the trinitarian self-giving, which allows Benedict to respond to the question: how can a third person intervene if the fires of purification relate a person to the Lord? It is worth citing the answer in full, for it emphasizes the communitarian nature of salvation, such that it may even be the case that, if one is lost, none will be saved:

> When we ask such a question, we should recall that no man is an island, entire of itself. Our lives are involved with one another, through innumerable interactions they are linked together. No one lives alone. No one sins alone. No one is saved alone. The lives of others continually spill over into mine: in what I think, say, do and achieve. And conversely, my life spills over into that of others: for better and for worse. So my prayer for another is not something extraneous to that person, something external, not even after death. In the interconnectedness of Being, my gratitude to the other – my prayer for him – can play a small part in his purification. And for that there is no need to convert earthly time into God's time: in the communion of souls simple terrestrial time is superseded. It is never too late to touch the heart of another, nor is it ever in vain. In this way we further clarify an important element of the Christian concept of hope. Our hope is always essentially also hope for others; only thus is it truly hope for me too. As Christians we should never limit ourselves to asking: how can I save myself? We should also ask: what can I do in order that others may be saved

> and that for them too the star of hope may rise? Then I will have done my utmost for my own personal salvation as well. (2007, 49)

Second, my solution suggests the integration of the doctrines of the limbo of the just and purgatory, which actually relate the two doctrines to Christ and the church, through the "descent into hell." An objection to my solution may come from Pitstick, whose research leads her to suggest:

> It is reasonable to believe that purgatory existed also prior to the accomplishment of Christ's redeeming work, but was preparatory for the limbo of the Fathers so long as heaven was closed. (2007, 50)

This reverses my solution, but is open to two objections. First, purgatory in this construal is unrelated to Christ, for purgatory is best understood as a form of Christological purification as has been suggested above, whereas the thesis advanced by Pitstick makes its Christological nature only implicit. This makes it similar to the limbo of the just when it has always been distinguished from this limbo. Second, if purgatory exists before Christ prior to baptism, then this involves a major change in the formal teaching of the church that purgatory is a place that is related only to venial sin or temporal penalties not yet satisfied, not to mortal sins (as would be implied in Pitstick's solution) or the stain of original sin, the latter of which must be erased through baptism, not entry into purgatory (see Denzinger 456, 570s, 693, 840, 983, 998, 2147a). My own solution allows purgatory its proper Christological and post-messianic purificatory status as found in scripture (2 Maccabees 12:43–6; Matthew 12:32; I Corinthians 3:11–15) and interpreted in the tradition (see especially Ambrose's commentary on 1 Corinthians 3:11–15, and Sermons 20 on Psalms 117; Jerome's commentary in *Amos* C. 5; Augustine's commentary on Psalms 37 and in *The City of God* XXI, 24, 2; and Origen in *Homilies* 6 on Exodus). If Pitstick were to argue that 2 Maccabees 12:43–6 indicates a pre-Christian notion of purgatory, it would be difficult to maintain this position in the light of official teachings of the church related to the nature of purgatory and original sin. I tentatively suggest that my second argument here is more decisive in terms of keeping with the majority tradition on these matters.

It is admittedly difficult in these matters to make clear chronological distinctions, for we are speaking of states beyond location but not technically without or beyond time (for neither purgatory nor the limbo of the just are perduring). Even so, as soon as we speak of "after death," as Ratzinger argues, this "time" is admittedly

> not eternal, but a transition, and yet trying to qualify it as of "short" or "long" duration on the basis of temporal measurements derived from physics would be naive and unproductive. (1988a, 230)

While Pitstick's suggestion makes sense of why those in the limbo of the just can be redeemed immediately, it significantly lacks biblical and patristic support. While my own suggestion about the movement from the limbo of the just to purgatory also lacks biblical and patristic support, it keeps Christologically centered to a greater extent than Pitstick's solution. How does my solution keep purgatory intact more than Pitstick's and, I might add, more than DiNoia's? Against Pitstick one might ask: how could non-Christians before the time of Christ go through purgatory, which is fundamentally Christological, if they must then wait in a limbo of the just because they do not yet know Christ? Against DiNoia one might say: in erasing original sin in the non-Christian before their entering purgatory (as its erasure is a condition of entering purgatory), DiNoia posits an erasure that is not explained in his theory and, in his opposition to Rahner's *in voto* solution, cannot properly be explained. My solution in placing the limbo of the just conceptually before purgatory in relation to the question of how the non-Christian might be saved, both before and after the time of Christ, overcomes problems found in Pitstick's and DiNoia's solutions.

I could technically stop here, as the question about Jane has now been answered by drawing on the doctrinal resources of "he descended into hell." But, in dealing with the matter through Christ's "descent into hell," certain other issues have arisen that require treatment. What of non-Christian children in the children's limbo (baby Jane in this version)? And what of Oakes' claim that Balthasar's solution of Christ's descent into hell proper best solves our question regarding the fate of the non-Christian? To attend to these further two questions, we must proceed, first to the children's limbo, next to hell.

The Children's Limbo

I want to focus on two issues in this section. First, since unbaptized infants include non-Christians, the fate of the unbaptized infant bears upon the question of baby Jane. Second, as unbaptized infants underscore the issue of original sin and the requirement for baptism to overcome sin, which has been central to my question regarding the church as a means, both of necessity and of precept, this will be my second concern. After briefly sketching the background to the children's limbo, I shall focus on these two issues by means of a critical engagement with the International Theological Commission's (ITC) report of 2007: *The Hope of Salvation for Infants Who Die Without Being Baptised*, published through the office of the Congregation of the Doctrine of the Faith.

For Augustine, entry into heaven is dependent upon the cleansing of the stain of original sin, through baptism, and in the Western tradition this precise requirement generated the controversial solution of the children's limbo. If unbaptized infants were not saved, would a just God allow them to be damned, even though they were innocent (in their lack of mortal or personal sins)? Before Augustine, Tertullian opposed infant baptism on the grounds of their innocence and Ambrose argued that original sin is an inclination to evil, not guilt proper, which requires personal sin. The Eastern tradition differed from Augustine in refusing to hold that Adam's sin incurred hereditary guilt or that Adam's act was the responsibility of all humans. However, the effects of Adam's sin meant the East still required baptism as the condition for salvation, as all were affected by Adam's sin. Augustine was influential in the Council of Carthage's (418) condemnation of "an intermediate place, or of any place anywhere at all, in which children who pass out of this life unbaptized live in happiness" (Denzinger 102). If happiness was denied to them, torment was not the only other option. Carthage did not endorse all of Augustine's views on unbaptized infants. Nevertheless, this early tradition clearly implied that unbaptized infants share a place with the damned insomuch as they are not saved, but with the mildest of punishments possible, so that non-existence would be less preferable than the mild degree of damnation (Augustine, *Original Sin* 1, 21; *Against Julian* 5, 44).

Albertus has the children's limbo next door to hell, for the reason that the souls from the limbo of the just and purgatory would eventually migrate to heaven. The latter two would not perdure. Abelard was the first to resist this line, rejecting any punishment of the senses for children (*poena sensus*). Abelard insisted on only the punishment of loss of the beatific vision (*poena damni*) for unbaptized children. This was ratified by Pope Innocent, but he asked whether such a loss would entail spiritual torment. Aquinas was bold in going a step further to deal with this torment, which would anguish thousands of parents throughout the ages. Drawing on the Greek tradition and Pseudo-Dionysius, Thomas argued that, because natural human ends were unaffected by the fall, which cut us off from our supernatural end, the children's limbo was a place of perfect natural happiness: perfect, because of their innocence; natural, because they had been denied the supernatural end; and happiness, as the proper end of the natural (*Sent.* II, 33, q. ii, a. 2). Aquinas later added that these souls do not suffer inner torment as they are unaware of the heavenly destiny, and therefore do not crave what they do not know (*De Malo* V, article 3). This last step was important in securing what seemed to many as a "just" settlement of the problem, although some did not agree with Aquinas' solution.

Thomas' view generally prevailed until the Reformation when there was a revival of the Augustinian position on this matter, which never gained a very strong following in Catholic circles. The Council of Florence (1438) taught that "the souls of those dying in actual mortal sin or in original sin alone go down at once into Hell, to be punished, however, with widely different penalties" (Denzinger 697). To some these widely differing penalties seemed to imply that the children's limbo was consolidated and definitive in magisterial teaching, but this is contestable. Vatican I did not pronounce on the matter, although a statement was prepared with this intention (that the destiny of the unbaptized was between that of the damned and the souls in purgatory and the blessed). The Central Preparatory Commission of Vatican II could not find a clear common view of the faithful (*sensus fidelium*), nor was there agreement among the bishops of the council. The matter was thus excluded from the agenda, leaving it for further theological debate. The 1994 *Catechism* cites 1 Timothy 2.4, and comments on "the great mercy of God who desires that all men should be saved," and then very oddly co-joins this verse with Mark 10:14, "Let the children come to me, do not hinder them." It then comments that the conjunction of these two verses "allows us to hope that there is a way of salvation for children who have died without Baptism" (1261). This indicates the need for better biblical arguments and proper exploration, but the door had been clearly opened for rethinking the matter. Pope John Paul II commissioned a study on this question.

In October 2005 the ITC started work on this question, presenting its final text to the Congregation for the Doctrine of Faith in 2007, and gaining the approval of the pope in January 2007. Far from "abolishing limbo," as some headlines ran, we instead find subtle arguments that there are grounds for hope for the salvation of all unbaptized infants. The document allows for diverging views. I want to turn to the arguments of the ITC. They have no authoritative teaching status, but nevertheless reflect a view authorized as legitimate speculation insomuch as the document is published by the Congregation for the Doctrine of the Faith.

After surveying the history of this question, the ITC poses three important objections to the children's limbo. First, it is Christologically weak, as "it is unclear whether the souls there have any relationship to Christ" (90) contrary to *GS* 22, where it is said that "by his incarnation, he, the Son of God, has in some way (*quodammodo*) united himself with every person." Second, regarding the maxim, "where sin abounded, grace superabounded," the children's limbo, following Augustine, constrains the superabundance of grace and subordinates it to sin. It is "a restrictive conception of the ways by which human beings benefit from solidarity with Christ" (91). Third, the supposed impossibility of baptism *in voto* for infants has not been properly decided and remains an open issue (94). The ITC then develops arguments for its alternative solution, opening with six preliminary points that help establish a new semantic field for thinking through the issues. It also contextualizes all magisterial statements relating to the matter that might be presented as objections to its own solution, trying to show that there is no definitive magisterial teaching regarding the status of the infant limbo. Let me turn to the six preliminary points to explicate the preferred alternative.

First, the Holy Innocents who were killed at the birth of Jesus are in heaven, as is attested in their feast day in the church's liturgy. They were unbaptized (86). They are venerated as martyrs as they were killed on account of Christ (5, and 86). Liturgically, the *Roman Missal* of 1970 also introduced a funeral for unbaptized infants and the ITC concludes from this that: "We do not pray for those who are damned" (5). Hence, along with other liturgical evidence and a growing *sensus fidelium*, they suggest this rethink is in order. Second, baptism is a necessity, but not an absolute necessity as is the saving action of God. The ITC qualifies this in saying: "What is absolute is humanity's need for the *Ursakrament* which is Christ himself. All salvation comes from him and therefore, in some way, through the Church" (82). Third, according to *GS* 22, Christ is related to all persons in "some way" (*quodammodo*) and the children's limbo obscures this relationship by implicitly suggesting three possible final destinies, which is impermissible (88–90). This repeats an objection. Fourth, the status of the children's limbo was not binding as an article of faith, nor was it proclaimed as such by any magisterial teaching. When it was defended by the magisterium, it was done so on the basis of it being falsely associated with Pelagianism, as in the Council of Carthage. Fifth, there is baptism *in re* (in actuality, by water) – and also baptism *in votum* (by desire, through the Spirit, *flaminis*). There is also a third category, baptism by blood (*sanguinis*), that is, "baptism" through joining in Christ's sufferings and martyrdom, without requiring baptism by water. This last was the circumstance of some martyrs who had not yet been baptized, and these martyrs were venerated and could not be excluded from salvation. The ITC argues for the possibility of these two latter categories being applied to unbaptized infants. How?

If baptized infants go to heaven, they go there not out of any free will exercised by them, but by the will of the parents, and more specifically the church, which carries out the baptism. "Thus original sin, which is contracted without consent is remitted without consent by the power of the sacrament [of Baptism]" (83). From this, it is argued that if infants are baptized without their consent in common baptism through the action of the church (and through the action of their parents' consent), then surely if the church were to pray for all unbaptized infants' "baptism" this would suffice as a condition for *in voto* baptism.

> [The] Church might be able to intercede for the infant and express a *votum baptismi* on his or her behalf that is effective before God. Moreover, the Church effectively does express in her liturgy just such a *votum* by the very charity towards all that is renewed in her in every celebration of the Eucharist. (98)

Here we have a similar argument to the one I have already developed above regarding the prayers in the Eucharist for classes of people rather than individuals (non-theists, theists), and in this case this is extended to the class of unbaptized infants rather than particular unbaptized infants. I think this is the strongest argument presented in the ITC report. But what of the third form of baptism?

To analogically relate martyrdom to unbaptized infants, an interesting line of argument is advanced by the ITC in its sixth point. The ITC argues that some

> infants who suffer and die do so as victims of violence. In their case, we may readily refer to the example of the Holy Innocents and discern an analogy in the case of these infants to the baptism of blood which brings salvation. Albeit unknowingly, the Holy Innocents suffered and died on account of Christ; their murderers were seeking to kill the infant Jesus. Just as those who took the lives of the Holy Innocents were motivated by fear and selfishness, so the lives particularly of unborn babies today are often endangered by the fear or selfishness of others [referring to the widespread act of abortion]. In that sense, they are in solidarity with the Holy Innocents. (86)

And, thus, in solidarity with Christ. In this last case, note the move away from the prayerful intention of the church to that of baptism in blood, in the reality of the death suffered, not in the intention of the infant, their parents, or the church.

Are the arguments employed by the Commission persuasive? I think they provide some grounds for optimism, but they are certainly not decisive and the debate on this matter is still open, as is officially accepted by the ITC. Some of the arguments are actually quite weak. For example, to argue that "where sin abounded, grace superabounded" leads to a criticism of the Augustinian position, as it is deemed that a constraint on God's superabundance is implausible. Indeed, the outcome the ITC wishes to circumvent ("a restrictive conception of the ways by which human beings benefit from solidarity with Christ" – 91) might equally lead us to Aquinas' solution in terms of a natural fulfillment of the infant's state rather than the ITC's answer. Aquinas' solution can mitigate Augustine's restrictivism, but retains the essential bottom line: original sin must be removed prior to salvation. The only reason to move away from Aquinas' solution is the force of the first Christological argument employed by the ITC: that limbo is unrelated to Christ. However, even here, if the ITC's own maxim is taken seriously, it would amount to an argument for the removal of hell from the teaching of the church, for the "*quodammodo*" of *GS* 22 would also be compromised if a single person was in hell. Furthermore, it is arguable that the relation to Christ need not only be expressed positively, but can also be negatively expressed (hell) or neutrally expressed (children's limbo) and both constitute a "relation," even if not the highest term of that relation. These different modes of relation keep *GS* 22 intact. Too much weight is placed on *GS* 22, which on its own cannot be stretched to the ITC's conclusion.

The argument from the murder of the Holy Innocents being analogous to the murder of innocent infants through fear and selfishness is interesting but fails to address three factors. First, if mere fear and selfishness as motivating factors for infant murder suffice for an analogy to be drawn regarding the victims, then would this analogy not also apply to adults who had been murdered out of fear and selfishness? This extends the ITC's argument in a direction it does not address and certainly has little precedence in the tradition, although it is an interesting path worth exploring, and I shall return to this briefly below. Second, the death of the messiah was the specific intention of the murder of the Holy Innocents, and on that there is no analogy in the murder of infants through fear and selfishness. This latter suggests a *sui generis* motivation involved in the murder of the Holy

Innocents that cannot be easily extended. Third, to extend baptism by blood developed in relation to unbaptized adult martyrs who died for their faith to infants, when there is no intentionality present in the infant who is not being martyred for their faith, is problematic. One can see a possible argument for extending such an argument to unbaptized infants whose parents intend their baptism but are martyred on their way to the ceremony, along with their children whom they intended to baptize. But to analogize a category when the key analogue is missing (the intention of the martyred) is problematic. This is not to suggest that such arguments as the ITC presents could not be made, but rather to indicate that they require more elaboration.

Conclusions

The *in voto* arguments regarding the prayers of the church are very plausible and are already part of the argument that I have deployed above. They alone are enough to secure the hope that all unbaptized infants will be saved, given that the ITC has established that there is no magisterial teaching in support of the limbo of the infants. Once this bridgehead argument is established, we can clearly apply the argument to non-Christian unbaptized children. Baby Jane is included in this hope that applies to all unbaptized non-Christian infants. Paragraph 2 of the ITC document acknowledges the inclusion of non-Christians as belonging to the general category of the "unbaptized." In reality billions of children are being included. Further, this argument has some support in the Reform tradition and is thus, like the previous conclusion, commended as a possible ecumenical solution. The Reform theologian William Shedd argues that unbaptized infants are elect as a class, which amounts to a stronger version of the ITC's argument. Crisp objects to Shedd for the paucity of biblical evidence (see Crisp 2007, chapter 4), but the argument for unbaptized infants might be developed from the ITC's basis, not as a class of elect, but saved through the prayers of the church. This solution also underwrites and explains the instrumental causality of the church through the Eucharistic sacrifice for all and, thus, this is a promising avenue to defend and develop.

The baptism by blood prompts a research question as to whether these reflections might be analogically applied to adult Jane who, in following her religion and conscience, dies for the good, true, beautiful, and holy. For example, if Jane is brutally murdered by the secret police, or state army, or death squads, in struggling non-violently for the basic human dignity of her people, or in seeking to save the lives of innocent people from a form of cruel injustice, is this not a better analogical situation to the baptism by blood? Here at least the analogue of intentionality is present. For both the unbaptized martyr and adult Jane killed by the secret police, the cause of death is personal sacrifice for a truth contained within the gospel. Further, if this argument is allowed, it analogically points to "elements" within a non-Christian religion that may provide preparatory bridges upon which many a noble and heroic non-Christian walks, sometimes alone and sometimes with their community, toward Christ.

The ITC's conclusions certainly support my argument about the descent into hell as a doctrine bearing upon the salvation of baby Jane and adult Jane. The infant limbo, or at least the legitimate arguments against it, indicate interesting conclusions in relation to unbaptized non-Christian infants, and provide further arguments for understanding the nature of a baptism in blood in the case of adult non-Christians. These are enormously significant lines of inquiry and there is much more discussion required for a resolution of the problems, but I hope to have indicated the way in which the descent into hell, in its third circle, also relates to the question at hand. What of the final pit of hell?

The Descent into Hell

Traditionally, the "descent into hell" had not been understood to imply descent into hell proper, except in teaching that Christ's victory on the cross reaches and permeates the entire cosmos, which includes hell. But in the writings of Hans Urs von Balthasar we find something different, even quite novel in the history of the dogma. His reflections are to be found mainly in *Heart of the World* (1979), *Mysterium Paschale* (1990), and volume four of the *Theo-Drama: The Action* (1994b). Edward Oakes (2007) makes the case that Balthasar's radicalization of the doctrine of the descent is vital in addressing the fate of non-Christians. He further argues that Balthasar's solution overcomes the problems of other solutions. Oakes only cites Rahner and DiNoia in this respect. I concur with his judgment on Rahner, not DiNoia. Oakes rightly acknowledges that the salvation of non-Christians "only works . . . if the dilemma of the scandal of particularity is resolved eschatologically" (2007, 187). We have seen the arguments he presents for dismissing DiNoia above, and now Oakes presents Balthasar's solution as superior. Why?

In Balthasar,

> both the universality of God's saving will and the centrality of Christ are preserved without our having to insist that the non-baptized have somehow received a grace that lets them escape hell and get into purgatory. Not that there are no signs of grace outside the boundaries of Christianity (far from it); rather one no longer need *require* that grace, in the manner of Karl Rahner. All one need know is that Christ, by means of his descent into hell, can bestow grace eschatologically on whom he will. (2007, 188)

This is claimed because Jesus, in descending into the hell of damnation, takes human damnation upon himself, such that no one will have to undergo this damnation, for it is borne by Christ. For Balthasar, damnation is taken into the life of God and transformed. In effect, Oakes hangs the issue of non-Christians on the bigger argument for quasi-universalism in Balthasar's theology.

Let me briefly outline Balthasar's doctrine before critically attending to Oakes' usage of it. The best expositions of Balthasar's position are to be found in Lauber, who is sympathetic to him, and in Pitstick, who is deeply critical. Balthasar argues that the limbos and purgatory are irrelevant, as Christ's death on the cross precludes his "activism," for death brings about passivity (1990, 149). In this passivity, the Son descends into the depths of damnation, the stark meaning of death, which is humanity's fate due to sin. Like Barth, Balthasar refuses to downplay the wrath of God, which is the proper aspect of God's profound and terrifying love, not a separate aspect of God. Death and damnation are the outcome of sin, which expresses the furthest distance possible from God. For Balthasar, the redemption on the cross is the beginning of the process of our salvation, for Christ passively accepts in obedience the fate that is humanity's through his descent into hell, the deepest pit of Godforsakenness. This passive obedience begins in his active obedience at Gethsemane, where Jesus gives up any desire other than to follow the Father's will. He must accept not only death but also damnation, utter separation from God, even including the loss of the "beatific vision," which is normally considered proper to Christ's human soul. Jesus cannot know that this is the route to a victorious end. He cannot even know that this is anything other than a desperate Godforsakenness. He can only know that he must do the Father's will.

> Perverse finite freedom casts all its guilt onto God, making him the sole accused, the scapegoat, while God allows himself to be thoroughly affected

> by this, not only in the humanity of Christ but also in Christ's trinitarian mission. The omnipotent powerlessness of God's love shines forth in the mystery of darkness and alienation between God and the sin-bearing Son; this is where Christ "represents" us, takes our place. (Balthasar 1994b, 336)

Only in this damnation is God able to undergo what is our desert, not only as the man Jesus, but also in his divine nature, "in Christ's trinitarian mission." Balthasar closely follows Nicholas of Cusa in ascribing a *visio mortis* (a vision of death) to Christ, although in fact Balthasar changes the content of Nicholas who only attributes the *poena sensus* (pain of the senses) to Christ in his descent. Balthasar wants to argue that the Son is identified with the absence of God, which is hell, so that Christ's *visio mortis* means he incorporates that which is not God. In this act there can no longer be an eternal exclusion of the presence of God anywhere as Godforsakenness, which is humanity's destiny after the fall, has been taken into God by God and overcome.

At this very point, where Balthasar seems to be in real danger of making the inner life of God dependent on human history, he is critical of Jürgen Moltmann's trinitarian Hegelianism, which he rightly thinks drives separation into the Godhead. I raise this point because Balthasar's position would seem to be veering close to Moltmann's position, which does make the inner life of God dependent on history, highlighting Moltmann's crippling Hegelianism. Of course, Balthasar is wanting to say, unlike Moltmann, that this action of Christ, this utter self-emptying, is what God has always been doing from eternity, so in that sense he conceptually can be distinguished from Moltmann. But this introduces a tension between the economic and immanent trinity that is not properly resolved. Balthasar insists that the drama of separateness and Godforsakenness in the economic trinity

> does not entangle the immanent Trinity in the world's fate, as occurs in mythology, but it *does* lift the latter's fate to the level of the economic trinity, which always presupposes, the immanent. This is because the Son's eternal, holy distance from the Father, in the Spirit, forms the basis on which the unholy distance of the world's sin can be transposed into it, can be transcended and overcome by it. (1994b, 362)

For Balthasar, the glory of the cross is beheld in the loss and abjection undertaken by God for us. The resurrection is not re-ascent, but the overcoming of utter desolation and Godforsakenness within God's life of love, within the trinity:

> By going all the way to the outermost alienation, God himself has proven to be the Almighty who also is able to safeguard his identity in non-identity, his being-with-himself in being lost, his life in being dead. . . . There is no "reascent" after the descent; the way of love "to the end" (John 13:1) is itself love's self-glorification. (Balthasar 1995, 413)

This understanding of the descent draws Balthasar into quasi-universalism, which he carefully nuances so that it is expressed as a hope, not a certainty (which is why I call it quasi). When I use the term universalism from now on, I mean this qualified hope, a quasi-universalism, not a certainty that would overrule the biblical witness and render a profound biblical tension between damnation and salvation prematurely resolved. Balthasar draws upon a cloud of witnesses to support his conclusions regarding his universalism, from Origen, Gregory of Nyssa, Maximus the Confessor, to Karl Barth, and also an important group of women mystics: Mechtild of Hackerborn, Mechtild of Magdeburg, Angelina of Foligno, Catherine of Siena, Julian of Norwich, Terese of Avila, Marie Des Vallées, Thérèse of Lisieux, and of course Adrienne von Speyr, who is the primary inspiration for Balthasar's reflections on Holy Saturday. In these women's writings, Balthasar argues that their sense of the intolerability of a single person being lost is grounded in the infinite divine mercy, and like Paul in Romans 9:3 ("For I could wish that I myself were accursed and cut off from Christ for the sake of my brethren, my kinsmen by race"), these women mystics would willingly forgo their salvation for the sake of another. In Balthasar's view these women's voices are deeply in tune with the prayers of the church that we have seen in the Good Friday liturgy and in the Eucharistic prayers desiring the salvation of all. However, it should be noted that Balthasar's universalism is a result of his understanding of the descent and the representative nature of the atonement. Clearly, universalism *per se* is not dependent upon this understanding of the descent, as the descent is not found in the sources cited above, with the single exception of Speyr. This should alert us to a possible problem, for Balthasar secures what he believes he has in common with these thinkers through a means that they all, with one exception, reject.

Before turning to Balthasar's proposal, I need to register two reservations I have regarding Oakes' presentation of the case. First, Oakes argues for Balthasar's solution for the descent into hell in relation to non-Christians, for it allows Christ to "bestow grace eschatologically on whom he will" (2007, 188); which means that all non-Christians might be saved. In the tradition, God's radical freedom is central to a wide variety of theologians, so that the descent is not logically or theologically required to establish the outcome that God can "bestow grace eschatologically on whom he will." This is not to say that Balthasar is thus wrong, but rather to question Oakes' claim that Balthasar's solution is superior because it secures this vital outcome. Second, Oakes suggests a solution for a problem that is not quite present. You will recall Oakes criticized DiNoia for conferring Christian grace upon religions that were not Christian. But the effect of Oakes' solution is actually to argue that non-Christians are damned, through no fault of their own, but the descent into hell ensures they will all be saved. This construal implies there is no value to non-Christian religions, no *preparatio evangelica* function. It implies that there is no value to Israel and the Greeks before the time of Christ, and this is in part because the limbo of the just is discarded by Balthasar, as that would require "activity," not "passivity" – which is the true property of death. It also implies that there is no sense in which the world religions might actually be "inchoate" responses to grace, as is the teaching of the magisterium.

However, Oakes is too Catholic to deny "signs of grace outside the boundaries of Christianity (far from it!)" (2007, 188). Rather, he is concerned to reject any ideological leveling out between religions, which he equates with Rahner. Hence, he finishes the previous sentence just cited: "rather, one no longer need *require* that grace, in the manner of Karl Rahner" (2007, 188). But Rahner's alternative is not the only one, and is in fact robustly criticized by DiNoia on similar grounds (1992, 98–103). Thus, Oakes is led into the anomalous position of objecting to DiNoia for conferring Christian grace on those who do not want it, but then doing the same in his own solution. He also admits that grace is to be found in the non-Christian religions, but at the same time identifies the issue of non Christians and salvation purely with Jesus' identity with the damned. Further, when we speak about the damned *per se* from Balthasar's perspective we are speaking about everyone, Christian and non-Christian alike, without distinction; we are speaking about the destiny that we all "merit," were it not for Christ's atonement. Hence, Oakes' argument that Balthasar's solution is better than DiNoia's is unconvincing on three counts. It is not the only way to base the claim of God's free choice to save whom he will; and it actually does not address non-Christians *per se*, but all humanity, both Christian and non-Christian. Further, it is also weak regarding the inappropriateness of his criticism of DiNoia as seen above. But the positive part of his thesis is very significant, regarding the actual contents and claims made by Balthasar, which Oakes is championing.

What then of Balthasar's remarkable theology of Holy Saturday? Oakes is right to the extent that, insomuch as it does bear upon non-Christians, it is worthy of serious attention when addressing this question. Much could be said here, and Pitstick has covered these problems very adequately, but I would like to focus on three particular critical issues. First, is Balthasar's solution within the bounds of orthodoxy? Second, does Balthasar's account cause a rupture in the divine life that makes it less than divine and thus inadequate to the task? Third, is the descent into hell actually required to attain the fruits it delivers?

The first question is difficult to answer. Pitstick, you will recall, set down four elements as definitive orthodoxy in the teaching of the "descent":

> First, Christ descended in His soul united to His divine Person only to the limbo of the Fathers. Second, His power and authority were made known throughout all of hell, taken generically. Third, He thereby accomplished the two purposes of the Descent, which were to "liberate the just" by conferring on them the glory of heaven and "to proclaim His power." Finally, His descent was glorious, and Christ did not suffer the pain proper to any of the abodes of hell. (2007, 342)

She argues that Balthasar cannot be reconciled to the first and fourth, and he dramatically reinterprets the second and third. Her conclusion is that Balthasar cannot strictly be called a Roman Catholic theologian, as he manifestly contradicts the teachings of the church.

Edward Oakes registers Pitstick's judgment and in response advances the argument that Balthasar's theology can be viewed as a legitimate doctrinal development. Oakes invokes Newman's seven tests for doctrinal development and focuses on two of them in terms of "internal logic" and "developmental consistency" to argue that Balthasar's position is both novel and orthodox. Pitstick's robust response (2008) to Oakes carefully outlines all seven of Newman's tests and shows the opposite: Balthasar cannot be seen to be carrying out legitimate doctrinal development but corrupts a true doctrine. He is involved in contradicting previous magisterial teachings (for example: the tradition holds the redemption was completed at the moment of Christ's death on the cross, thus Christ's descent concerned an application of its fruits, whereas Balthasar holds that Christ's descent, not his crucifixion, is the moment of "supreme dramatic intensity," thus the redemption was accomplished in hell, not on the cross). He also teaches novel doctrines that are, by implication, contrary to already held teachings (the example above suffices for both these cases). Pitstick's case is robust, but there is still a question of the magisterial authority by which some teachings are affirmed in the faith of the church. And on this point she has been challenged.

The Catholic philosopher Paul Griffiths suggests that Pitstick is premature in claiming *de fide* status to her four points. He does not make a judgment as to the veracity of the four points themselves, but the status attributed to them by Pitstick. Griffiths undermines Pitstick's claim that Balthasar is beyond the pale. This is because

> her four-point summary of the doctrine of the descent uses technical language which has never been the subject of definition by any council, which appears in no creed, and which, so far as I can tell, is almost entirely absent from ordinary magisterial teaching. (2008)

I think Griffiths' criticism correct in the precise sense regarding the doctrinal formula employed by Pitstick. However, it is difficult to deny that, if a particular term or concept is used in magisterial teachings to assert X, and if someone asserts Y by employing concepts that are not explicitly related to X but that by logical implication would contradict X, we would surely deduce that Y is not acceptable to hold. While Griffiths' point is legitimate in one restricted sense, I do not think it finally holds against Pitstick's criticism. But it is still important to make a judgment on Balthasar's theology in terms of its implications and its inner logic, not only because this position is advanced by such a distinguished theologian who has been so influential in recent Catholic theology, but because this is also the way theses must be tested. Clearly, this process will take time. Even when the formal teaching of the *Catechism* states that "Jesus did not descend into hell to deliver the damned, nor to destroy the hell of damnation, but to free the just who had gone before him" (633), Cardinal Schönborn, in presenting the *Catechism*, commented on this passage, with specific reference to Balthasar in an interesting manner. He said:

> The brief paragraph on Jesus' descent into hell keeps to what is the common property of the Church's exegetical tradition. Newer interpretations, such as that of Hans Urs von Balthasar . . . however profound and helpful they may be, have not yet experienced that reception which would justify their inclusion in the Catechism. (Ratzinger and Schönborn 1994, 7)

It is in this spirit of reception that Balthasar is to be critically evaluated, even if Pitstick has given good grounds for rejecting his reception.

There are two deeply problematic issues in Balthasar's proposals. There is a tendency toward both a Christological and a trinitarian rupture within the divine life in Balthasar's argument. I say "tendency" because there are statements in Balthasar's corpus that seem to rectify this impression, but then these modifications are in danger of undermining the goals to be secured by his original proposals. The Christological problem is nicely stated by John Saward:

> Balthasar's presentation of Christ's dereliction is beautiful but very difficult. First, he seems to me to distinguish insufficiently between the *feeling* of abandonment and its *reality*. . . . The experience of Godforsakenness, according to Balthasar, is all-consuming, enveloping and penetrating the whole of our Lord's soul, excluding, *at any level*, joy or beatitude. This runs counter to the Scholastic view that from his conception, even during his Passion, Jesus as man was *simul viator et comprehensor*, at once pilgrim and beholder, sufferer and seer, enjoying the beatific vision of his father, and yet feeling a sorrow surpassing all suffering endured or endurable by men in this present life. (1990, 55–6)

What is at stake is the unity of the trinity and the unity of Christ. If Christ's human soul is ontologically alienated from his divine nature when Christ is Godforsaken, there is also a rupture in the divine trinitarian life that destroys the nature of God, for at that point the second person of the divine trinity either has no divine identity, or has no relation with the man Jesus if Balthasar is serious in what he is asserting. If Christ is truly Godforsaken, in the ontological manner constantly implied by Balthasar, then it would be impossible to overcome the very lack that hell represents, the distance from God, as the lack/distance is greater than God if that is what constitutes Christ's identity in the descent.

It consequently appears that the unity of the very Godhead is rent asunder in Balthasar, as happens in Moltmann's trinity during the "descent," where the trinity is really a "binity." Moltmann is actually criticized for this by Balthasar himself. Lauber outlines Moltmann's position very fairly and shows how both Barth and Balthasar are deeply critical of Moltmann's Hegelian historicizing of the trinitarian life (2004, 113–45). Lauber delicately captures the precarious distance between Balthasar and Moltmann on this particular issue:

> Although Balthasar criticizes Moltmann for speaking univocally regarding human suffering and divine suffering, for identifying the internal divine processions with salvation history, and for locating the suffering and forsakenness of the cross directly in the Trinitarian life of God, he insists that we must not distinguish to the point of separating the saving mission of Jesus Christ and the procession of the Son from the Father (1994b, 322). While Moltmann's position includes the danger of identifying missions and processions, Balthasar worries that Barth risks espousing the latter position of separating God's internal processions from God's economic mission, and, as a consequence, stops short of affirming that the events of the passion really affect the internal life of God. (2004, 142)

The knife-edge on which Balthasar's position is balanced must be appreciated, for he is navigating a precarious path between Barth and Moltmann, but there is a real problem: does such a path actually exist?

Balthasar certainly tries to mend the rupture that takes place at the economic level. First, he rightly distinguishes between the economic and immanent trinity. Like Barth, he refuses the Rahnerian low road of collapsing the economic and immanent trinity into a single identity, a road that Moltmann eventually walks. Balthasar argues that the relationship of the Son and Father is always intact at the level of the immanent missions, even at the point where the relationship is utterly broken at the level of economic processions. But there is a clear question that needs answering: is the Son's divinity ontologically separated and ruptured from the unity with the Father in the Son's identification with hell? If yes, then there is a rupture in the Godhead that compromises the immanent Trinity; if no, then Balthasar's identification of the Son with damnation in hell is undermined. If both, which is what it seems, the latter goal fails entirely, which is the unique content of Balthasar's doctrine. God can "experience" suffering through the taking on of flesh in the Son in his human nature. Further, death can be known uniquely in the Godhead through the Son's human death. But all that is entirely different from saying that death actually penetrates the divine nature, which is what Balthasar has to say to attain the fruits of his theology of the descent. I cannot press this point further without examining the impassibility of God, and that would take me too far from my goal. I draw the reader's attention to Weinandy's excellent studies arguing against claiming the passibility of God (1985; 2000).

I would conclude that Balthasar's descent into hell teaching is both in danger of contradicting the teachings of the Catholic church to which Balthasar belongs (and here I agree with Pitstick), and in danger of advancing a deeply problematic Christology and trinitarian doctrine of God. On both grounds it does not actually help address the question about Jane, despite Oakes' claims. But there is a further question: is the descent into hell actually required to attain the fruits it delivers in Oakes' rendition? The short answer is no, one can address the fate of non-Christians, as I claim to have done above, without requiring resort to such a problematic speculation. Christ's descent into the limbo of the just facilitates an answer that is nearly complete and becomes more fully satisfactory if taken along with the doctrine of purgatory. The pastoral pressure regarding the fate of Jane and her relatives and friends is utterly relieved, while at the same time upholding a high doctrine of Christ and his church. This is an important advance in the theology of religions.

Conclusion

In this chapter I have tried to show how the "descent into hell," understood primarily in terms of the limbo of the just, purgatory, and the children's limbo, is profoundly helpful in addressing the question we started with: how can Jane be saved after this life if she dies a good Theravadin Buddhist? The force of this question has led various theologians to argue that all religions must be salvific mediators, to a greater or lesser extent, but this solution has been disallowed if one is working as a Catholic theologian as am I. Instead, I have proposed a solution that goes back to the earliest days of the Christian church, but which has fallen out of use. Whether this is a satisfactory solution will be up to others to decide, but I hope it has answered the question that *DI* suggests is in urgent need of attention by theologians: what is the *way* in which the salvific grace of God – which is always given by means of Christ in the Spirit and has a mysterious relationship to the church – comes to individual non-Christians? This inquiry has been in the spirit of paragraph 21:

> Theologians are seeking to understand this question more fully. Their work is to be encouraged, since it is certainly useful for understanding better God's salvific plan and the ways in which it is accomplished.

The solution I have offered is to be commended for the following reasons, despite its many shortcomings. First, it addresses the doctrinal questions that exercised us: how can the instrumental efficient causality and final causality of Christ and his church be understood in terms of the claim that the good and just unevangelized people and communities might yet be saved? It gives a fully Christological and ecclesiological answer to the problem. Second, it avoids the avenue which seems to be logically required when admitting this possibility: that the religions of such non-Christians must be "salvific mediators," of varying, but adequate quality. Third, it draws out implications from within the tradition to reflect upon the question, and while there are elements of novelty in my thesis, I have suggested these novelties are an organic unfolding of the implications of what has been received in the tradition as legitimate possibilities. Fourth, my solution explains the significance of the church's teaching regarding the *preparatio evangelica* that these religions might in part embody. Fifth, it allows for the real variety of religious ends in the world's religions, while still recognizing that within these differences there may be sufficient elements of *preparatio evangelica* that allow God's grace to work toward the final salvation of such persons. Sixth, it allows the religions to be viewed as a complex and dynamic process, which may be judged to be pure idolatry, the best thinking and imagination of human persons in a particular context, a movement inspired by the Holy Spirit and moving toward Christ, a moment when the kingdom of God becomes inchoate in history, a context that has produced wonderful holy and just people, and a mixture of all these and more, without ever claiming salvific mediation for these religions, which is deemed inadmissible. And in doing the latter, it does not consign these children of God to damnation. Seventh, it frees Christians to engage in vigorous and critical dialogue, keeping mission to the forefront, but without the worry about the salvation of the non-Christian. This, fortunately, is in the hands of God. Eighth, such a solution integrates the doctrines of the limbo of the just, the children's limbo, and purgatory to show how Christian eschatology and the "descent into hell" are good news to all women, men, and children, for it is no less than the story of the glorification of the most Blessed Trinity.

Bibliography

Adams, Robert Meerihew (1977) Middle knowledge and the problem of evil. *American Philosophical Quarterly*, 14, 2, 109–17.

Akhavi, Shahrough (1980) *Religion and Politics in Contemporary Iran*. State University of New York Press, Albany.

Asad, Talal (1986) *The Idea of an Anthropology of Islam*. Center for Contemporary Arab Studies, Georgetown University, Washington DC.

Asad, Talal (1993) *Genealogies of Religion: Discipline and Reasons of Power in Christianity and Islam*. Johns Hopkins University Press, Baltimore & London.

Asad, Talal (2003) *Formations of the Secular: Christianity, Islam and Modernity*. Stanford University Press, Stanford.

Askari, Hasan (1985) Within and beyond the experience of religious diversity. In: John Hick & Hasan Askari (eds.), *The Experience of Religious Diversity*, pp. 191–218. Avebury, Aldershot.

Ayoub, Mahmoud (1999) Pope John Paul II on Islam. In: Byron L. Sherwin & Harold Kasimow (eds.), *John Paul II and Interreligous Dialogue*, pp. 171–86. Maryknoll, New York.

Balthasar, Hans Urs von (1979) *Heart of the World*. Ignatius Press, San Francisco, trans. Erasmo S. Leivà.

Balthasar, Hans Urs von (1990) *Mysterium Paschale*. T. & T. Clark, Edinburgh, trans. Aidan Nichols.

Balthasar, Hans Urs von (1994a) *The Moment of Christian Witness*. Ignatius Press, San Francisco, trans. Richard Beckley.

Balthasar, Hans Urs von (1994b) *Theo-Drama: The Action*, vol. 4. Ignatius Press, San Francisco, trans. Graham Harrison.

Balthasar, Hans Urs von (1995) *Explorations in Theology: Spirit and Institution*, vol. 4. Ignatius Press, San Francisco, trans. Edward T. Oakes.

Barrett, David B. (1991) The status of the Christian world mission in the 1990s. In: G. Anderson (ed.), *Mission in the Nineteen Nineties*, pp. 28–41. W. B. Eerdmans, New Haven and Grand Rapids.

Barrett, David B., Kurian, George T., & Johnson, Todd M. (eds.) (2001) *The World Christian Encyclopedia: A Comparative Survey of Churches and Religions in the Modern World.* Oxford University Press, New York.

Barth, Karl (1970) *Church Dogmatics* I.2. T. & T. Clark, Edinburgh.

Bastian, R.J. (1981) Purgatory. In: *New Catholic Encyclopedia*, vol. 11, pp. 1034–9. Heraty, Palatine.

Bauman, Zygmunt (1989) *Modernity and the Holocaust.* Cornell University Press, Ithaca.

Baumgold, Deborah (1988) *Hobbes's Political Theory.* Cambridge University Press, Cambridge.

Beattie, Tina (2008) *Rowan Williams and sharia law* [WWW document]. URL www.opendemocracy.net/article/faith_ideas/europe_islam/sharia_law_uk [accessed on September 16, 2008].

Beiting, Christopher (2004) The nature and structure of limbo in the works of Albertus Magnus. *New Blackfriars*, 85, 999, 492–509.

Benedict XVI, Pope (2006) *Three stages in the program of de-Hellenization* [WWW document]. URL www.zenit.org/article-16955?1=english [accessed on September 16, 2008].

Benedict XVI, Pope (2007) *Spe salvi* [WWW document]. URL www.vatican.va/holy_father/benedict_xvi/encyclicals/documents/hf_ben-xvi_enc_20071130_spe-salvi_en.html [accessed on September 16, 2008].

Bodin, Jean ([1576] 1967) *Six Books of the Commonwealth.* Blackwell, Oxford, trans. and abridged by M. J. Tooley.

Boff, Leonardo (1985) *Church, Charism and Power: Liberation Theology and the Institutional Church.* SCM, London, trans. John W. Diercksmeier.

Bonner, Hypatia Bradlaugh (1895) *Charles Bradlaugh*, vol. 1. Watts, London.

Boros, Ladislaus (1965) *The Moment of Truth: Mysterium Mortis.* Burns & Oates, London.

Brerwood, Edward (1674) *Enquiries Touching the Diversity of Languages and Religions through the Chief Parts of the World.* Samuel Mearne, London.

Bretherton, Luke (2008) Translation, conversation and hospitality? Approaches to theological reasons in public deliberation. In: Nigel Biggar & Linda Hogan (eds.), *Religious Voices in Public Places.* Ashgate, Aldershot.

Bruce, Stephen (ed.) (1992) *Religion and Modernization: Sociologists and Historians Debate the Secularization Thesis.* Oxford University Press, Oxford.

Brunner, Emil (1949) *The Christian Doctrine of God.* Lutterworth, London.

Buckley, Michael J. (1987) *At the Origins of Modern Atheism.* Yale University Press, New Haven.

Burrell, David (2004) *Faith and Freedom: An Interfaith Perspective.* Blackwell, Oxford.

Catholic Church (1994) *Catechism of the Catholic Church.* Geoffrey Chapman, London.

Cavanaugh, William (2002) *Theopolitical Imagination*. T. & T. Clark, Edinburgh.

CDF (2001) *Notification on the Book Toward a Christian Theology of Religious Pluralism* [WWW document]. URL www.vatican.va/roman_curia/congregations/cfaith/documents/rc_con_cfaith_doc_20010124_dupuis_en.html [accessed on September 16, 2008].

Cesari, Jocelyne (2004) *When Islam and Democracy Meet: Muslims in Europe and in the United States*. Palgrave Macmillan, Basingstoke.

Chadwick, Owen (1964) *The Reformation*. Penguin, Harmondsworth.

Clooney, Francis X. (1990) Reading the world in Christ. In: Gavin D'Costa (ed.), *Christian Uniqueness Reconsidered*, pp. 63–80. Orbis, Maryknoll.

Clooney, Francis X. (1993) *Theology after Vedanta: An Experiment in Comparative Theology*. State University of New York Press, Albany.

Cobb, John B. (1982) *Beyond Dialogue: Towards a Mutual Transformation of Christianity and Buddhism*. Fortress Press, Philadelphia.

Coles, Romand (2005) Democracy, theology, and the question of excess: a review of Jeffrey Stout's *Democracy and Tradition*. *Modern Theology*, 21, 2, 301–22.

Congar, Yves (1969) *The Church That I Love*. Dimension Books, New Jersey.

Cornille, Catherine (ed.) (2002) *Many Mansions: Multiple Belonging*. Orbis, Maryknoll.

Craig, W. Lane (1989) No other name: a middle knowledge perspective on the exclusivity of salvation through Christ. *Faith and Philosophy*, 6, 2, 172–88.

Crisp, Oliver (2007) *An American Augustinian: Sin and Salvation in the Dogmatic Theology of William G. T. Shedd*. Paternoster Press/Wipf and Stock, Bletchley.

Crocker, Lester (1968) *Rousseau's Social Contract: An Interpretive Essay*. Press of Case Western Reserve University, Cleveland.

Dalton, William Joseph (1989) *Christ's Proclamation to the Spirits: A Study of 1 Peter 3:18–4:6*, 2nd edn. Editrice Pontifico Instituto Biblico, Rome.

Daniélou, Jean (1957) *Holy Pagans of the Old Testament*. Longmans, Green & Co., London, trans. Felix Faber.

Daniélou, Jean (1964) *The Theology of Jewish Christianity*. Darton, Longman & Todd, London, trans. John A. Baker.

Davidson, Donald (1984) *Inquiries into Truth and Interpretation*. Oxford University Press, Oxford.

Davies, Michael (1992) *The Second Vatican Council and Religious Liberty*. Neumann Press, Long Prairie.

Davis, Stephen T. (1990) Universalim, hell, and the fate of the ignorant. *Modern Theology*, 6, 2, 173–86.

D'Costa, Gavin (1991) A Christian reflection on some problems with discerning "God" in the world religions. *Dialogue and Alliance*, 5, 1, 4–17.

D'Costa, Gavin (2000) *The Meeting of Religions and the Trinity*. T. & T. Clark, Edinburgh.

D'Costa, Gavin (2005) *Theology in the Public Square: Church, Academy and Nation*. Blackwell, Oxford.

D'Costa, Gavin, Gill, Sean, & King, Ursula (eds.) (1995) *Religion in Europe: Contemporary Perspectives*. Kok Pharos, Kampen.

Deleuze, Gilles (2004) *Difference and Repetition*. Continuum, London, trans. Paul Patton.

Denzinger, Henry (1955) *The Sources of Catholic Dogma*, 30th edn. Loreto Publications, New Haven, trans. Roy J. Deferrari.

DiNoia, Joseph A. (1992) *The Diversity of Religions: A Christian Perspective*. Catholic University Press of America, Washington DC.

Duffy, Stephen (1999) A theology of religions and/or a comparative theology? *Horizons*, 26, 1, 105–15.

Dunn, Richard S. (1970) *The Age of Religious Wars: 1559–1689*. W. W. Norton & Co., New York.

Dupuis, Jacques (1997) *Toward a Christian Theology of Religious Pluralism*. Orbis, Maryknoll.

Eagleton, Terry (2000) *The Estate Agent: Review of* The Trouble with Principle *by Stanley Fish* [WWW document]. URL www.lrb.co.uk/v22/n05/eagl01_.html [accessed on September 16, 2008].

Eliade, Mircea (1969) *The Quest: History and Meaning in Religion*. Chicago University Press, Chicago.

Ellis, Marc H. (1989) *Toward a Jewish Theology of Liberation: The Uprising and the Future*. Orbis, Maryknoll.

Esack, Farid (1997) *Qu'ran, Liberation and Pluralism: An Islamic Perspective of Interreligious Solidarity Against Oppression*. One World, Oxford.

Fackre, Gabriel (1995) Divine perseverance. In: John Sanders (ed.), *What About Those Who Have Never Heard? Three Views on the Destiny of the Unevangelised*, pp. 13–48. IVP, Downers Grove.

Fathers of the Church: all texts without dates and publication details are available from URL www.newadvent.org/fathers/ [accessed on September 16, 2008].

Fenn, Richard K. (1995) *The Persistence of Purgatory*. Cambridge University Press, Cambridge.

Ferguson, Niall. Eurabia. *New York Times*, April 4, 2004.

Fitzgerald, Timothy (2000) *The Ideology of Religious Studies*. Oxford University Press, Oxford.

Flanagan, Kieran (1966) *The Enchantment of Sociology: A Study of Theology and Culture*. Macmillan, London.

Flood, Gavin (1999) *Beyond Phenomenology: Rethinking the Study of Religion*. Cassell, London.

Foucault, Michel ([1966] 1970) *The Order of Things: An Archaeology of the Human Sciences*. Tavistock, London.

Fourest, Caroline (2008) *Brother Tariq: The Doublespeak of Tariq Ramadan*. Encounter Books, New York.

Fredericks, James L. (1999) *Faith among Faiths: Christian Theology and Non-Christian Religions*. Paulist Press, New York.

Fromkin, David (1989) *A Peace to End All Peace*. Deutsch, London.

Fromkin, David (2004) *Europe's Last Summer: Who Started the Great War in 1914?* Alfred A. Knopf, New York.

Fuller, Graham (2003) *The Future of Political Islam*. Palgrave Macmillan, New York.

Giddens, Anthony (1987) *A Contemporary Critique of Historical Materialism: The Nation State and Violence*. University of California Press, Berkeley.

Gill, Sam (1998) No place to stand: Jonathan Z. Smith as *homo ludens*, the academic study of religion *sub specie ludi*. *Journal of the American Academy of Religion*, 66, 2, 283–312.

Goddard, Hugh (2001) *A History of Christian–Muslim Relations*. New Amsterdam Books, Amsterdam.

Gray, John (2007) *Black Mass: Apocalyptic Religion and the Death of Utopia*. Allen Lane, London.

Gregory, Alan P. R. (1998) Review of Richard K. Fenn, *The Persistence of Purgatory*. *Anglican Theological Review*, Fall, 107.

Griffin, David Ray (ed.) (2005) *Deep Religious Pluralism*. John Knox, Westminster.

Griffiths, Paul (2008, in press) Response to Pitstick. *Pro Ecclesia*.

Grudem, Wayne (1991) He did not descend into hell: a plea for following scripture instead of the Apostles' Creed. *Journal of the Evangelical Theological Society*, 34, 103–13.

Habermas, Jürgen (1987) Some questions concerning the theory of power: Foucault again. In: *The Philosophical Discourse of Modernity: Twelve Lectures*, pp. 238–65. Polity Press, Oxford, trans. Frederick Lawrence.

Hacker, Paul (1980) *Theological Foundations of Evangelization*. Steyler Verlad, St Augustin.

Haight, Roger (1999) *Jesus, Symbol of God*. Orbis, Maryknoll.

Halliday, Fred (1996) *Islam and the Myth of Confrontation: Religion and Politics in the Middle East*. I. B. Tauris, New York.

Harris, Elisabeth J. (2002) Double belonging in Sri Lanka: illusion or liberating path? In: C. Cornille (ed.), *Many Mansions: Multiple Belonging*, pp. 76–92. Orbis, Maryknoll.

Harrison, Peter (1990) *"Religion" and the Religions in the English Enlightenment*. Cambridge University Press, Cambridge.

Hasker, William (1986) A refutation of middle-knowledge. *Nous*, 20, 545–57.

Hauerwas, Stanley (2007) *The State of the University: Academic Knowledges and the Knowledge of God*. Blackwell, Oxford and Malden.

Heim, S. Mark (2001) *The Depth of the Riches: A Trinitarian Theology of Religious Ends*, W. B. Eerdmans, Grand Rapids.

Helm, Paul (1991) Are they few that be saved? In: Nigel M. de S. Cameron (ed.), *Universalism and the Doctrine of Hell*, pp. 256–81. Paternoster Press, Carlisle.

Henry, Carl (1991) Is it fair? In: W. Crockett & J. Sigountos (eds.), *Through No Fault of Their Own? The Fate of Those Who Have Never Heard*, pp. 245–56. Baker Books, Grand Rapids.

Hick, John (1977) *God and the Universe of Faiths*. Collins, London.

Hick, John (1989) *An Interpretation of Religion*. Macmillan, Basingstoke.

Holyoake, George Jacob (1870) *The Principles of Secularism*. Austin & Co., London.

Holyoake, George Jacob (1896) *English Secularism: A Confession of Belief*. Open Court, Chicago.

Hooker, Richard ([1593] 1632) *On the Lawes of Ecclesiastical Politie*. William Stanbye, London.

Huntington, Samuel (1997) *The Clash of Civilizations and the Remaking of the World Order*. Touchstone, New York.

Insole, Christopher (2004) *The Politics of Human Frailty: A Theological Defense of Political Liberalism*. SCM, London.

Iran (1979) *Islamic Republic of Iran constitution* [WWW document]. URL www.iranonline.com/iran/iran-info/Government/constitution.html [accessed on September 16, 2008].

ITC (2007) *The hope of salvation for infants who die without being baptised* [WWW document]. URL http://www.vatican.va/roman_curia/congregations/cfaith/cti_documents/rc_con_cfaith_doc_20070419_un-baptised-infants_en.html [accessed on September 16, 2008].

James, Montague Rhode (1924) *The Apocryphal New Testament*. Clarendon Press, Oxford.

Jantzen, Grace (1984) Human diversity and salvation in Christ. *Religious Studies*, 20, 579–80.

Jathanna, Origen (1981) *The Decisiveness of the Christ Event and the Universality of Christianity in a World of Religious Plurality*. Herbert Lang, Berne.

Jenkins, Philip (2007) *God's Continent: Christianity, Islam, and Europe's Religious Crisis*. Oxford University Press, Oxford.

John Paul II, Pope (1991) *Centesimus annus* (*On the hundredth anniversary of Rerum Novarum*) [WWW document]. URL www.vatican.va/holy_father/john_paul_ii/encyclicals/documents/hf_jp-ii_enc_01051991_centesimus-annus_en.html [accessed on September 16, 2008].

John Paul II, Pope (1993) *Veritatis splendor* (*The splendor of truth*) [WWW document]. URL www.vatican.va/holy_father/john_paul_ii/encyclicals/documents/hf_jp-ii_enc_06081993_veritatis-splendor_en.html [accessed on September 16, 2008].

John Paul II, Pope (1995) *Evangelium vitae* (*The gospel of life*). [WWW document]. URL www.vatican.va/holy_father/john_paul_ii/encyclicals/documents/hf_jp-ii_enc_25031995_evangelium-vitae_en.html [accessed on September 16, 2008].

Kenny, Anthony (2006) *An Illustrated Brief History of Western Philosophy*. Blackwell, Oxford.

Khodr, George (1991) An Orthodox perspective on interreligious dialogue. *Current Dialogue*, 19, 1, 25–7.

Knitter, Paul (1987) Dialogue and liberation. *Drew Gateway*, 58, 1, 1–53.

Knitter, Paul, Cobb, John Jr, Swidler, Len, & Hellwig, Monica (1990) *Death or Dialogue?* Orbis, Maryknoll.

Kuhn, Thomas (1970) *The Structure of Scientific Revolutions*, 2nd edn. Chicago University Press, Chicago.

Lake, Donald (1975) He died for all: the universal dimensions of the atonement. In: Clark H. Pinnock (ed.), *Grace Unlimited*, pp. 31–51. Bethany, Minneapolis.

Lamberth, David C. (2008) Assessing Peter Ochs through Pierce, pragmatism and the logic of scripture. *Modern Theology*, 24, 3, 459–67.

Lauber, David (2004) *Barth on the Descent into Hell: God, Atonement and the Christian Life*. Ashgate, Aldershot.

Legenhausen, Muhammad (1997) Extended book review of *Whose Justice? Which Rationality? Al-Tawhid*, 14, 2, 158–76.

Legenhausen, Muhammad (1999) *Islam and Religious Pluralism*. Al-Hoda, London.

Legenhausen, Muhammad (2002) Democratic pluralism in Islam? A critique. *Transcendent Philosophy*, 3, 4, 107–13.

Legenhausen, Muhammad (2006) *A Muslim's proposal: non-reductive religious pluralism* [WWW document]. URL www.uibk.ac.at/theol/leseraum/texte/626.html [accessed on September 16, 2008].

Le Goff, Jacques (1990) *The Birth of Purgatory*. Scolar Press, Aldershot, trans. Arthur Goldhammer.

Lindbeck, George (1984) *The Nature of Doctrine: Religion and Theology in a Postliberal Age*. SPCK, London.

Lindbeck, George (2002) *The Church in a Postliberal Age*. SCM, London.

Locke, John (1689) *A letter concerning toleration*, trans. William Popple [WWW document]. URL http://jim.com/tolerati.htm [accessed on September 16, 2008].

Lombardi, Riccardo (1956) *The Salvation of the Unbeliever*. Burns & Oates, London, trans. Dorothy M. White.

MacIntyre, Alasdair (1990) *Three Rival Versions of Moral Enquiry*. Duckworth, London.

MacIntyre, Alasdair (1991) Incommensurability, truth, and the conversation between Confucians and Aristotelians about the virtues. In: Eliot Deutsch (ed.), *Culture and Modernity: East–West philosophic perspectives*, pp. 104–22. University of Hawaii Press, Honolulu.

March, Andrew (2007) Reading Tariq Ramadan: political liberalism, Islam, and "overlapping consensus." *Ethics and International Affairs*, 21, 4, 399–413.

Masuzawa, Tomoko (2005) *The Invention of World Religions, Or, How European Universalism Was Preserved in the Language of Pluralism*. University of Chicago Press, Chicago.

McCutcheon, Russell T. (1999) *The Insider/Outsider Problem in the Study of Religion.* Cassell, London.

McGrane, Bernard (1989) *Beyond Anthropology: Society and the Other.* Columbia University Press, New York.

Milbank, John (1990a) *Theology and Social Theory: Beyond Secular Reason.* Blackwell, Oxford.

Milbank, John (1990b) The end of dialogue. In: Gavin D'Costa (ed.), *Christian Uniqueness Reconsidered*, pp. 174–91. Orbis, Maryknoll.

Milbank, John (2007) *Geopolitical theology: economy, religion and empire after 9/11* [WWW document]. URL www.theologyphilosophycentre.co.uk/papers.php#milbank [accessed on September 16, 2008].

Modood, Taqiq (2008) *Multicultural citizenship and the anti-sharia storm* [WWW document]. URL www.opendemocracy.net/article/faith_ideas/europe_islam/anti_sharia_storm [accesssed on September 16, 2008].

Murray, John Courtney (1965) *The Problem of Religious Freedom.* Newman Press, Westminster.

Neusner, Jacob (ed.) (2006) *Religious Foundations of Western Civilization: Judaism, Christianity and Islam.* Abingdon Press, Nashville.

Neville, Robert Cummings (2002) *Religion in Late Modernity.* State University of New York Press, Albany.

Newbigin, Lesslie (1981) The basis, purpose and manner of inter-faith dialogue. In: Richard W. Rousseau (ed.), *Interreligious Dialogue*, pp. 13–31. University of Scranton Press, Montrose.

Oakes, Edward T. (2007) The internal logic of Holy Saturday in the theology of Hans Urs von Balthasar. *International Journal of Systematic Theology*, 9, 2, 184–99.

Ochs, Peter (2005) Judaism and Christian theology. In: David F. Ford & Rachel Muers (eds.), *The Modern Theologians*, 3rd edn., pp. 645–62. Blackwell, Oxford.

Packer, J. I. (1983) Introductory essay. In: John Owen (ed.), *The Death of Death in the Death of Christ*, pp. 1–25. Banner of Truth, Edinburgh.

Palmer, Michael (1997) *Freud and Jung on Religion.* Routledge, London.

Panikkar, Raimundo (1964; 1981) *The Unknown Christ of Hinduism.* Darton, Longman & Todd, London.

Panikkar, Raimundo (1973) *The Trinity and the Religious Experience of Man.* Darton, Longman & Todd, London.

Panikkar, Raimundo (1987) The Jordan, the Tiber, and the Ganges. In: John Hick & Paul Knitter (eds.), *The Myth of Christian Uniqueness: Towards a Pluralistic Theology of Religions*, pp. 98–116. Orbis, Maryknoll.

Pannenberg, Wolfhart (1971) Towards a theology of the history of religions. In: *Basic Questions in Theology*, pp. 65–118. Fortress Press, Philadelphia.

Pennington, Brian K. (2005) *Was Hinduism Invented? Britons, Indians, and the Colonial Construction of Religion.* Oxford University Press, Oxford.

Perry, Marvin, & Schweitzer, Frederick M. (2005) *Antisemitism: Myth and Hate from Antiquity to the Present.* Palgrave Macmillan, Basingstoke.

Petrushevsky, Il'ia Pavlovich (1985) *Islam in Iran.* Athlone, London, trans. Hubert Evans.

Philip's (2004) *Philip's Guide to the State of the World.* Philip's, London.

Pieris, Aloysius (1988) *An Asian Theology of Liberation.* Orbis, Maryknoll.

Pinnock, Clark H. (1992) *A Wideness in God's Mercy: The Finality of Jesus Christ in a World of Religions.* Zondervan, Grand Rapids.

Pinto, Henrique (2003) *Foucault, Christianity and Interfaith Dialogue.* Routledge, London.

Piscatori, James P. (1983) Ideological politics in Sa'udi Arabia. In: J. P. Piscatori (ed.), *Islam in the Political Process*, pp. 56–72. Cambridge University Press, Cambridge.

Pitstick, Alyssa Lyra (2007) *Light in Darkness: Hans Urs von Balthasar and the Catholic Doctrine of Christ's Descent into Hell.* W. B. Eerdmans, Grand Rapids.

Pitstick, Alyssa Lyra (2008, in press) Development of doctrine, or denial? Balthasar's Holy Saturday and Newman's *Essay. International Journal of Systematic Theology.*

Pius XII, Pope (1943) *Mystici corporis* (*On the mystical body of Christ*) [WWW document]. URL www.vatican.va/holy_father/pius_xii/encyclicals/documents/hf_p-xii_enc_29061943_mystici-corporis-christi_en.html [accessed on September 16, 2008].

Polanyi, Michael (1962) *Personal Knowledge: Towards a Post-Critical Philosophy.* Harper & Row, New York.

Race, Alan (1983) *Christians and Religious Pluralism.* SCM, London.

Rahner, Karl (1963a) Concerning the relationship between nature and grace. In: K. Rahner (ed.), *Theological Investigations*, vol. 1, pp. 297–318. Darton, Longman & Todd, London.

Rahner, Karl (1963b) Membership of the church according to the teaching of Pius XII's encyclical "Mystici Corporis." In: K. Rahner (ed.), *Theological Investigations*, vol. 2, pp. 1–88. Darton, Longman & Todd, London.

Rahner, Karl (1965) *Theology of Death.* Darton, Longman & Todd, London.

Rahner, Karl (1966) Christianity and the non-Christian religions. In: K. Rahner (ed.), *Theological Investigations*, vol. 5, pp. 115–34. Darton, Longman & Todd, London.

Rahner, Karl (1967) The eternal significance of the humanity of Christ for our relation to God. In: K. Rahner (ed.), *Theological Investigations*, vol. 3, pp. 35–46. Darton, Longman & Todd, London.

Rahner, Karl (1968) *Spirit in the World*, 2nd edn. Sheed & Ward, London.

Rahner, Karl (1969) Reflections on the unity of the love of neighbour and the love of God. In: K. Rahner (ed.), *Theological Investigations*, vol. 6, pp. 231–53. Darton, Longman & Todd, London.

Rahner, Karl (1973) On the official teaching of the church today on the subject of indulgences. In: K. Rahner (ed.), *Theological Investigations*, vol. 10, pp. 166–98. Darton, Longman & Todd, London.
Rahner, Karl (1984) Purgatory. In: K. Rahner (ed.), *Theological Investigations*, vol. 14, pp. 181–91. Darton, Longman & Todd, London.
Ramadan, Tariq (1999) *To Be a European Muslim*. Islamic Foundation, Leicester.
Ramadan, Tariq (2000) *Islam, the West and the Challenges of Modernity*. Islamic Foundation, Leicester.
Ramadan, Tariq (2004) *Western Muslims and the Future of Islam*. Oxford University Press, Oxford.
Ratzinger, Joseph (1988a) *Eschatology: Death and Eternal Life*. The Catholic University Press of America, Washington DC, trans. Michael Waldstein.
Ratzinger, Joseph (1988b) *Church, Ecumenism and Politics: New Essays in Ecclesiology*. Crossroads, New York.
Ratzinger, Joseph, & Schönborn, Christoph Cardinal (1994) *Introduction to the Catechism of the Catholic Church*. Ignatius Press, San Francisco.
Rawls, John (1993) *Political Liberalism*. Columbia University Press, New York.
Rawls, John (2001) *The Law of Peoples*. Harvard University Press, Cambridge.
Rengger, Nick (2007) The exorcist? John Gray, apocalyptic religion and the return to realism in world politics. *International Affairs*, 83, 5, 951–9.
Rorty, Richard (1979) *Philosophy and the Mirror of Nature*. Princeton University Press, Princeton.
Rorty, Richard (1999) Religion as a conversation-stopper. In: R. Rorty (ed.), *Philosophy and Social Hope*, pp. 168–74. Penguin, London.
Rothenberg, Gunther E. (1973) The Habsburg army in the Napoleonic wars. *Military Affairs*, 37, 1, 1–5.
Rousseau, Jean-Jacques (1762) *The Social Contract*, trans. G. D. H. Cole [WWW document]. URL www.constitution.org/jjr/socon.htm [accessed September 16, 2008].
Ruether, Rosemary Radford (1980) *Faith and Fratricide: The Theological Roots of Anti-Semitism*. Seabury Press, New York.
Runnymeade Trust (1997) *Islamophobia: A Challenge for Us All*. Runnymeade Trust, London.
Sachedina, Abdulaziz (2001) *The Islamic Roots of Democratic Pluralism*. Oxford University Press, Oxford.
Said, Edward (1995) *Orientalism*. Penguin, London.
Saldanha, Chrys (1984) *Divine Pedagogy: A Patristic View of Non-Christian Religions*. Libreria Ateneo Salesiano, Rome.
Salvatore, Armando (2007) *The Public Sphere: Liberal Modernity, Catholicism, Islam*. Palgrave Macmillan, New York.
Salvatore, Armando, & Eickelman, Dale F. (eds.) (2006) *Public Islam and the Common Good*. Brill, Leiden.

Sanders, John (1994) *No Other Name: Can Only Christians be Saved?* SPCK, London.

Sanneh, Lamin (1987) Christian mission and the Western guilt complex. *Christian Century*, 8 (April), 330–4.

Saward, John (1990) *Mysteries of March: Hans Urs von Balthasar on the Incarnation and Easter*. The Catholic University of America Press, Washington DC.

Schmaus, Michael (1975) *Dogma: The Church as Sacrament*, vol. 5. Sheed & Ward, London.

Schmidt-Leukel, Perry (2008) *God Without Limits: A Christian and Pluralistic Theology of Religions*. SCM, London.

Shah-Kazemi, Reza (2006) *The Other in the Light of the One: The Universality of the Qur'ân and Interfaith Dialogue*. The Islamic Texts Society, Cambridge.

Shaklar, Judith (1984) *Ordinary Vices*. Harvard University Press, Cambridge.

Sharpe, Eric (1986) *Comparative Religion: A History*, 2nd edn. Duckworth, London.

Skinner, Quentin (1978) *The Foundations of Modern Political Thought*, vol. 2. Cambridge University Press, Cambridge.

Skotnicki, Andrew (2006) God's prisoners: penal confinement and the creation of purgatory. *Modern Theology*, 22, 1, 85–110.

Smart, Ninian (1978) Beyond Eliade: the future of theory in religion. *Numen*, 25, 2, 171–83.

Smart, Ninian (1988) Religious studies in the United Kingdom. *Religion*, 18, 1–9.

Smith, Jonathan Z. (1978) *Map Is Not Territory: Studies in the History of Religions*. E. J. Brill, Leiden.

Smith, Wilfred Cantwell (1962) *The Meaning and End of Religion: A Revolutionary Approach to the Great Religious Traditions*. Macmillan, New York.

Smith, Wilfred Cantwell (1978) *The Meaning and End of Religion: A Revolutionary Approach to the Great Religious Traditions*, UK edn. SPCK, London.

Solzhenitsyn, Aleksander (1983) *Men have forgotten God: the Templeton address* [WWW document]. URL www.roca.org/OA/36/36h.htm [accessed on September 16, 2008].

Soroush, 'Abodolkarim (2000) *Reason, Freedom, & Democracy in Islam: Essential Writings of 'Abodolkarim Soroush*. Oxford University Press, Oxford, trans. Mahmous Sadri & Ahmad Sadri.

Stanley, Brian (1990) *The Bible and the Flag*. Intervarsity Press, Leicester.

Stott, John, & Edwards, David (1988) *Essentials: A Liberal–Evangelical Dialogue*. Hodder & Stoughton, London.

Stout, Jeffrey (1981) *The Flight from Authority: Religion, Morality, and the Quest for Autonomy*. University of Notre Dame Press, Notre Dame.

Stout, Jeffrey (2004) *Democracy and Tradition*. Princeton University Press, Princeton.

Strange, Daniel (2002) *The Possibility of Salvation Among the Unevangelised: An Analysis of Inclusivism in Recent Evangelical Theology*. Paternoster Press, Carlisle.

Strynkowski, John (1971) The descent of Christ among the dead. STD Dissertation, Pontificia Universita Gregoriana, Rome.

Sullivan, Francis A. (1992) *Salvation Outside the Church? Tracing the History of the Catholic Response*. Paulist Press, New York.

Sullivan, Francis A. (2002) Introduction and ecclesiological issues. In: Stephen J. Pope & Charles Hefling (eds.), *Sic et Non: Encountering Dominus Iesus*, pp. 47–56. Orbis, Maryknoll.

Surin, Kenneth (1990) A politics of speech: religious pluralism in the age of the Macdonald's hamburger. In: Gavin D'Costa (ed.), *Christian Uniqueness Reconsidered*, pp. 192–212. Orbis, Maryknoll.

Surin, Kenneth (1998) "Many religions and the one true faith": an examination of Lindbeck's chapter three. *Modern Theology*, 4, 2, 187–209.

Tanner, Norman (1990) *Decrees of the Ecumenical Councils, Volume Two: Trent to Vatican II*. Sheed & Ward and Georgetown University Press, London & Washington DC.

Thomas, Scott M. (2005) *The Global Resurgence of Religion and the Transformation of International Relations: The Struggle for the Soul of the Twenty-First Century*. Palgrave Macmillan, Basingstoke.

Tilley, Terrence W., Albarran, Louis T., Birch, John F. *et al.* (2007) *Religious Diversity and the American Experience*. Continuum, New York.

Tracy, David (1981) *The Analogical Imagination*. Crossroads, New York.

Van Bragt, Jan (2002) Multiple religious belonging of the Japanese people. In: C. Cornille (ed.), *Many Mansions: Multiple Belonging*, pp. 7–19. Orbis, Maryknoll.

Vatican documents: all texts without dates and publication details are available from URL www.vatican.va/ [accessed on September 16, 2008].

Waldron, Brian (2003) Locke. In: David Boucher & Paul Kelly (eds.), *Political Thinkers: From Socrates to the Present*, pp. 181–97. Oxford University Press, Oxford.

Walker, D. P. (1964) *The Decline of Hell: Seventeenth Century Discussion of Eternal Torment*. University of Chicago Press, Chicago.

Walls, Jerry L. (2000) *Heaven: The Logic of Eternal Joy*. Oxford University Press, Oxford.

Weigel, George (2005) *The Cube and the Cathedral: Europe, America, and Politics without God*. Basic Books, New York.

Weinandy, Thomas G. (1985) *Does God Change? The Word's Becoming in the Incarnation*. St Bede's Publications, Still River.

Weinandy, Thomas G. (2000) *Does God Suffer?* T. & T. Clark, Edinburgh.

White, Matthew (2005) *Source list and detailed death tolls for the twentieth century hemoclysm* [WWW document]. URL http://users.erols.com/mwhite28/warstat1.htm#Second [accessed on September 16, 2008].

Wilfred, Felix (1991) *Sunset in the East: Asian Challenges and Christian Involvement*. University of Madras Press, Madras.

Williams, Rowan (2008) *Archbishop's lecture – civil and religious law in England: a religious perspective* [WWW document]. URL www.archbishopofcanterbury.org/1575 [accessed on September 16, 2008].

Wolterstorff, Nicholas (1996) *Religion in the Public Square: Debating Church and State.* Rowman & Littlefield Publishers, Lanham.

Young, Iris Marion (1996) Communication and the other: beyond deliberative democracy. In: Seyla Benhabib (ed.), *Democracy and Difference*, pp. 120–36. Princeton University Press, Princeton.

Zaman, Muhammad Qasim (2002) *The Ulama in Contemporary Islam: Custodians of Change.* Princeton University Press, Princeton.

Subject Index

Index of Works

Scriptural Quotations

Non-Canonical Works